Criminal Circumstance

Dear Kate,
Please read the
whole thing!!

Pamela Wiley

NEW LINES IN CRIMINOLOGY
An Aldine de Gruyter Series of Texts and Monographs

SERIES EDITOR
Thomas G. Blomberg, *Florida State University*

Thomas G. Blomberg and Stanley Cohen
Punishment and Social Control: *Enlarged Second Edition*

Thomas G. Blomberg and Karl Lucken
American Penology: *A History of Control*

Bruce A. Jacobs
Robbing Drug Dealers: *Violence Beyond the Law*

David J. Rothman
Conscience and Convenience: *The Asylum and Its Alternatives in Progressive America*

David J. Rothman
The Discovery of the Asylum: *Social Order and Disorder in the New Republic*

Pamela Wilcox, Kenneth C. Land, and Scott A. Hunt
Criminal Circumstance: *A Dynamic Multicontextual Criminal Opportunity Theory*

Criminal Circumstance

A Dynamic Multicontextual Criminal Opportunity Theory

Pamela Wilcox
Kenneth C. Land
Scott A. Hunt

Aldine de Gruyter
New York

About the Authors

Pamela Wilcox is Associate Professor of Sociology at the University of Kentucky.
Kenneth C. Land is the John Franklin Crowell Professor of Sociology and Director of the Center for Demographic Studies at Duke University.
Scott Hunt is Associate Professor of Sociology at the University of Kentucky.

ALDINE DE GRUYTER
A division of Walter de Gruyter, Inc.
200 Saw Mill River Road
Hawthorne, New York 10532

This publication is printed on acid free paper

Library of Congress Cataloging-in-Publication Data

Wilcox, Pamela, 1968–
   Criminal circumstance : a dynamic multicontextual criminal
opportunity theory / Pamela Wilcox, Kenneth C. Land, Scott A. Hunt.—
Rev. ed.
      p. cm. — (New lines in criminology)
Includes bibliographical references and index.
   ISBN 0-202-30720-4 (alk. paper) — ISBN 0-202-30721-2 (pbk. : alk.
paper)
   1. Criminology. I. Land, Kenneth C. II. Hunt, Scott A., 1960- III.
Title. IV. Series.

HV6018 .W475 2002
364—dc21

                                                                    2002014275

Manufactured in the United States of America
10 9 8 7 6 5 4 3 2 1

CONTENTS

List of Figures

List of Tables

Acknowledgments

Much of this book was written during Pamela Wilcox's sabbatical leave, cofunded by the University of Kentucky's College of Arts and Sciences and NIDA grants DA-11317 and DA-05312.

In addition, all three authors are indebted to a number of friends and colleagues for their support throughout the various stages of writing of this book. Several colleagues at University of Kentucky, in particular, deserve our thanks. Richard Clayton, director of University of Kentucky's Center for Prevention Research, along with his entire Center staff, provided many resources helpful toward the completion of this project, including additional office space, administrative support, as well as scholarly advice. Graham Ousey, Tom Janoski, and Bill Skinner, all in the Department of Sociology at University of Kentucky, also provided helpful advice and resources at various stages of the project. Michael Rosenberg, of University of Kentucky's Counseling and Testing Center, provided invaluable guidance in effectively managing such a large-scale project. Both Lawrence E. Cohen (University of California, Davis) and Philip J. Cook (Duke University) read initial drafts of the manuscript and provided helpful feedback for revision purposes. We also thank Thomas G. Blomberg, Richard Koffler, and Mai Shaikhanuar-Cota for their encouragement and suggestions for improving our manuscript. Finally, we want to express our appreciation for all of our colleagues in the scholarly community of criminology, who earnestly labor at puzzling out the causes and consequences of criminal acts. We are particularly grateful for the work of our colleagues who have contributed to the social control and routine activities traditions. While too numerous to list here, their influences on our thoughts and work are readily apparent on every page of this volume.

In sum, we benefited from the quality scholarship, generous resources, and meaningful friendships provided by many people. While we accept full responsibility for any errors appearing herein, we are quite certain that we share ownership of the strengths of our work with each of them.

Preface

In this volume, we seek to further the development of criminal opportunity theory by identifying and addressing six areas revolving around theory, empirical research, and policy.

We offer a general clarification and fine-tuning of central theoretical assumptions, concepts, and propositions found in criminal opportunity theory. This base-level work will facilitate our present efforts to make theoretical advancements as well as illuminate paths for innovative empirical tests.

We emphasize the ecology of crime, seeking to develop a fuller understanding of individual-environment effects. Criminal opportunity theory seems inherently well-suited for multicontextual exploration (i.e., explaining criminal acts in terms of individuals embedded in particular environments). However, most tests of the theory remain single-level (either micro or macro, individual or environmental). Additionally, to date, there has not been a systematic attempt to delineate abstract principles that specify exactly how individual and environmental influences interact to produce criminal opportunities.[1]

We explore the linkages among various types of crime, victimization, and reactions to crime. Contemporary research has indicated that the criminal opportunity model is not only applicable to various kinds of crime but to reactions to crime as well (e.g., perceived risk, fear, and constrained behavior). What is left to be done, and a task we take up here, is to provide an explicit demonstration of the interrelationships between crime, victimization, and reactions within a comprehensive theoretical framework.

We highlight temporal effects associated with criminal opportunity contexts. In addition to being well-suited for multicontextual exploration, criminal opportunity theory provides a solid foundation upon which to more fully understand the temporal dimensions of criminal opportunity contexts, i.e., rhythm, tempo, and timing of activities. In addition to these

temporal dimensions, criminal opportunity theory has the capacity to provide rich analyses of the interplay between individual and ecological
influences across time, even though most tests of criminal opportunity
theory use cross-sectional data. Further, even though it has not done so
thus far, criminal opportunity theory can provide age-graded, develop-
mentally appropriate constructs to understand criminal acts across the life
course.

   We discuss the possibilities for empirically testing our modified criminal opportunity theory. Given that we propose a rather complicated con-
stellation of causal factors—i.e., there are effects on criminal acts that are
purely environmental and purely individual as well as influences that are
products of environmental-individual interactions—it is incumbent that
we clearly demonstrate that our perspective is amenable to empirical
investigation. We suggest that recent advances in statistical techniques
equipped to handle hierarchical linear models or nested data provide
some of the tools necessary for testing our propositions. We also consider
how qualitative methods could be employed in multicontextual, opportunity analyses of criminal acts.

   We conclude by considering implications for legal and extralegal crime
prevention and intervention. Again, given that our modified theory adds
dynamic multicontextual complexities to the basic criminal opportunity
perspective, we are compelled to comment upon the practical utility of our
perspective.

NOTES

   1. Vila and Cohen's (1993) evolutionary ecological theory provides a provoca-
tive exception.

1

Theory Generally and a General Theory of Crime

Some Preliminary Considerations

The main objective of this book is to propose an alternative criminal opportunity theory. We build upon social control and routine activities theories to develop a dynamic, multicontextual criminal opportunity theory. Emphasizing the importance of contextual explanations of criminal acts, we propose two levels of analysis: individual and environmental. At each level, the theory pivots on three broad organizing constructs—offenders motivated to commit criminal acts, targets (persons or property) suitable as objects of criminal acts, and the presence or absence of individuals or other defensive mechanisms capable of serving as guardians against criminal acts. Our efforts are intended to more fully explore criminal opportunity theory's potential as a multilevel, general theory of crime.

This advancement of a multilevel criminal opportunity theory has its origin in a series of collaborative, empirical studies by Pamela Wilcox and Kenneth Land.[1] These studies revolved around a straightforward, two-pronged empirical question: What are the antecedents and consequences of criminal victimization? Puzzling out this line of inquiry, we confronted some intriguing theoretical and methodological issues. We discovered that even the most compelling individual-level explanations of the antecedents and effects of criminal victimization were unsatisfactory because they tended to neglect the influences of social context (e.g., neighborhoods). At the same time, we determined that potent contextual explanations tended to gloss over individual factors. Following groundbreaking work by Sampson and Wooldredge (1987), Miethe and Meier (1990, 1994), as well as Miethe and McDowall (1993), we concluded that an adequate account of criminal victimization must involve a theory that is multilevel, incorporating both individual and environmental concepts. To move toward a

1

more satisfying explanation of victimization, we borrowed from social control and routine activities theories to form a framework that maintains that the *amount or rate of occurrence, location, and distribution of criminal acts across social and physical space can best be explained in terms of criminal opportunity contexts—the circumstances surrounding the convergence in time and place of motivated offenders, suitable targets, and the absence of capable guardians*. Methodologically, we found a relatively new statistical tool that fit our desire to study individual-environmental contextual effects. Multilevel or hierarchical linear models (HLM) provided the means to examine nested data (e.g., individuals embedded in particular social environments such as schools or neighborhoods) in such a way that individual effects, environmental effects, and the interaction between the two could be isolated with precision.

These initial theoretical and methodological developments opened up a productive line of inquiry that has consistently contributed to an understanding of the rate, location, and distribution of criminal acts in dynamic, multilevel terms. Pursuing this multilevel, criminal opportunity research agenda, Wilcox and Land noticed that advances in the methodological techniques used to study nested data outstripped theoretical developments that could explain multilevel phenomena. HLM could detect individual-environmental main and interaction effects, but a theoretical framework that could systematically explain the origins and consequences of these effects was lacking. The impetus for this book thus rests in a desire to contribute to the development of a theoretical framework of the ecology of criminal acts that is explicitly centered around multilevel analysis.

WHY BOTHER?

This is often the first question anyone claiming to advance a theory of anything must face. This is especially true for theories about serious concerns such as crime. Crime is profoundly real, possessing qualities that make its occurrence and prevention pressing and persistent matters for individuals and societies. Theory, in contrast, is seen as highly abstract and removed from the seriousness of "real life." Theory almost seems to be a peculiar sport of an academic class. The practically minded—including undergraduates, graduate students, practitioners, and even some academic criminologists—are often perplexed with the seeming obsession some scholars have with theory, which, after all, is nothing more than an explanation of facts. The practically minded, seeing a compelling need to identify the crucial factors that could be used to predict and prevent crime, wonder why anyone would invest precious time and energy into speculating about the abstract, underlying details of why crime occurs when and where it does.

Sometimes those who place little value on theory suggest that it is a purely "academic" (read "useless") exercise. Akers sums up this problem nicely:

> To many students, criminal justice practitioners, and other people, theory has a bad name. In their minds, the word "theory" means an irrelevant antonym of "fact." Facts are real, while theories seem to involve no more than impractical mental gymnastics. Theories are just fanciful ideas that have little to do with what truly motivates real people. (1997:1)

From this perspective, theories are nothing more than elaborate opinions professed by quixotic intelligentsia. Further, theorizing is seen to be very similar to (if not exactly the same as) the zealous professing of religious or political ideologues. It even seems that theoreticians who espouse views most removed from common sense earn the greatest praises. From this perspective, theory masquerades as science and is irrelevant at best; at worst, theory is seen to impede or even work against efforts to deal with very real problems such as violence, theft, and recidivism.

Without completely dismissing the likelihood that theoreticians have earned some part of their negative reputations among students, practitioners, and others, we take exception to the notions that theory is a useless and unnecessary enterprise. Again, we agree with Akers in his assessment of the scientific and practical importance of theory:

> Theory, if developed properly, is about real situations, feelings, experience, and human behavior. An effective theory helps us to make sense of facts that we already know and can be tested against new facts. . . . [Theory refers] to statements about relationships between actual events; about *what is* and *what will be*. They are not answers to questions of *what ought to be,* nor are they philosophical, religious, or metaphysical systems of beliefs and values about crime and society. . . . Criminological theories are abstract, but they entail more than ivory-tower or arm-chair speculations. They are part of the broader social science endeavor to explain human behavior and society. . . . Moreover, [theoretical] understanding is vital for those who plan to pursue specialized careers in the law or criminal justice. Virtually every policy or action taken regarding crime is based on some underlying theory or theories of crime. (ibid.:1–2)

We bother with theory because it has scientific and practical utility when done properly. When done properly, theory can help us to test supposed relationships between facts. Such testing sometimes confirms suspected relationships between variables. At other times, theory testing reveals that supposed associations between crime and other variables do not exist or exist in a manner very different from what was suspected. Further, theory can be used to identify new factors that could be associated with the occurrence of crime; or it can be used to more precisely specify the nature of the relationships already established between crime and the factors that produce it. We bother with theory—we bother with explaining the abstract, underlying causes of crime—because such exercises can help to better understand and predict the occurrence of crime. Also, we bother with theory because it is a practical matter. Every intervention, prevention, and policy is based on some theoretical explanation of the causes of human behavior. The improvement of interventions, preventions, and policies is directly related to the improvement of theoretical understandings of the abstract, underlying details of the causes of crime. We engage in theorizing simply because the development of theory, when it is properly done, is a crucial component to understanding and possibly improving the "real world."

WHAT IS THEORY?

The foregoing introduction presumes knowledge of a number of key concepts and terms. We now slow down the pace of description to provide definitions and descriptions of these key elements. The first of these is the term "theory" itself.

In order to have a means of assessing when theory is properly done, it is necessary to consider what constitutes a theory and upon what criteria it can be evaluated. A useful place to begin is an examination of what is meant by *theory*. Even those with only passing familiarity of the social sciences probably know that raising the question of what is meant by theory opens up a number of philosophy of science issues. Given that our emphasis revolves around crime and not theory per se, we might be justified in not broaching this perplexing topic at all. In fact, leading works in criminological theory tend to avoid this subject altogether. However, we believe that an explication of our general orientation toward theory will facilitate a more complete understanding of our multicontextual opportunity theory of crime.

Consensus does not exist on what constitutes a theory.[2] Given this lack of consensus, we desire to have a working definition of theory that is compatible with our objective of developing a multicontextual explanation of criminal opportunity across time and space. We find Cohen's definition to be useful:

> A theory is a set of interrelated universal statements, some of which are definitions and some of which are relationships assumed to be true, together with a syntax, a set of rules for manipulating the statements to arrive at new statements. (1989:178)

This definition highlights several key aspects of properly done theory that require brief elaboration.

First, theoretical statements are *universal*. By universal we mean that theoretical statements are abstract assertions taken as general truths about concepts and relationships between concepts that transcend time and space. In contrast to universal statements, idiographic statements are limited to the particulars of a specific time and place. In its most extreme form, idiographic explanation is merely a microscopic depiction of the unfolding of the actions of specific individuals moving in certain space-time contexts (e.g., an explanation of how and why J. Smith came to murder T. Jones in a bar in Wahoo, Nebraska, in 1909). In a less extreme form, idiographic explanations attempt to describe how and why a type of event occurs in a specific time and place in history (e.g., an explanation of serial killings in the United States in the first-half of the twenty-first century). Idiographic statements are descriptions of actions in particular times and spaces; they are not intended to be general explanations of behavior across time and space (i.e., they are not universal statements).

From our view, theory cannot be limited to particular time and space situations. It seems to us that, by definition, situational explanations of events do not constitute "theories." A properly done theory of crime would try to explain the rate, location, and distribution of criminal acts in all times and places. The requirement of being universal does not mean that theory is ahistorical and unable to incorporate cultural variations or context specificity. For instance, to say that increased social control decreases the likelihood of criminal acts occurring universally does not preclude the fact that social control has taken different forms across time—e.g., consider the movement from nineteenth-century private policing to modern public professional police forces to the recent growth in private security efforts.[3] Also, such a universal statement about the relationship between social control and crime does not overlook the fact that social control has distinctive cultural features across societies—e.g., consider the differences in shaming practices in Japan and the United States.[4] These examples suggest that theories with universal statements are not necessarily ahistorical and ethnocentric. Our multicontextual opportunity theory of crime provides universal statements that have the capacity to account for human behavior across time and cultural contexts.

A second key feature of our working definition of theory is that theoretical statements are *interrelated*. Statements must be interrelated in a couple of different ways. First, the statement that "increased social control decreases the likelihood of criminal acts occurring" would not be useful at all if there were not definitions of social control and criminal acts. In this sense, statements that posit relationship between concepts (e.g., social control and criminal acts) must be interrelated with definitions of those concepts. Another way in which theoretical statements are interrelated is that statements of relationships between concepts are connected by common terms. For instance, these statements are interrelated because they share a common term:

- Increased informal social control (e.g., neighborhood watches) decreases the likelihood of the occurrence of criminal acts.
- The more social ties in a neighborhood (e.g., regular interactions between neighbors) the greater the informal social control.

Disparate statements about some phenomenon, even if empirically true, do not constitute a theory about that phenomenon. For example:

- Increased levels of poverty in a neighborhood increases the likelihood of the occurrence of criminal acts.
- Higher percentages of male residents in a neighborhood increases the likelihood of the occurrence of criminal acts.

Disparate statements such as these do not constitute a theory because they are not logically connected to one another. In elaborating our multi-contextual opportunity theory of crime, we provide definitions for all our key concepts and develop propositions with interrelated terms.

Logic, or *syntax* in Cohen's (1989) words, is the third key component of our working definition of theory. Logic in essence is a set of rules for advancing theoretical arguments. That is, the structure and forms of theoretical arguments must conform to the rules of logical reasoning. Logical arguments can be either inductively generated (from facts to theory) or deductively derived (the application of a theory to a particular case).[5]

ASSESSING THEORY

Regardless of whether a theory employs inductive or deductive reasoning, its statements must be both connected and consistent logically. Thus, *logical* consistency is one criterion for evaluating theory.[6] That is, the explicit statements of a theory must avoid logical contradiction. Akers makes this point when he writes:

> A theory which proposes that criminals are biologically deficient and that deficiency explains their criminal behavior cannot also claim that family socialization is the basic cause of criminal behavior. (1997:6)

A more difficult task than avoiding logical contradiction among explicit theoretical statements is to eliminate contradictions among tacit theoretical assumptions. This task is more difficult in that the existence and logic of underlying assumptions are not readily apparent. In our multicontextual opportunity theory of crime we not only strive to develop explicit statements that are logical, but we also reconcile potential contradictions in opportunity theory's tacit premises about offender motivation.

Another important criterion for assessing theory is that it must be *empirically testable*. In other words, theoretical propositions have to be advanced in such a fashion that objective evidence could be gathered that would either support or refute them. This criterion that a theory be amenable to empirical tests is more demanding than merely marshaling evidence in support of stated propositions. An adequate theory must be *falsifiable*.[7]

There are several ways in which theories can be unfalsifiable. One way a theory can be unfalsifiable is if its definitions and propositions are tautological (i.e., they are true by definition). When properly formulated, a theory avoids unconscious circular reasoning. To illustrate tautology, the following argument is true by definition, and is therefore unfalsifiable:

1. An antisocial personality trait is defined as violent behavioral expressions.
2. The antisocial personality trait causes violence.

Such an argument could never be proven to be false because the cause (antisocial personality trait) is defined by the very thing it is said to explain (violence).

Akers provides a couple of keen examples of tautological reasoning that have clear ramifications for practical applications of theory:

> A variation on a tautology that is true by definition is seen in the practice of placing a label on some behavior, then using that label to explain the same behavior. For instance, one may label serial killers as psychopaths then assert that people commit serial murder because they are psychopathic. Such a statement does no more than repeat the label. Similarly, we may observe that a person drinks excessively and has problems with alcohol, so we theorize that the person overdrinks because he is alcoholic. How do we know he is an alcoholic? We know because he drinks excessively and has problems with alcohol. We have come full circle. (1997:8)

Tautologies not only lead to bad theories, but they can also produce vacuous diagnoses in the "real world."

Another way a theory can be unfalsifiable is if "its propositions are so open-ended that any contradictory empirical evidence can be interpreted or re-interpreted to support the theory" (ibid.). To illustrate, a theory could posit that burglary of commercial establishments is the result of alienation engendered by capitalist economies. For those burglars who indicate that they burglarized a commercial establishment because they felt estranged from the capitalist system, the theory is supported. For those burglars who offer other explanations (e.g., they wanted to make a fast buck), the theory could reinterpret those explanations as examples of "false consciousness," which is itself a result of alienation. Such a theory is unfalsifiable because any evidence can be used to support its proposition and none can be mustered to refute it.

A third way in which a theory can be unfalsifiable is if its concepts are not observable and reportable events. As Akers observes:

> If a theory proposes that people commit crimes because they are possessed by invisible demons, there is no way to prove whether or not such demons are responsible for the crime. (ibid.)

This is unfalsifiable and tautological because what is to be explained (crime) cannot be measured separate from the proposed cause (demons). Recognizing the vital importance of being able to falsify theoretical statements, we take care to ensure that our multicontextual opportunity theory is constructed in a manner that makes it susceptible to empirical evidence that could refute its propositions.

Without a doubt, the most important criterion for assessing a theory is its *degree of empirical validity*.[8] However, no amount of empirical evidence could ever really prove a theory to be true. Rather, systematically gathered evidence that is congruent with a theory's propositions can be said to support that theory. Likewise, no single empirical test could ever be used to entirely disprove a theory. Instead, when findings are incongruent with a theory's propositions, researchers can only safely say that their results failed to support that theory. This suggests that the empirical validity of a theory is relative. That is, empirical validity is a matter of degree; empirical research can fail to support, provide weak support, or lend strong support.[9] Our multicontextual opportunity theory of crime draws upon research findings to refine its concepts and propositions. Further, we specify our theory to such an extent that researchers could design crucial empirical tests of our propositions. In addition, we provide a methodological discussion to facilitate empirical tests of our theory.

The *usefulness* of a theory can be another criterion for assessment. Once again we turn to Akers for a cogent discussion of the relationship between theory and practice:

> All major criminological theories have implications for, and have indeed been utilized in, criminal justice policy and practice. Every therapy, treatment program, prison regimen, police policy, or criminal justice practice is based, either explicitly or implicitly, on some explanation of human nature in general or criminal behavior in particular. Every recommendation for

changes in our legal and criminal justice system has been based on some underlying theory that explains why the laws have been enacted, why the system operates as it does, and why those who are in the system behave as they do. The question, then, is not where policy can be or should be based on theory—it already is guided by theory—but rather how well is policy guided by theory and how good is the theory on which the policy predicated? (1997:11)

As researchers who are not practitioners, we take as our task the provision of a solid theory that is logically constructed and sound enough to stand up to the rigors of empirical testing. At the same time, we desire to offer a theory that could prove useful in terms of policy and practice. Since we believe that the utility of a theory is an important criterion in its overall assessment, we conclude our book with a consideration of the policy and practice implications of our theory.

The final criterion we wish to consider can be understood in terms of *theoretical scope*, which is the range of the phenomenon to be explained (ibid.:7). A theory can be rather narrow in scope (e.g., an explanation of multiple-offender robbery) or broad (e.g., an explanation of all criminal acts). The theories that can successfully explain the broadest range of phenomena are more desirable. Related to this issue of scope is the notion of *parsimony*, which pertains to the conciseness and abstractness of a theory. Parsimonious theory is desirable because it is more potent—that is, it is able to account for the widest range of phenomena with the fewest statements.

While the issue of theoretical scope is an important one for contemporary criminology, a definitively "correct" resolution of this matter does not exist. The diversity of approaches to theoretical scope is reflected in the fact that criminological theories vary considerably as to what is to be explained. Some focus on "deviance"; some concentrate on "crime"; some center on specific types of crime; and some revolve around reactions to crimes. Not only do criminological theories differ on what is to be explained, they also diverge in terms of the breadth and complexity of their causal principles.

To illustrate, Tittle's (1995) "control balance" perspective is a "general theory of deviance." In this theory, Tittle seeks to explain all forms of deviance captured in the broad conceptual categories of "predation," "exploitation," "defiance," "plunder," "decadence," "submission," and "conformity." His conceptual framework used to explain deviance is equally wide-ranging. Tittle (ibid.:172) provides a complicated web of constructs that incorporates human biological drives, social desires (including a desire for autonomy), control imbalance, predisposition toward motivations to be deviant, situational provocation, situational risk, feelings of debasement, seriousness of deviance, constraint, motivation, and opportunity. Another example of a wide-ranging perspective is Gottfredson and

Hirschi's (1990:15–42) "general theory of crime," which seeks to explain all acts of "force or fraud undertaken in pursuit of self-interest," including burglary, robbery, homicide, auto theft, rape, white-collar crime, drug and alcohol abuse, as well as "events analogous to crimes" such as accidents. In fact, Gottfredson and Hirschi boldly assert that their theory "is meant to explain all crime, at all times, and, for that matter, many forms of behavior that are not sanctioned by the state" (ibid.:117). Gottfredson and Hirschi posit that low self-control, which is the result of ineffective child-rearing and social control in families and schools, is the factor that explains acts of force and fraud. Another wide-ranging theory is Akers's (1998) social learning approach, which is a "general theory of crime and deviance." The basic explanatory principle is that crime and deviance are products of social learning, which consists of differential association, differential reinforcement, imitation, definitions, and discriminative stimuli. While Akers (1998) concentrates on deviance and crime exclusively, his theoretical approach is a variant of learning theory that has also been developed to explain human behavior generally.[10]

In contrast to these examples of wide-ranging theories, other perspectives are much more narrowly focused. For instance, Wilson and Herrnstein believe that crime is too broad of a concept, contending that "crime is as broad of a category as disease, and perhaps as useless" (1985:21). They therefore choose to restrict their explanation to universal "serious crimes such as murder, theft, robbery, and incest." For Wilson and Herrnstein these serious crimes are the result of a complex interaction of constitutional or biological traits and familial factors, and, after one takes these into consideration, there is little variation left to explain. Another example of a perspective that takes a more restricted approach to theory is Hagan's (1997:288) developmental approach to "street crime in America." Hagan's explanation revolves around historically specific constructs that include "capital disinvestment and recapitalization, social and cultural capital, criminal capital and embeddedness, and deviance service centers and ethnic vice industries" (ibid.:289). Clarke and Cornish make a much more explicit and emphatic argument that criminology theory should rest upon crime-specific models:

> Recent preoccupation with offender pathology and the desire to construct general statements about crime, deviancy, and rule breaking have consistently diverted attention from the important differences between types of crime—the people committing them, the nature of the motivations involved, and the behaviors required. Whatever the purposes and merits of academic generalization, it is essential for policy goals that these important distinctions be maintained. And, moreover, it will usually be necessary to make even finer distinctions between crimes than those provided by legal cate-

gories. For instance, it will not usually be sufficient to develop models for a broad legal category such as burglary. Rather it will be necessary to differentiate at least between commercial and residential burglary . . . and perhaps even between different kinds of residential and commercial burglaries. (1985:165)

These examples suggest that among criminologists there is not agreement as to what constitutes "appropriate" theoretical scope. Gottfredson and Hirschi point out:

In criminology it is often argued that special theories are required to explain female and male crime, crime in one culture rather than another, crime committed in the course of occupation as distinct from street crime, or crime committed by children as distinct from crime committed by adults. (1990:117)

Further, they argue that a broader, more general theory of crime is preferred to crime-specific theories:

Limits on the range of a theory should not be taken too seriously unless those stating the limits provide evidence that it will not work outside the narrow domain they specify. (Put another way, modesty per se is not a virtue in theory.) (ibid.)

Yet, some would suggest that concepts as broad as "crime" or "deviance" do not lend themselves to empirical investigation.[11]

Lacking clear guidelines within the discipline, we choose to develop a perspective that is akin to a general theory of crime. We take as our task the theoretical explanation of the rate, location, and distribution across social and physical space of "criminal acts," which we define in greater detail below. In terms of parsimony, some might point out that our general theory of criminal acts is relatively less parsimonious than the perspectives upon which we most heavily rely. After all, by positing a multilevel theory we specify individual-, environmental-, and cross-level propositions. This is clearly more complex than either an exclusively individual- or environmental-level theory would entail. Indeed, our view is more complex than a theory that would simply combine individual- and environmental-level propositions (without considering cross-level interactions). Plus, we more fully integrate temporal factors into all levels of our theory. Considering all this, it would be easy to see why someone might conclude that our theory is wanting in terms of parsimony. In our defense, we contend that even though our theory is admittedly more complex than extant criminal opportunity perspectives, it retains a high degree of parsimony because we advance a single causal principle for all levels of analysis. Namely, criminal acts are a function of the convergence in time and space of motivated offenders, suitable targets, and a lack of capable guardians. Because our approach attempts to explain multiple levels of a phenomenon with one causal principle that consists of only five key concepts (time, space, motivated offenders, suitable targets, and capable guardians), we would argue that parsimony is a strength, not a weakness, of our theory.

HOW DO MODELS FIT IN?

Later in this book, after defining the components of our theory of criminal contexts and criminal acts, we describe how statistical models, specifically multilevel or hierarchical linear models, can be used to test and evaluate the applicability of the theory to explain various properties of criminal acts and their consequences. Our effort to offer models derived from our theory represents a significant and rather unique contribution to criminology. We say this because it seems that criminological theories are typically advanced without derived models; they thus provide few, if any, clear guides for empirical tests. On the other hand, criminological models are often put forward without being clearly related to a coherent theoretical system that has logically consistent and integrated principles, concepts, and propositions. By specifying a theory with derivative models we hope to more fully satisfy the demands of criminology as a science. Just as a previous section described how we are using the term "theory" in this book, we now address the question of how we use the term "models."

Following Land (2001:382), we use the term "models" most generally to refer to the tools by which individuals order and organize experiences and observations. Note that one implication of this definition is that many verbal characterizations of crime phenomena are properly regarded and respected as models. Many of these *verbal* models have stimulated much research in criminology over many years and will continue to do so.

But for the analysis of observations in the form of quantitative data, it often is useful to utilize formal models. If models most generically are tools for ordering our experiences, what are "formal models"? Briefly, *formal* models encapsulate some slice of experiences/observations within the confines of the relationships constituting a formal system such as formal logic, mathematics, or statistics (Land 2001:383). Thus, a formal criminological *model* is a way of representing data on crime within the framework of a formal apparatus, such as a statistical model, that provides us with a means for exploring the properties of crime mirrored in the model. Why construct formal criminological models? Why not just use verbally stated models? Basically, we construct formal models to assist in bringing a more clearly articulated order to quantitative data on criminal acts and their

contexts, as well as to make more precise predictions about certain properties of criminal acts and their interactions with contexts.

What differentiates models from theories? These terms sometimes are
distinguished and sometimes are used interchangeably. Usually, however,
scientific theories are regarded as more general than scientific models.
Models typically are specified with a particular set of observations or data
in hand. The purpose of the model is to order and organize the observations in accordance with a particular theory. On the other hand, scientific
theories typically can be applied to many different sets of observations or
data. Thus, as Land (2001:386) notes, a *theory* can be viewed as a family of
related models, whereas a *model* is a formal manifestation of a particular
theory to be applied to a particular set of observations or data.

TOWARD A DYNAMIC MULTICONTEXTUAL CRIMINAL
OPPORTUNITY THEORY

Thus far we have provided a general overview of the importance, nature,
and assessment of theory. We now outline the basic contours of our multicontextual criminal opportunity theory. A brief explication of criminal acts
begins this discussion. We then provide an overview of the fundamental
logic and conceptual framework underlying our multicontextual criminal
opportunity perspective.

On the surface, it seems rather obvious what a criminological theory
seeks to explain: crime. However, any serious attempt to specify what is to
be explained in a precise, scientific manner exposes a tangled web of conceptual problems. If "crime" refers to any violation against the law, then a
theory that purports to explain it would include such diverse acts as double
parking and premeditated murder. Limiting "crime" to violations of the
law would mean that the very same act (e.g., marital rape) could be classified as both criminal and not criminal in two different cultural, geopolitical
contexts. Likewise, the very same act (e.g., smoking marijuana) could be
classified as both criminal and not criminal in two different historical
moments in the same cultural, geopolitical context. Gottfredson and
Hirschi consider how this problem is typically identified and "addressed"
by modern criminologists:

> Criminologists often complain that they do not control their own dependent
> variable, that the definition of crime is decided by political-legal acts rather
> than by scientific procedures. The state, not the scientist, determines the
> nature or definition of crime. After registering this complaint, the modern
> criminologist proceeds to define crime as "behavior in violation of the law"
> and to study the phenomenon as defined by others. (1990:3)

We suspect that criminologists typically settle for studying behaviors that are violations of the law on pragmatic grounds—i.e., while not perfect, such a definition of what is to be explained is relatively clear and manageable in terms of empirical examination.

Shifting the focus from violations of the law to violations of norms or "deviance" does not offer an obvious remedy. For instance, a theory of "deviance" could include explanations of such diverse acts as chewing gum in school and premeditated murder. Expanding what is to be explained to "deviance" would still pose cultural and historical oddities. As with a theory of "crime," a theory "limited" to explanations of "deviance" would mean that the very same act (e.g., marital rape) could be classified as both deviant and not deviant in two different cultural, geopolitical contexts. And, the very same act (e.g., smoking marijuana) could be classified as both deviant and not deviant in two different historical moments in the same cultural, geopolitical context. An additional complexity raised by defining what is to be explained in terms of "deviance" is that it suggests that in any given cultural, temporal context consensus exists as to what constitutes norm violations. While near-consensus might exist in a given population concerning the "deviance" of certain behaviors (e.g., cannibalism), such taboos are probably very few. It is likely that in most modern, industrialized societies there is not near-consensus on what behaviors are "deviant" or to what degree and under what circumstances behaviors become "deviant." It is unlikely that nearly everyone would agree that such behaviors as premarital sex, taking supplies from work, women wearing makeup, men wearing makeup, or ingesting LSD are truly "deviant." Consensus probably breaks down even when considering more grave actions. For example, consider the debate that might ensue if a group of people were asked under what conditions is it deviant or not deviant to take a human life. In short, shifting the analytical focus from "crime" to "deviance" does not present an obvious "solution" to our problem of what is to be explained.

It seems clear that a perfect solution to the problems surrounding what is to be explained does not exist. However, the subject matter of "crime" is simply too important to be completely paralyzed by this dilemma. At the same time, the conceptual and practical implications revolving around this very thorny issue are also too important to ignore or dismiss. How insightful can a theory be that fails to identify, at least in broad terms, the domain of behaviors it seeks to explain? How useful could such a theory be in the real world? One imperfect solution to this dilemma, which was alluded to in our discussion of theoretical scope, is to restrict a theory's analytical focus to a very narrow range of behaviors, e.g., predatory crimes. As we implied in our earlier discussion, such a maneuver is ultimately unsatisfactory for a theory, such as ours, that seeks to be a "general theory." Our imperfect solution to this knotty problem is to take properties of "criminal acts" pertaining to their amount or rate of occurrence, location, and distribution across social and physical space as the thing to be explained. It is our intention that this choice of what is to be explained encompass a broad range of like phenomena. We also believe that this choice provides a pragmatic solution in that our definition of what is to be explained lends itself to empirical investigation.

By *criminal acts,* we refer to *actions that involve force, fraud, and/or activities prohibited by law.* While not as encompassing as deviance generally (e.g., our definition excludes violations of conventional social etiquette), criminal acts can be understood as a broad concept in that it includes interests in both offending—i.e., criminal acts that are crimes—and victimization—i.e., "criminal acts that begin the victimization experience" (Miethe and Meier 1994:xiii). While borrowing from Gottfredson and Hirschi's (1990) conception of crime, our definition does not include accidents or other behaviors analogous to crimes as their self-control theory does. Our definition is flexible enough to allow for examinations of *mala in se* crimes, even if their status as crimes is ambiguous under the law (e.g., domestic abuse or marital rape). It also captures crimes that are *mala prohibita*, thus allowing for general examinations of rule-breaking behaviors as defined in particular space-time contexts (e.g., status offenses or substance use/abuse behaviors). Our definition is practically amenable in that it lends itself to the use of a variety of means to measure properties of criminal acts, especially their rate of occurrence, location, and distribution across social and physical space, including official crime statistics and self-report data.

With our definition of criminal acts, we place analytical attention squarely on the contexts of criminal events. Although criminal acts encompass a relatively wide range of events, it is not necessary to identify a plethora of concepts to explain criminal acts. Rather, we believe that one critical construct, *criminal opportunity context,* is the key to explaining the amount or rate of occurrence, location, and distribution across social and physical space of criminal acts. From our view, criminal opportunity context can be elegantly conceptualized as individual and ambient characteristics related to offenders, targets, and guardianship.

A grounding orientation of our perspective is the recognition that both individual and environmental factors across time affect criminal acts. Treating individual and environmental factors in isolation from one another (i.e., not in a multicontextual manner) and as static (i.e., without regard for temporal influences) is ultimately inadequate. From our view, an adequate theory of crime requires an exposition of the separate, direct effects individual and environmental factors have on the rate of occurrence, location, and distribution across social and physical space of criminal acts as well as an elaboration of a framework that understands how individual and environmental characteristics interact over time to produce criminal acts. The importance of the individual-environmental-temporal nexus grounds our most basic premise. *The amount or rate of occurrence, location, and distribution of criminal acts across social and physical space can best be explained in terms of criminal opportunity contexts. Criminal opportunity contexts* refer to the social and physical individual and environmental circumstances that affect the convergence in time and place of a motivated offender, a suitable target, and absence of capable guardianship.[12] Thus, criminal opportunity contexts must be defined both temporally and spatially. Because all criminal acts require some degree of criminal opportunity, an adequate theory must incorporate characteristics of individuals, targets, temporal settings, and sociocultural environments.

By seeking to explain properties of criminal acts as a function of circumstantial determinants created by the temporal and spatial convergence of motivated offenders and suitable targets in the absence of capable guardians, our approach builds upon the criminal opportunity perspective in criminology.[13] A fundamental premise of criminal opportunity theory is that contexts are more or less favorable for offending and victimization. Criminal opportunity theory, with its emphasis on the spatial and temporal requirements for successful criminal events, has refocused attention on the crime as opposed to the criminal. Analytic attention is thereby riveted upon the characteristics of criminal acts, and not the features of the criminal or victim. This means that criminal opportunity theory has emphasized the "normality" of criminal acts, arguing that offending and victimization emerge from social organization and social interaction rather than individual pathology.[14] This insistence on the "normality" of criminal acts, that "the criminal act, not criminals or victims, is the appropriate dependent variable of criminological investigation" (Miethe and Meier 1994:xiii), is captured in the traditional downplay of individual motivations for offending in criminal opportunity theory. That is, the criminal opportunity perspective traditionally does not ask, What drives some individuals to crime? which ultimately yields answers that revolve around individual motivation in one or more of its many guises (e.g., economic deprivation, cultural values, frustration, and psychological predispositions). Rather, it maintains that criminal acts emerge from the circumstances in which individuals find themselves.

Nonetheless, it should be noted that some criminal opportunity scholars incorporate motivation for individual criminal acts into their explanations. For instance, Cohen and Machalek (1988) applied an evolutionary ecological approach to generalize opportunity theory in such a way as to incorporate motivation. They argued that recent discoveries about the evolution of behavioral diversity within biological populations (human or otherwise)—such as competition, conflict, cooperation, and deviance—lend themselves to this analysis. To the extent that constitutional or biological (e.g., height, weight, physical strength) psychological (e.g., intellectual ability, self-control), or sociological (e.g., age, race/ethnicity, gender, socio-economic class), traits and variables are seen as influencing a person's *resource holding potential* (a means of exploiting valued resources or targets from the environment), Cohen and Machalek argue that they can be viewed as altering the probability that individuals will adopt an illegal strategy as a means of improving his/her position in the environment. This approach has the advantage of explaining the origin of nonbiological differences among individuals that significantly influence the kinds of strategies they adopt, while at the same time demonstrating that the interactive dynamics of social systems (sociological variables) are more important than other variables in determining crime participation rates in a given social location. While we indicate that the generalized crime opportunity theory of Cohen and Machalek is similar to our perspective, we concentrate our theoretical efforts exclusively on the articulation of how characteristics of the criminal circumstances or contexts are related to the properties of criminal acts that we have identified.

With its focus on properties of criminal acts, the foundational theoriz-ing in the criminal opportunity tradition[15] offers a rather elegant, parsi-monious, and ambitious perspective that seeks to explain all types of crimes and victimization experiences as a function of key factors found in social contexts. This solid conceptual base has set an agenda that has enabled theoretical and empirical advancements in a number of areas, including situationally based criminal decision-making processes, victim-ization studies, crime prevention, ecological criminology, and micro-macro integration.[16]

While offering a perspective that is a general theory of criminal acts, we nonetheless recognize the validity of Clarke and Cornish's (1985) assertion that the specifics of particular crimes necessarily shape analyses of those criminal acts. Even though we acknowledge that researchers must be aware of the specific characteristics of the particular types of criminal acts they attempt to explain, we do not believe that such an awareness requires distinct concepts or theories for each and every distinct type of criminal act. To elaborate, what constitutes a "suitable target" for residential bur-glary is quite different from "suitable targets" for arson, assault, and auto theft. Clearly, the difference between these kinds of criminal acts would require different operationalizations of "suitable target" in their analyses. However, the differences between these kinds of criminal acts would not necessitate the development of distinct sets of concepts and theories. We contend that a complete explanation of *all* criminal acts must involve ele-ments of criminal opportunity, i.e., the convergence of motivated offend-ers, suitable targets, and the lack of capable guardians. From our view, while the specific operationalizations of motivated offenders, suitable targets, and capable guardianship will be influenced by the type of criminal act being analyzed, the concepts and the relationships between them will be the same.

In sum, while criminal opportunity theorists traditionally conceptualize and operationalize criminal opportunity as the routine activities of individuals or the sociodemographic characteristics of individuals and their environmental contexts (presumed to serve as proxies for routine activities), our theory presents many more varied—multicontextual and temporal—sources of criminal opportunity. Our revision of criminal opportunity theory thereby cultivates the inherent yet underdeveloped dynamic and multicontextual facets of criminal opportunity theory more explicitly while simultaneously expanding its scope. We explain how a variety of characteristics of individual-ecological contexts provide circumstances that either enhance or diminish criminal opportunity, thus affecting crime, victimization, as well as cognitive, emotional, and behavioral responses to crime and victimization. These characteristics provide opportunity simultaneously both in an additive fashion and an interactive fashion. In this sense, there is but one critical construct in our conceptual model, and that is criminal opportunity context, with context involving the nexus of space, time, individual, and environment. Simply put, contexts demonstrating criminal opportunity are susceptible to criminal acts. Our approach offers a parsimonious alternative to "integrated theories" that posit multiple causal processes leading to criminal acts. While we recognize the importance of a plethora of variables, these variables are important not in defining multiple causal mechanisms but in delineating the multiple and interactive dimensions of one particular causal mechanism: criminal opportunity. We do not mean to imply that our theory is a complete explanation of everything and anything criminal. Such a claim would be untenable. Our aspirations are much more modest. We believe that our multilevel criminal opportunity theory holds the potential to be a relatively more complete and thereby relatively more satisfying specification of the relationships between criminal acts and criminal opportunity contexts.

PLAN OF THE BOOK

We lay out our dynamic multicontextual criminal opportunity theory more systematically over the next eight chapters. Chapter 2 reviews the theoretical foundation upon which we build: criminal opportunity theory. In this chapter, we assert that opportunity is assumed to be a necessary (if not sufficient) condition for crime by all. Yet, for the most part, criminal

opportunity is a concept that has been undertheorized. Two notable exceptions to this are social control and routine activities perspectives. Chapter
2 therefore revolves around a presentation of the history and developments of criminal opportunity theory as they have been articulated in the
social control and routine activities perspectives. In addition, we identify
the undeveloped and underdeveloped aspects of criminal opportunity
theory, providing a brief overview of how our theory proposes to address
these heretofore neglected areas.

In Chapter 3, we more fully outline the proposed theory as a whole,
suggesting that criminal opportunity can be conceptualized and operationalized through multiple dimensions and at multiple levels of analysis.
Such a perspective necessitates borrowing from, yet problematizing and
reconceptualizing, elements from routine activities, and control criminological perspectives. More specifically, Chapter 3 discusses the profitabil-
ity of theoretical integration, key underlying assumptions surrounding
our integrated theory, definitions of our core concepts, and general propositions central to our theory.

Having introduced the overall theory, Chapter 4 begins a section of the
book in which we dissect various aspects of the theory more carefully. In
Chapter 4, we examine how criminal opportunity is presented at the individual and environmental levels, reviewing extant work in substantial
detail. We then present this work within the context of our theoretical
propositions, outlined in Chapter 3, thus illustrating how our concepts can
be operationalized.

Chapter 5 goes beyond the notion of simultaneous, independent effects
of individual-level and ambient opportunity discussed earlier and discusses interactions among the two. Special attention is paid to *how* the
indicators of opportunity within multiple contexts act and interact simultaneously in explaining crime and victimization.

Chapter 6 recognizes that dynamic, multicontextual criminal opportunity can affect not only criminal offending and victimization but also
reactions to crime/victimization, including cognitive risk perception,
emotionally based fear of crime, and risk- or fear-elated precautionary
behavior. The theoretical ideas addressed in Chapters 3 through 5 are
extended to show how criminal opportunity can be useful in understanding these various reactions to crime.

The next chapter, Chapter 7, pays particular attention to the temporal
dimensions of the theory, including the rhythm, tempo, and timing of
activities related to the emergence of criminal opportunity. Chapter 7 also
situates the multicontextual opportunity theory within a life-course or
longitudinal perspective, suggesting that the various dimensions of
opportunity may act and interact differently depending upon time.

Next, Chapter 8 discusses how the proposed theory could be empirically tested, with an emphasis on HLM statistical models. Also, Chapter 8 considers how qualitative methods can be fruitfully used in multilevel studies of criminal opportunity and criminal acts.

Finally, Chapter 9 concludes by discussing the compatibility between our dynamic multicontextual criminal opportunity theory and legal and extralegal crime prevention and intervention measures.

NOTES

1. See especially Wilcox Rountree, Land, and Miethe (1994) and Wilcox Rountree and Land (1996a, 1996b, 2000).

2. In discussing the varying definitions of theory, Gibbs remarks: "In sociology the diverse conceptions of theory virtually defy description" (1972:15). For understanding the diversity in orientations toward sociological theory compare Blalock (1969), Blumer (1969), Gibbs (1972), Homans (1967), Hooks (1984), Kaplan (1964), Lyotard (1984), Popper (1965), Schroyer (1970), Seidman (1994), Sjoberg and Nett (1997), Stinchcombe (1968), and Zetterberg (1965).

3. See Cunningham and Taylor (1984).

4. See Braithwaite (1989).

5. For discussions of reasoning and theory development see Beveridge (1950), Nagel (1961), and Pearl (2000).

6. See Gibbs (1972:58–79) for a discussion of "dissensus" revolving around the criteria for assessing sociological theory.

7. See Popper (1965).

8. See Gibbs (1989). The criteria for assessing the production and presentation of empirical research is a related matter of crucial concern, but one that is beyond the scope of a book on theory.

9. Issues surrounding "causation," "correlation," and "probabilistic explanation" are key topics related to empirical validity, but are beyond the scope of our book. Kaplan (1964) offers a classic treatment of these issues. For a more contemporary treatment see Pearl (2000).

10. For examples of general social learning theories see Bandura (1969) and Skinner (1953).

11. For an example of this position see Gibbs (1989:188–90).

12. This grounding principle stems form the pioneering work of Cohen and Felson (1979).

13. See Birkbeck and LaFree (1993).

14. See Durkheim ([1895] 1938).

15. For example, see Clarke (1980), Cohen and Cantor (1981), Cohen and Felson (1979), Cohen, Kluegel, and Land (1981), Cook (1986), Cornish and Clarke (1986), Felson and Cohen (1980, 1981), Hindelang, Gottfredson, and Garofalo (1978).

16. For example, see Birkbeck and LaFree (1993), Cohen and Land (1987), Miethe and Meier (1990, 1994), Wilcox Rountree (1994), Wilcox Rountree, Land, and Miethe (1994).

2

Criminal Opportunity

A Necessary Condition and Central Construct

Why *opportunity?* We have thus far suggested that theory development is a useful and desirable enterprise—it is worth the bother. However, why single out opportunity as the conceptual cornerstone of a multicontextual theory of crime? After all, many concepts could be said to be primary causes of crime. While it may be understandable that a desire for parsimony leads to the identification of a core explanatory factor, it is not transparent as to why opportunity would be selected over all other competitors.

One reason we focus on opportunity is because it is assumed by all theories to be a necessary (if not sufficient) condition of crime. Even though it is widely assumed to be an essential component of any explanation of crime, criminal opportunity is typically left unspecified. The concept of criminal opportunity functions as a deus ex machina; that is, crime is said to spring forth from opportunity (among other things) but systematic conceptualizations and theorizing about opportunity as such are largely absent. Given that opportunity is an assumed necessary condition for crime, and given that it is a theoretical black box in that the details of its inner workings are unspecified and unexamined, it seems reasonable to advance a conceptual framework that takes criminal opportunity as its central focus.

While the concept of criminal opportunity has largely been undertheorized, two broad theoretical traditions have explored some of the inner workings of criminal opportunity—routine activities and social control–disorganization theories. The purpose of this chapter is to discuss these two broad traditions to reveal the theoretical origins and foundations upon which we build our criminal opportunity theory. In so doing, we are able to identify criminal opportunity theory's basic assumptions, concepts, and propositions. In addition to considering the history and

21

basic contours of criminal opportunity theory, we identify areas that have
been undeveloped or underdeveloped, suggesting how our modified
approach can address those neglected concerns.

THE ORIGINS AND FOUNDATIONS OF CRIMINAL
OPPORTUNITY THEORY

The origins and foundations of criminal opportunity theory can be traced
to the birth of criminology in the eighteenth century. While it would be
possible to offer a detailed exegesis that documents the continual development of criminal opportunity from the eighteenth century to present,
we choose instead to focus on twentieth-century influences primarily. Our
sketch of criminal opportunity theory therefore focuses on two major
influences: routine activities and social control–disorganization theories.[1]
It is certainly true that routine activities and social control–disorganization
perspectives could be seen as *competing* approaches, rather than mere complementary variants within the same theoretical tradition. Indeed, within
the routine activities tradition itself, there are variations that suggest
incompatibility. However, we believe that criminal opportunity theory is
strengthened by considering simultaneously routine activities theory,
microlevel control theories, and the ecological orientation found in the
control variant of social disorganization theory. In the next chapter, we
argue that the apparent contradictions between and within the two traditions can be reconciled and integrated into a logically consistent, multicontextual criminal opportunity theory. Here, we review both traditions
because both are indispensable for our development of a criminal opportunity theory that is centered around the individual-environment-
temporal nexus.

The Routine Activities Tradition

The routine activities perspective does not focus on the emergence of
asocial tendencies in the *criminal*. Instead, the routine activities approach
stems from rational choice assumptions and emphasizes the circumstances under which *crime* is most likely. Criminal inclinations are taken as
given, and the theory instead focuses on the way in which the circumstances surrounding a criminal event are nonrandomly, socially structured.[3] In doing so, it stresses the interdependence between the activities
and behavior patterns of victims and the decisions and behaviors of
offenders.[4] By focusing on the circumstances of crime, routine activities
theory is well positioned to stress the complementary, symbiotic relationship between criminal offending and victimization experiences.[5] The
routine activities perspective is depicted in Figure 2.1, which illustrates

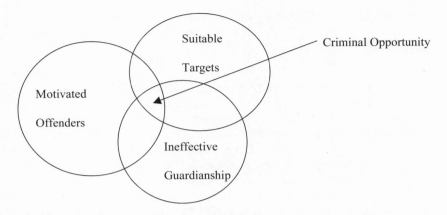

Figure 2.1.   Criminal opportunity according to routine activities theory.

that criminal opportunity exists in the intersection of motivated offenders, suitable targets, and ineffective guardianship.

Discussing the development of routine activities theory reveals both micro- and macrostrains of this perspective. A useful starting point for a discussion of routine activities theory is Hindelang, Gottfredson, and Garofalo's (1978) *Victims of Personal Crime*. Hindelang et al. were the first to propose the idea that victimization likelihood is a function of lifestyle characteristics. More specifically, their lifestyle exposure model suggests that there are strong sociodemographic correlates (e.g., age, race, sex, income, marital status) with victimization because they serve as indicators of lifestyles that expose one to crime. Hindelang et al. define lifestyle as "routine daily activities, both vocational activities (work, school, keeping house, etc.) and leisure activities" (ibid.:241). From this perspective, lifestyle variations "are important because they are related to the differential exposure to dangerous places, times, and others—i.e., situations in which there are high risks of victimization" (Miethe and Meier 1994:32). Miethe and Meier provide a succinct description of the lifestyle argument:

> Differences in lifestyles are socially determined by individuals' collective responses or adaptations to various role expectations and structural constraints. Under this theoretical model, both ascribed and achieved social characteristics (e.g., age, gender, race, income, marital status, education, occupation) are important correlates of predatory crime because these status attributes carry with them shared expectations about appropriate behavior and structural obstacles that both enable and constrain one's behavioral choices. Adherence to these cultural and structural expectations leads to the establishment of routine activity patterns and associations with others

similarly situated. These lifestyles and associations are expected to enhance one's exposure to risky or vulnerable situations that, in turn, increases an individual's chances of victimization. (ibid.)

In essence, Hindelang et al. (1978) represents a microlevel routine activities perspective that explains victimization at the individual level. In fact, most of the tests of routine activities theories have been examinations of this sort of microlevel choice approach. One could even argue that micro–routine activities theory has accounted for much of the explosion in studies of victimization occurring within the past several decades. Micro–routine activities theory's explicit inclusion of the pertinent role of the victim makes it a natural fit for those interested in understanding crime from the standpoint of victimization. In a microlevel application of routine activities theory, *individual* risk factors—including exposure to motivated offenders, proximity to offenders, guardianship of property, and level of target attractiveness—are integral in determining whether or not a *victimization* is likely.[6] These individual risk factors—presumed to be indicated by activities of daily living or lifestyle choices—affect one's likelihood of becoming a victim either by providing or inhibiting criminal opportunity in the form of the likely convergence in time and space of an offender and an unguarded and otherwise suitable target. Thus, though the focus of the micro–routine activities perspective is the act of crime or victimization, behavioral properties of individuals involved in this act (i.e., the victim, third parties) are integral in understanding the dynamics behind a successful criminal/victimization event.

Although the impetus for the development of a lifestyle perspective on victimization can be credited to the pioneering work of Hindelang et al. (1978), Cohen, Felson, Land, Cook, Miethe, and others have been largely responsible for refining such propositions into an explicitly sound, testable routine activities theory. To elaborate, Cohen and Felson (1979) construct an ecological interdependence model that sees individuals acting within particular spatial and temporal contexts. From Cohen and Felson's ecological interdependence perspective, routine activities are "any recurrent and prevalent activities which provide for basic population and individual needs" (ibid.:593). Routine activities encompass work and leisure, and "population and individual needs" include "food, shelter, and other basic needs or desires (e.g., companionship, sexual expression)" (Miethe and Meier 1994:36). Borrowing from Hawley's (1950) human ecology theory, Cohen and Felson (1979:590) see human beings situated in an ecological niche in which macropatterns of routine activities can be characterized by rhythm ("the regular periodicity with which events occur, as with the rhythm of travel"), tempo ("the number of events per unit of time, such the number of criminal violations per day on a given street"), and timing ("the coordination among different activities which are more or less interdependent, such as the coordination of an offender's rhythms with those of a victim").[7] Structural changes in routine activity patterns impact the convergence in time and space of motivated offenders, suitable targets, and capable guardians, which, in turn, influence crime rates. In other words, social changes in societal patterns of conventional routine activities impact criminal opportunity, which then affects the likelihood that criminal acts will occur. Cohen and Felson (1979) maintain that given offender motivation, routine activities that lead to the space-time convergence of suitable targets and the absence of capable guardians will result in increased crime rates.

Figures 2.2 and 2.3 illustrate several scenarios in which criminal opportunity is produced through this space-time convergence of motivated offenders, suitable targets, and ineffective guardianship. It is clear from these figures not only that criminal opportunity is a function of the amount of convergence (overlap) between a supply of motivated offenders, suitable targets, and ineffective guardianship, but it is important to recognize that the overlap itself is sometimes a function of the actual amount or supply of offenders, suitable targets, and ineffective guardianship. For instance, Figure 2.2 depicts a situation in which the amount of criminal opportunity varies across time 1, time 2, and time 3 as a function of the degree of overlap (in time and space) between motivated offenders, suitable targets, and ineffective guardianship. While the supply of each of the three elements of criminal opportunity is constant at all three time points, time 1 clearly provides the most criminal opportunity of the three scenarios, since the overlap in time and space is greatest. At time 2 there is substantially less convergence, and at time 3 there is no convergence of all three elements. In Figure 2.3, the convergence (in terms of size of overlap) is shown to be partly a function of the potentially changing size of the supply of motivated offenders, suitable targets, and ineffective guardianship.

Borrowing from both Hindelang et al. (1978) and Cohen and Felson (1979), Cohen, Kluegel, and Land (1981) incorporate individual-level lifestyle risk factors with a routine activities emphasis on the convergence of motivated offenders, suitable targets, and ineffective guardianship. Their resulting exegesis represents a significant step toward a criminal opportunity perspective of crime *and* victimization at the microlevel in particular. Specifically, Cohen et al. offer these foundational hypotheses:

1. All else being equal, the more one is exposed to motivated offenders (e.g., the more time one spends outside the home or participating in dangerous activities), the greater is the likelihood for crime/victimization.

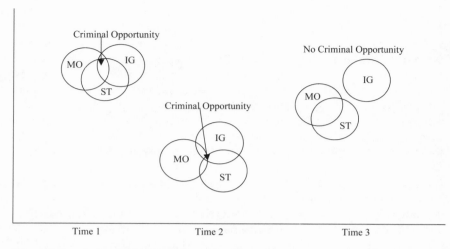

Figure 2.2.   A dynamic view of criminal opportunity.

2. All else being equal, the closer one is (in proximity) to areas with
   high rates of offending, the greater the likelihood for crime/victim-
   ization.
3. All else being equal, the less guarded (e.g., nobody home, no alarms,
   no neighborhood watch, no dog, living alone) a target for crime, the
   greater is the likelihood that crime will be committed against that
   target.
4. All else being equal, the more attractive (i.e., valuable) a target, the
   greater is the likelihood that a crime will be committed against that
   target.

When considered together, micro-[8] and macrolevel routine activities
approaches[9] provide a foundation for developing a multilevel theory of
criminal opportunity that incorporates both individual and ecological factors and that is capable of explaining both offending and victimization. We
use these different strains of routine activities theory as foundations in our
theoretical integration. We use them both in conjunction with several social
control-disorganization models—the component to which we now turn.

The Social Control-Disorganization Tradition

Considered in a very broad sense, the social control perspective in criminology views crime as a result of the exertion of inadequate control on the
part of one or more of various social institutions, including but not exclusive to family, school, community, and the criminal justice system. We

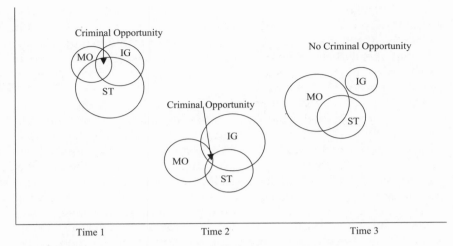

Figure 2.3. Another dynamic view of criminal opportunity.

view both formal and informal controls from both individual and environmental levels of analysis as important in defining criminal opportunity. Hence, our multilevel criminal opportunity theory draws upon a variety of control theories, including social bonding, social disorganization, and deterrence theories.

Social Bonding Theory. From a microlevel informal social-control perspective, Hirschi's (1969) ideas regarding social bonding are important. In his exposition of one of the most widely tested theories in criminology, Hirschi posited that delinquency resulted from the absence of a strong social bond. According to Hirschi, an effective social bond consists of four elements: attachment, commitment, involvement, and belief. Attachment refers to the affective ties between individuals and their significant others. Persons with strong attachment are concerned about the thoughts, feelings, and reactions of these significant others. This concern creates a stake in conformity; attached individuals do not want to disappoint those about whom they care. Commitment refers to the adherence to conventional, age-appropriate "ideals." Social norms dictate that school-age children should adhere to the goal of finishing high school and going to college; children with commitment aspire to do these things. Social norms dictate that young adults should strive to get a well-paying job and get married; adults who are committed share these aspirations. Commitment also provides a stake in conformity and thus enhances social control. Strongly bonded individuals do not want to jeopardize their ability to meet these aspirations. Involvement refers to the level of participation in conventional activities, such as

homework, school clubs, and athletics. It is the behavioral flip side of cog-
nitively based commitment. Hirschi assumed that greater involvement in
conventional activities created less time for nonconventional or criminal
activities. Finally, belief refers to the acceptance of the value and validity of
societal rules. If one believes the rules are "right," a stake in conformity is
again established.

Though there is conceptual overlap in Hirschi's concepts, causing
researchers to use similar measures to operationalize different concepts,
there is fairly consistent evidence in the empirical literature that a strong
social bond—especially regarding ties to family and school—does serve to
inhibit a variety of crimes.[10] Again, the theory is rooted in the idea that
individual-level informal social controls help identify the costs versus the
benefits of crime. It is compatible with other theories that emphasize crime
costs in the form of controls, including a social disorganization theory
emphasizing macrolevel informal social controls and a deterrence theory
emphasizing formal social controls. It is to these additional control theories that we now turn.

Social Disorganization Theory. The relationships between ecologically
based informal control factors and crime are systematically explored by
social disorganization theory, developed from the Chicago studies done in
the early part of the twentieth century.[11] Rooted firmly in the urban ecology
tradition, they provide a macrosociological or community-level model that
focuses on the characteristics of aggregates that lead to increased likelihood
of criminal acts. Shaw and McKay (1942) found that crime rates were differentially distributed across the city in a nonrandom fashion. The communities closest to the city's center were those where crime was most
pervasive. These neighborhoods were areas in transition, characterized by
aggregate-level low socioeconomic status, high ethnic/racial heterogeneity, and high residential mobility. Despite population succession, these
areas continually had the highest rates of crime in the city. From this finding, Shaw and McKay concluded that these elevated levels of crime were
not a function of the personal characteristics of the groups inhabiting the
communities. Rather, they posited that the structural factors of poverty,
high heterogeneity, and high mobility created "social disorganization,"
and it was community-level social disorganization that was presumed to
cause crime.[12]

As depicted in Figure 2.4a, the social disorganization perspective maintains that ecological characteristics of communities in transition produce
social disorganization, which then gives rise to criminal acts. It should be
noted that we adopt a classification and interpretation of social disorganization theory that entails viewing it as a type of control model—one rooted
in the notion that crime results from insufficient social controls. Kornhauser's (1978) seminal analysis of criminological theory revealed two

Figure 2.4a. Model implied by Shaw and McKay's social disorganization theory.

variants of social disorganization theory—a strain variant and a control variant. Kornhauser argued that "the intervening causes of delinquency are in varying pressures (strains) or varying constraints (controls) resulting from varying degrees of social disorganization" (ibid.:24). She ultimately supports the control conceptualization of social disorganization theory over the strain conceptualization, and we follow this lead in our conceptualization of social disorganization as a control model. Accordingly, as stated by Kornhauser:

> Delinquency is an omnipresent vulnerability, the resort to which is not of frustrated wants but of the ratio of its costs to its benefits. Thus differential vulnerability to delinquency is determined by variation in the strength of social controls, the sum of which account for the net costs of delinquency. (ibid.)

So, much like bonding theory, crime costs in the form of social controls are emphasized. Here, however, the controls are not in the forms of individual-level social bonds, but rather community-level ties. Weakened community-level attachment, commitment, involvement, and belief is analogous to social disorganization. A community in a state of social disorganization cannot establish or maintain consensus concerning values, norms, roles, or hierarchical arrangements among its members.[13] Such a community lacks the Durkheimian ([1893] 1964) notions of cohesiveness and social solidarity, and it can neither provide a sense of belonging nor easily achieve community goals.[14] With no realization of common values, informal social control is inoperative and opportunities for crime flourish.[15] While Shaw and McKay never actually measured social disorganization—the inability of a community to organize around common norms, achieve goals, and effectively control members—they assumed that the relationships between high crime and structural indicators such as ethnic/racial heterogeneity, residential mobility, and low SES resulted from that unmeasured concept.

During the second half of the twentieth century, criminologists began to dismiss general macrosociological approaches, including social disorganization theory specifically, in favor of social-psychological or individual-level explanations of criminal motivation and behavior. Such a disciplinary

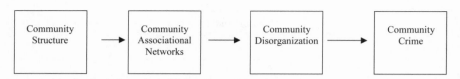

Figure 2.4b. Social disorganization theory based upon the systemic model of community attachment.

environment has generally been unfriendly to the social disorganization perspective, inasmuch as Shaw and McKay's theory resembles a group-level variant of control theory in which criminal motivation is assumed and accounting for conditions in which crime can successfully occur is emphasized.[16] Being group-level *and* amotivational has made the theory doubly unpopular during much of the most recent half-century (1950–2000). However, in the past several decades (since ca. 1980), social disorganization theory has been rejuvenated within the discipline, as scholars revamp Shaw and McKay's ideas in an attempt to compensate for an overemphasis on the individual. The contemporary community-crime models in this tradition have been based on the "systemic model of community attachment" as posited by Kasarda and Janowitz (1974). According to Kasarda and Janowitz, community represents "a complex system of friendship and kinship networks and informal and formal associational ties rooted in family life and ongoing socialization processes" (ibid.:328). This idea of systemic community attachment was very similar to Shaw and McKay's notion of social disorganization. In fact, many contemporary tests of social disorganization theory[17] rely upon the idea of systemic community attachment for operationalizing the process of social (dis)organization. While the idea of social networks is implicit in Shaw and McKay's ideas regarding "social disorganization," the systemic model of community attachment makes this process a more explicit part of the theory. Figure 2.4b shows that the systemic model of social disorganization theory posits that ecological characteristics of communities in transition disrupt community associational networks, thus producing social disorganization, which, in turn, produces criminal acts.

In recent empirical work, researchers have continued to find support for the social ecology of crime argument first put forth by Shaw and McKay and have extended its explanatory coverage in applying the theory to victimization risk as well. Since social disorganization theory focuses on the environmental or structural conditions necessary for criminal acts to occur—not necessarily for criminality to develop within individuals—this perspective is ideal for appropriately accounting for both crime and victimization, as both of these experiences are components of the same event. Further, social disorganization theory successfully explains crime rates and victimization risks associated with a diverse range of criminal acts—not just the officially recorded juvenile delinquency to which Shaw and McKay referred. Both instrumental and expressive acts—both property and violent events—which have a widespread impact upon the community as a whole, are suited for a social disorganization explanation. Bursik (1988), for instance, sees few exceptions to the breadth of crime falling within social disorganization theory's scope, arguing that inapplicability might only characterize crimes for which there is a low degree of community consensus regarding morality/immorality—such as petty crimes—and crimes for which there is no *general* threat involved—such as white-collar crime. In addition to an emphasis on the physical characteristics of environments (e.g., population density), it should be noted that this view incorporates a temporal dimension by suggesting that rapid social change (e.g., population mobility) is indicative of social disorganization. It should also be noted that this theory argues that social disorganization inhibits informal social control (i.e., guardianship) and thereby provides opportunities for criminal acts.

Deterrence Theory. In his seminal work, Gibbs (1975:2) defines deterrence as "the omission of an act as a response to the perceived risk and fear of punishment for contrary behavior." So, much like social bonding theory and the control variant of social disorganization theory, deterrence theory rests on the premise that crime occurs when it is not controlled—when the stake in conformity is diminished. But, deterrence theory deemphasizes informal social control exerted by institutions such as family, school, and community. Instead, it tends to emphasize the control exerted by formal agents, or those associated with the legal/criminal justice system. According to deterrence theory, social control occurs when formal punishments are perceived/feared to be certain, severe, and swift. It is assumed that certain, severe, and swift punishments will serve to both diminish future crime among those experiencing punishment (specific deterrence) and prevent potential offenders throughout society, who presumably are knowledgeable of the costs of crime, from engaging in criminal acts (general deterrence).

Because deterrence theory relies upon the assumption that it is perceived punishment that is important, skepticism surrounds earlier research[18] focusing on aggregate-level objective measures of certainty (e.g., arrest or clearance rates) and severity of punishment (e.g., time served, presence of the death penalty), including policy impact studies.[19] The aggregate-level studies have produced very mixed results and have introduced important methodological limitations surrounding aggregation bias and temporal ordering.[20] More recently, time series studies (e.g., ARIMA models) of aggregate patterns of control and crime have attempted to refine tests of deterrence theory. These also yield mixed results, though most fail to support the deterrence argument.[21]

Perhaps more consistent with the theory are more explicit measures of *perceived* certainty, severity, and celerity of punishment. Studies utilizing survey-based perceptual measures have, over the past several decades, also yielded mixed results.[22] A thorough recounting of this rather voluminous literature is beyond the scope of this book. In general, we offer that while some perceptual research supports the notion that perceived certainty of punishment, in particular, is important in deterring crime, other research suggests that it is the threat of informal sanctions that deters.[23] However, criticism surrounds the notion of incorporating informal sanctions (e.g., embarrassment, loss of relationships) into the study of deterrence. This criticism suggests that original formulations of deterrence theory clearly focus on the effects of formal sanctions, and therefore interest in informal sanctions represents entry into different theoretical territory.[24] As an alternative to incorporating informal controls into deterrence theory, we offer an integrative perspective that allows social controls of a variety of sorts—formal and informal, and from different levels of analysis—to serve as indicators of guardianship and thus be used in conjunction with routine activities theory in a more general, multicontextual criminal opportunity theory.

While the general criminal opportunity theory offered here tends to emphasize informal controls in the emergence of criminal opportunity contexts, we do not dismiss altogether the potential role of certain forms of formal social control, such as police surveillance. In fact, we suggest that the similar orientations of each of these strains of social control theory (deterrence, bonding, and disorganization) allow them to be used together, and used in conjunction with routine activities theory, in establishing a more comprehensive conceptualization of criminal opportunity.[25] Further, we propose to use this revised conceptualization to explain not only criminal offending, but victimization, and "responses" to crime including risk perception, fear, and constrained behavior. Some very recent work hints at these integrative and extension possibilities. There have been recent lines of inquiry that have served to extend the two traditions of routine activities and social control in new, simultaneous directions. We present two of these recent lines of inquiry here: multilevel opportunity models of crime/victimization and opportunity models of reactions to crime/victimization.

MULTILEVEL OPPORTUNITY MODELS OF CRIME/VICTIMIZATION

Recent studies of criminal victimization have moved away from an exclusive focus on *either* micro- *or* macrolevel processes. Instead, rooted in the routine activities and social control-disorganization theoretical traditions, multilevel studies have emerged that incorporate *both* micro- *and* macrolevel factors. More specifically, these multilevel analyses integrate individual- and neighborhood-level variables within traditional linear or logistic regression models to examine the effects criminal opportunity and informal community control have on crime and victimization. Furthermore, studies have begun to examine the simultaneous effects of "opportunity"—conceptualized as individual exposure and proximity to offenders, target vulnerability, and diminished guardianship—and criminogenic ecological context—conceptualized as weakened informal social control, or more recently, diminished "collective efficacy."[26]

For instance, in a study of individuals and households within 238 neighborhoods (electoral wards) in England and Wales, Sampson and Wooldredge (1987) found individual-level activity patterns, especially those related to exposure and guardianship (e.g., living alone and frequency with which one "goes out" or leaves a home unoccupied), to be important determinants of burglary victimization risk. However, aggregate characteristics of the British neighborhoods-percentage of single-person households, percentage of single-parent households, percentage of unemployed, housing density, and social cohesion—were also directly related to burglary victimization risk.

In their study of fifty-seven U.S. neighborhoods (across Rochester, St. Louis, and Tampa–St. Petersburg), Smith and Jarjoura (1989) also found that household characteristics related to exposure and guardianship *as well as* neighborhood contextual factors such as racial heterogeneity, residential instability, population age structure (percentage aged twelve to twenty), percentage of single-parent households, social integration, and median income affected household burglary victimization.[27]

Similarly, Kennedy and Forde (1990), analyzing data from the Canadian Urban Victimization Survey, found increased exposure and low guardianship to have positive effects on both property and violent victimization. In addition, Kennedy and Forde found that characteristics of the census metropolitan areas (CMAs), such as percent unemployed and percentage of families with low incomes, were consistent determinants of victimization across many offense categories. With respect to breaking and entering victimization specifically, Kennedy and Forde found that lifestyle characteristics such as the frequency with which one went walking or driving at night or the frequency with which one attended bars, sporting events, movies, work, or class—all suggestive of diminished guardianship and/or heightened exposure—increased victimization risk. In addition, community-level unemployment—thought to increase neighborhood guardianship—decreased breaking and entering victimization, while percentage of low-income families (an indicator of proximity) increased risk.

Fisher, Sloan, Cullen, and Lu's (1998) study of victimization among over three thousand college students across twelve different institutions incorporated individual-level, institution-level, and census tract–level measures of exposure, proximity, target attractiveness, and guardianship into logistic regression models of both theft and violent victimization. Most of the significant effects in their models were at the individual-level. Fisher et al. state:

> Contextual variables suggested by the lifestyle-routine activities approach, however, had only limited effects in predicting property victimization—a finding that was obtained for violent victimization as well. None of these factors was related to violent victimization and only two were related to property victimization. (ibid.:700)

Nonetheless, Fisher et al. speculate that a larger sample of institutions might have revealed greater contextual variation. Another explanation offered for the weak contextual effects—especially at the census tract level—is that college campuses may indeed be "ivory towers" impervious to the effects of the broader social context in which they are situated.

Thompson and Fisher (1996) examined individual- and community-level influences on household larceny. Their findings suggest higher risks for households with children, households in nonurban areas, households with shorter tenure within a neighborhood, and households with low informal social control in terms of neighborly surveillance.

Miethe and McDowall (1993) extended the contextual study of victimization by examining micro-macro interactions. In their study of residents in three hundred Seattle neighborhoods, Miethe and McDowall found target attractiveness (e.g., owning expensive, portable goods) and guardianship measures (e.g., living alone and taking safety precautions) to have neighborhood-specific effects. These routine activity risk factors were weak predictors of burglary victimization risk in socially disorganized areas. Yet, within neighborhoods with high-SES, less mobile populations, these same factors were key predictors.[28]

While the contextual studies reviewed above have advanced knowledge in terms of delineating the mutual effects of micro- and macro-processes as well as the embeddedness of individual-level effects within community-level dynamics, the hierarchical nature of the multilevel data under study—with individuals clustered nonrandomly into neighborhoods—calls for nontraditional modeling methods that would avoid the violation of important assumptions of traditional regression procedures (e.g., assumptions related to independence of errors). To address this issue, Wilcox Rountree et al. (1994) integrated individual-level routine activity variables and neighborhood-level social disorganization variables into hierarchical logistic regression models of violent and property (burglary) victimization using the same Seattle data analyzed by Miethe and McDowall (1993). More complex contextual findings were portrayed in such hierarchical models. For instance, using traditional logistic regression methods, Miethe and McDowall concluded that the likelihood of violent-crime victimization did not vary significantly across Seattle neighborhoods. Further, these researchers found no evidence of variation in the predictors of violent victimization across neighborhood contexts. However, the Wilcox Rountree et al. (1994) study revealed that risk for violent victimization, in fact, differed significantly across Seattle neighborhoods. In addition, the effects that individuals' race and protective behavior had on violent victimization were conditional upon neighborhood context. Key community characteristics that accounted for the variable effects included neighborhood incivility, neighborhood density or traffic, and neighborhood-level ethnic heterogeneity. Similarly, in comparison to Miethe and McDowall (1993), the Wilcox Rountree et al. (1994) study revealed more dramatic contextual effects for ethnic heterogeneity and community incivility on variability of burglary victimization across neighborhood units.

Sampson, Raudenbush, and Earls (1997) also integrate individual and community characteristics within hierarchical models in their study of violent crime across 343 Chicago neighborhoods. Using reports of violent victimization as one measure of violence, Sampson et al. found community-level collective efficacy to decrease violent victimization risk, controlling for individual-level risk factors. In addition, collective efficacy mediated much of the effects of structural disadvantage and residential stability, though immigrant concentration remained a significant (positive) predictor of violent victimization risk while controlling for collective efficacy as well as individual-level risk factors. Sampson et al. did not estimate these models with respect to burglary victimization.

Finally, in one of the only studies to date to examine the question of generalizability in multilevel models of victimizations, Wilcox Rountree and Land (2000) compare such models across Rochester, St. Louis, and Tampa–St. Petersburg. Wilcox Rountree and Land (2000) conclude that their findings make a case for the generalizability of opportunity-based multilevel victimization models, as they found substantial consistency across the three cities studied. For instance, mean burglary victimization risk varied significantly across neighborhoods in all cities examined, while the individual-level, opportunity-related covariates of victimization (e.g., family income, living alone) did not vary in their effects across neighborhood or city contexts. Second, much of the variability in burglary victimization risk across neighborhoods was accounted for by the inclusion of neighborhood-level covariates, including average income, ethnic heterogeneity, residential mobility, and social ties.

OPPORTUNITY MODELS OF REACTIONS TO
CRIME/VICTIMIZATION

Further developments in opportunity theory have extended social control-disorganization and routine activities theories to explanations of *reactions* to crime as opposed to crime and/or victimization per se. In his 1986 article, "The Demand and Supply of Criminal Opportunities," Philip Cook delineates a limitation of extant routine activities models such as those used in the research reviewed above. According to Cook, "one important element that is lacking from the life-style model is a 'feedback loop' by which the individual's exposure to risky circumstances is influenced by his concern with being victimized" (ibid.:6). Such a view is built around the assumption that individuals choose their routine activities rationally—they are neither socially constrained nor circumstantial phenomena (ibid.). Thus, individuals base their choice of activities on their perceptions regarding threat of criminal victimization. Furthermore, this perception of threat is rationally conceived on the part of an individual based upon such things as vulnerability and perceived risk, perceived seriousness, actual incidence of victimization, or neighborhood/city conditions.[29] Therefore, if individuals perceive themselves to be vulnerable targets (physically, emotionally, economically, etc.), or if they have been victimized previously or reside in socially disorganized neighborhoods, they will probably engage in compensatory self-protection efforts, thus influencing routine activities.

Liska and colleagues addressed certain aspects of Cook's "feedback loop" in research examining the effects of fear of crime and routine activities.[30] In particular, Liska et al. (1988) demonstrated reciprocity between fear of crime and constrained behavior. They found that fear of crime constrained social behavior in the sense that fearful individuals engaged in fewer activities outside the home or more frequently changed activities because of crime. Liska et al. (1988) also found that constrained social activities increased fear of crime. Later, Liska and Warner (1991) modeled the relationship between fear of crime, routine activities (constrained behavior), and crime across cities using nonrecursive structural equation systems. Their findings indicate that a "feedback loop" is evident; while urban crime rates affected routine activities by constraining behavior through fear, the constrained activities, in turn, influenced subsequent crime/victimization rates (decreasing them), presumably by limiting criminal opportunities. Such findings suggest that opportunity not only affects crime but reactions to crime (such as fear), and these reactions can, in turn, affect subsequent activities and future crime.

Social disorganization theory in the control tradition has also been extended into the literature on reactions to crime. While some "fear of crime" and "risk perception" studies focus on aspects of the social context such as novelty versus familiarity, darkness versus daytime, and being alone versus bystander density,[31] other studies have used structural indicators resembling more closely the social disorganization tradition. In their seminal works, Skogan and Maxfield (1981) and Skogan (1990) test models in which social integration, neighborhood-level crime, and community disorder (boisterousness, drunkenness, untidiness, etc.) are thought to affect levels of fear, and they find that such structural covariates are indeed important in predicting anxiety about crime. Numerous works by Taylor, Ferraro, and their colleagues also suggest strong effects on fear for perceptions of neighborhood problems, or "disorder."[32] Finally, Lewis and Salem (1986) provide evidence from their aggregate study across ten neighborhoods that fear is more than simply a function of crime/victimization within an area; concern about incivility and available networks of social control (e.g., social integration and organizational strength) are also found to be of importance in understanding community levels of concern about crime. Lewis and Salem point out that "the fact that fear levels exceed those measuring both crime awareness and crime concern might be due in most neighborhoods to the compounding effect of the other incivility concerns" (1986:76). So, more general problems of disorder or disorganization which are perhaps perceived by many to be indicative or symbolic of "more trouble to come" (i.e., in the form of crime) increase fear among respondents in studies that include such measures. These findings seem to be consistent with James Q. Wilson and George Kelling's ideas regarding "broken windows":

> But the link between order-maintenance and crime-prevention, so obvious to earlier generations, was forgotten. That link is similar to the process whereby one broken window becomes many. The citizen who fears the ill-smelling drunk, the rowdy teenager, or the importuning beggar is not merely expressing his distaste for unseemly behavior, he is also giving voice to a bit of folk wisdom that happens to be a correct generalization—namely, that serious street crime flourishes in areas in which disorderly behavior goes unchecked. (1982:34)

Disorder and incivilities within an area, then, serve to indicate inadequate social control, and the idea is that if a community can not control the sobriety of its members, the tranquility and tidiness of its streets, etc., it is inevitable that it will also be unable to control crime. The limited research done on disorder seems to support the notion that residents of disorderly communities do correctly perceive the relationship between incivility and crime—neighborhood disorder is a significant predictor of anxiety about victimization. Such findings also support the idea originally conceived by Garofalo and Laub (1979)—that "fear of crime" may be more than "fear" of "crime." Rather, "fear of crime" may represent a more general concern about problems within a community—problems that perhaps often accompany crime-ridden areas and are thus perceived of in a manner similar to crime. In fact, Garofalo and Laub suggest that "fear of crime" may really refer to "urban unease." Thus when people say that they are fearful of crime, they may not only be concerned about crime itself, but also about the contextual conditions conducive to crime.

Beyond the focus on community disorder, other studies of risk perception and fear of crime have suggested that additional contextual variables related to "social disorganization" are important, including population density, poverty, and proportion nonwhite.[33] These studies, which incorporate contextual variables to account for variations in levels of fear, have added substantially to our understanding of this phenomenon. These research findings have forced us to recognize factors that affect fear beyond the psychological level. Further, these studies have expanded the usefulness of social control-disorganization theory, implying that indicators of social disorganization at the aggregate level not only serve to increase crime and victimization in an area, but also to heighten concern over crime.

Recent multilevel work addresses the link between routine activities, structural conditions, victimization, and reactions to crime.[34] Wilcox Rountree and Land's (1996a) secondary analysis of Miethe's (1992) Seattle-based survey data suggest that individual-level routine activities and indicators of ambient disorganization not only affect victimization, but also have direct effects on perception of risk, which, in turn, affects subsequent individual-level precautionary measures. Their subsequent work has attempted to disentangle the effects of routine activities on different types of reactions to crime/victimization, including cognitive risk perception and crime-specific emotionally based "fear." For instance, Wilcox Rountree and Land (1996b) found that indicators of exposure, target attractiveness, and guardianship—including ownership of portable household goods, safety precautions, guardianship barriers on property, access routes to house, and having a corner residence—increased worry (fear) of burglary; similar but fewer effects were found with respect to general, cognitive risk perception. In terms of environmental influences, Wilcox Rountree and Land (1996b) found that incivilities heightened both risk perception and fear of crime. Social integration also increased fear of burglary, but it had a negative effect on crime risk perception.

Though risk perception, as opposed to fear, is thought to be the more rationally driven reaction to crime, the findings of Wilcox Rountree and Land (1996b) suggest that even emotionally based "fears" are often rationally situated within contexts of perceived criminal opportunity. Wilcox Rountree (1998) extended these findings in showing that different crime-specific fears (including fear of burglary and fear of violence) are influenced by criminal-opportunity-related risk factors at both individual and neighborhood levels, even controlling for previous victimization and perceived risk. Ferraro's (1995) analysis of data from the Fear of Crime in America Survey also shows lifestyle/routine activities characteristics to affect cognitive risk perception, and, in turn, fear of both property and violent victimization and subsequent activities (constrained behavior).

In sum, extant contextual crime and victimization research has found significant direct effects of both individual- and neighborhood-level indicators of criminal opportunity and social control. The more recent studies have shown further that these two types of indicators interact in determining victimization risk, such that neighborhood factors condition or contextualize the effects of individual-level criminal opportunity.[35] Finally, recent research has extended routine activities theory and social control-disorganization theory such that micro- and macroindicators of criminal opportunity are presumed to structure more than just crime/victimization; they can also structure reactions to crime/victimization.

The new developments discussed above—including multilevel work and extensions to reactions to crime/victimization—have typically been rather piecemeal. The evolutionary ecological theory of expropriative crime proposed by Cohen and Machalek (1988) and extended by Vila and Cohen (1993) perhaps comes closest to a more holistic synthesis. The causal model outlined by this perspective (Cohen and Machalek 1988:494) is shown in Figure 2.5. As suggested by Figure 2.5, this perspective posits that selection of alternative behavioral strategies—including production and expropriation—is largely a function of resource holding potential (the whole set of characteristics pertinent to a particular contest), the value placed upon a contested resource, and opportunities for expropriation. Furthermore, these three key variables are all affected by more exogenous biological, psychosocial, and environmental factors, including—as just a few examples—sex, IQ, cognition, and culture. Finally, a key component of the evolutionary ecological approach is that strategy selections (e.g., production versus expropriation) are largely interdependent. For instance, expropriative crime is often countered with target-hardening or victim-resistance strategies, which lead to further evolution in expropriative strategies, and so on. As pointed out by Vila and Cohen, this dynamic approach "allows them to explain how strategies can influence their own proliferation" (1993:874).

This evolutionary ecological approach has several obvious strengths. First, it is explicitly multicontextual. It recognizes that factors from a variety of domains—e.g., constitutional factors, social-psychological states, and individual and group-level behaviors—affect expropriative crime. As such, it is able to synthesize into one model a multitude of variables from

40

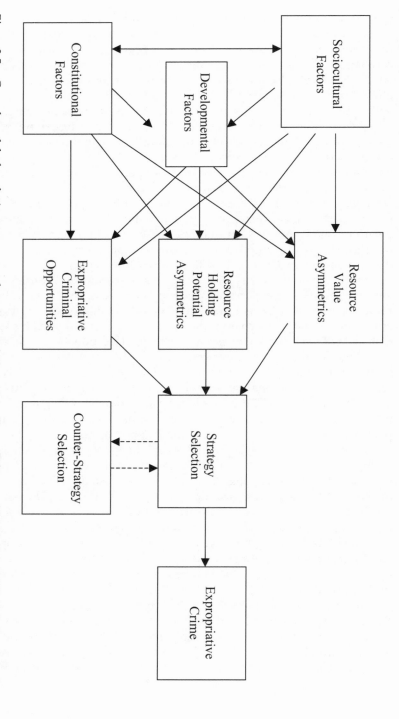

Figure 2.5. Causal model of evolutionary approach to expropriative crime. From Cohen and Machalek (1988:494). Reprinted with permission.

a range of extant criminological theories. Second, it clearly has a dynamic element, with its recognition that changes in expropriative crime occur in reaction to counterstrategies. Thus, societal reactions to crime—including risk perception, fear, and fear-related precautionary behavior—play an important role in explaining the evolution of expropriate crime.

Despite its appeal, this approach also has limitations. While the theory makes great headway in terms of synthesizing current explanations of crime, it is still not as parsimonious as it could be. For instance, as suggested by Figure 2.5, the theory's conceptual model distinguishes "criminal opportunities" as a construct distinct from the exogenous constitutional, developmental, and sociocultural factors as well as resource value and resource holding potential. Our theory, as summarized in Chapter 3 and as detailed further in subsequent chapters, suggests that, instead, criminal opportunity can be indicated by each of these additional variables in the evolutionary ecological perspective. Second, the theory is clearly intended for macrolevel analysis, with the explanation of expropriative rates of crime across societies as its key objective. As suggested by Cohen and Machalek (1988:492):

> It is useful to think of populations as composed of various combinations and frequencies of strategy types, rather than individuals. . . . This better enables us to understand how the properties of a particular strategy influence the probability that it will succeed or fail when pitted against other kinds of strategies in various combinations and proportions. Consequently, we are able to take a step forward specifying the relative advantage of a particular strategy in a given social context, independent of differences among individuals with respect to their ability or propensity to execute this choice. (1988:492)

While cross-context differences in strategy selection are certainly of sociological interest, intracontext individual differences in strategy selection are and will remain of great interest. Perhaps an even more transdisciplinary approach would recognize nonrandom, cross-contextual variation in strategy selection, thus estimating contextual effects, yet also recognizing intracontext, interindividual differences in strategy selection. Such is the concern of our theory, to which we now turn.

NOTES

1. Even though some may contend that aspects of the modern criminal opportunity perspective can be traced to Cloward and Ohlin's (1960) approach, we omit a discussion of this perspective because we believe that their differential opportunity perspective is not compatible with the criminal opportunity tradition upon which we seek to build. Cloward and Ohlin's differential opportunity perspective

represents a "mixed model" in that criminal opportunity (an amotivational component) allows for subcultural value transmission (suggesting motivation). Cohen and Felson maintain that criminal opportunity "differs considerably from the traditional sociological usage of the *differential opportunity* concept" (1979:593). In a footnote Cohen and Felson argue: "Cloward and Ohlin (1960) employed [differential opportunity] in discussing how legitimate and illegitimate opportunities affect the resolution of the adjustment problems leading to gang delinquency. From their view, this resolution depends upon the kind of social support for one or another type of illegitimate activity that is given at different points in the social structure (Cloward and Ohlin 1960:151). Rather than circumstantial determinants of crime, they use differential opportunity to emphasize structural features which motivate offenders to perpetrate certain types of crimes. Cloward and Ohlin are largely silent on the interaction of this motivation with target suitability and guardianship as this interaction influences crime rates" (ibid.).

2. Chapter 3 considers the assumption of motivated offenders in greater detail.

3. See Felson and Cohen (1980).

4. See Cohen and Felson (1979), Cohen and Machalek (1988), Felson and Cohen (1980), and Maxfield (1987a. 1987b).

5. See Cohen and Felson (1979) and Felson and Cohen (1980).

6. See Cohen et al. (1981) and Cook (1986).

7. It is worth emphasizing at this point that Cohen and Felson's (1979) work provides, at least implicitly, the conceptual foundations for a dynamic multicontextual criminal opportunity perspective with its emphasis on individuals acting within spatial and temporal settings. The centrality of the individual-environmental-temporal nexus is suggested in Cohen and Felson's discussion of Hawley's (1950) work: "While criminologists traditionally have concentrated on the *spatial* analysis of crime rates within metropolitan communities, they seldom have considered the *temporal* interdependence of these acts. In his classic theory of human ecology, Amos Hawley (1950) treats the community not simply as a unit of territory but rather as an organization of symbiotic and commensalistic relationships as human activities are performed over both space and time" (ibid.:589).

8. For example, see Hindelang et al. (1978) and Cohen et al. (1981).

9. For example, see Cohen and Felson (1979).

10. See Chapter 4 for a review of some of this literature.

11. See Shaw and McKay (1942).

12. For more contemporary illustrations see Messner and Golden (1992) as well as Shihadeh and Ousey (1996, 1998).

13. See Kornhauser (1978) and Shaw and McKay (1942).

14. For example, see Crutchfield, Geerken, and Gove (1982) as well as McGahey (1986).

15. See Bursik (1986, 1988), Bursik and Webb (1982), Heitgard and Bursik (1987), Kapsis (1978), Lynch and Cantor (1992), Sampson (1987), Sampson and Castellano (1982), Schuerman and Kobrin (1986), Skogan (1990), Warner and Pierce (1993), Warner and Wilcox Rountree (2000), and Wilson (1987, 1996).

16. See Bursik (1988) and Kornhauser (1978).

17. These are reviewed in Chapter 4.

18. See Nagin (1978) for a comprehensive review.

19. See Cook (1980) for an excellent review.

20. For example, see Decker and Kohfield (1985) as well as Greenberg, Kessler, and Logan (1981).

21. For example, see Bailey and Peterson (1990), Bursik, Grasmick, and Chamlin (1990), and Loftin and McDowall (1982).

22. For example, see Klepper and Nagin (1989), Paternoster, Saltzman, Chiricos, and Waldo (1983), and Saltzman, Paternoster, Waldo, and Chiricos (1982).

23. For example, see Williams and Hawkins (1986).

24. See Akers (1997).

25. See Cook (1980).

26. See Sampson et al. (1997).

27. While Smith and Jarjoura (1989) examine a multilevel model of victimization, their focus was to expose the individual and neighborhood influences on victimization, *not* to examine the generalizability of these micro- and macroeffects across the cities in their sample. Therefore, Smith and Jarjoura do not run separate analyses for each city, nor do they control for "city" in their models.

28. Smith, Frazee, and Davison's (2000) recent study is not multilevel (the unit of analysis is the face block only), so it is not reviewed here. Nonetheless, its findings have implications for the integration of routine activities theory and social control-disorganization theory. They found that land use characteristics indicative of exposure and target attractiveness interacted with indicators of social disorganization. As mentioned earlier, the positive effects of motels/hotels and hot spots on street robbery were exacerbated in areas with many single-parent households (presumably indicating weakened informal social control) and tempered in areas with few single-parent households.

29. For example, see Balkin (1979), Bursik and Grasmick (1993), Chiricos, Hogan, and Gertz (1997), Cook (1986), Garofalo (1981), LaGrange, Ferraro, and Supancic (1992), Liska, Lawrence, and Sanchirico (1982), Perkins and Taylor (1996), Skogan and Maxfield (1981), Stafford and Galle (1984), and Warr and Stafford (1983).

30. For example, see Liska et al. (1988) as well as Liska and Warner (1991).

31. See Warr (1990).

32. For example, see Ferraro (1995), LaGrange et al. (1992), Perkins and Taylor (1996), Taylor (2001), Taylor and Covington (1993), as well as Taylor and Hale (1986).

33. For example, see Chiricos et al. (1997), Lee and Ulmer (2000), Liska and Baccaglini (1990), Liska et al. (1982), as well as Taylor and Covington (1993).

34. For example, see Wilcox Rountree and Land (1996a, 1996b), Wilcox Rountree (1998), as well as Ferraro (1995).

35. For example, see Miethe and McDowall (1993) and Wilcox Rountree et al. (1998).

3

A Multicontextual Approach

In this chapter, we outline our dynamic, multicontextual criminal opportunity theory. To move this agenda along, we first discuss the utility of integrating the social control and routine activities perspectives summarized previously into a more general criminal opportunity model. This discussion leads us to consider and take a stance toward the key assumption about the nature of criminal motivations. By clarifying this fundamental assumption, we are then able to identify and define individual- and environmental-level concepts central to our dynamic, multicontextual criminal opportunity perspective. Our intent is to attend to these basic theoretical tasks in order to develop a theory that has enhanced analytical utility and that possesses sound logical consistency. The chapter concludes with a rendering of core propositions for an emerging dynamic, multilevel criminal opportunity theory.

INTEGRATING SOCIAL CONTROL AND ROUTINE
ACTIVITIES THEORIES

As suggested in the previous chapter, the development of routine activities theory has included both a macro and micro focus. The macro concentrates on the space-time production of criminal opportunity that results from broad patterns of routine activities within a society, while the micro fixes its attention on the space-time emergence of criminal opportunity that stems from individual-level routine activities and lifestyle choices. Also, we outlined a control variant of social disorganization theory, with its emphasis on the space-time ecology of groups or aggregate units. In addition, we outlined two additional control theories—social bonding and deterrence—that explain the differential emergence of crime across time and place as a function of formal and informal controls. We believe that these traditions are complementary perspectives that can be

integrated to create a more general and robust criminal opportunity theory. Each of the routine activities and social control approaches focus on
the conditions necessary for an *act* of crime or victimiz
event—to occur. Both of these approaches can be used to
offending and victimization risks. Both of these approach
explain the relationships between criminal acts and react
agree with Sampson and Wooldredge, who argue that:

> the more general opportunity model (Cohen et al. 1981), wh
> lifestyles and routine activities with a more explicit focus on
> imity and macrosociological processes . . . provides the mos
> for future multilevel . . . research. (1987:391)

A necessary step toward bringing these two approach
single theory that is logically consistent is to establish that they are indeed
suitable for theoretical integration.

Theoretical Integration: Definitions and Criteria

Thornberry defines theoretical integration as "the act of combining two
or more sets of logically interrelated propositions into one larger set of
interrelated propositions, in order to provide a more comprehensive
explanation of a particular phenomenon" (1989:52). Liska, Krohn, and
Messner simplify this considerably, saying that "to integrate theories is to
formulate relationships between them" (1989:1). The nonspecificity characterizing these definitions resembles the ambiguity surrounding most
issues pertaining to integration of criminological theory. Albeit general
agreement as to the need to further develop our existing theories exists,
there is an overwhelming lack of consensus regarding what constitutes
"true integration" as opposed to "theoretical elaboration," or even "theoretical imperialism."[1]

Often this conflict revolves around differences of opinion concerning
the theoretical logic of the integration despite empirical viability. In other
words, it is quite conceivable that joining two theories into one model
empirically can yield greater explanatory power. But whether it makes *theoretical sense* to do so is often another matter. Reconciling assumptive differences among constituent theories involved in any integration is a must
according to some criminologists,[2] while others have more relaxed standards and seem mainly interested in the empirical advancements made by
such attempts.[3] So there does seem to be a recognition in criminology that
our conventional theories are rather noncomprehensive—they tend to
focus on one condition or process that underlies crime. Yet not all criminologists are in agreement as to the value of linking elements of existing

theories, especially if the theories to be integrated have different orienting strategies or underlying assumptions regarding human nature and social reality.

Since our efforts revolve fundamentally around theoretical integration, an elaboration of reconciling assumptive differences seems warranted. As mentioned above, some, but certainly not all, criminologists maintain that integrative theories face the danger of inconsistent internal logic stemming from joining contradictory and competing assumptions.[4] Hirschi (1989), the leading proponent of this position, contends that the integrated theory movement[5] represents a mistaken move away from logical consistency as a requisite of adequate theory. For Hirschi, integrated perspectives usually patch together components of two or more theories without regard for the assumptions that ground those theories and hence create frameworks that are conceptually flawed.[6]

Illustrating the possible difficulty facing theory integration, Hirschi states: "If theory A asserts X and theory B asserts not-X, it would seem impossible to bring them together in a way pleasing and satisfactory to both, and also pointless to try" (ibid.:29). To delineate further, if a theorist wants to incorporate aspects of a theory that claims that motivation is a key factor in the etiology of crime with elements from another theory that claims that motivation is irrelevant in the etiology of crime, something needs to be done to remove or reconcile claims that are clearly opposed to one another.

According to Hirschi there are several kinds of maneuvers around this dilemma. One such tactic is to deny that the assumptions are indeed opposed by simply repudiating the oppositional assumption tradition. Hirschi adeptly describes this strategy that allows theorists to claim both X and not-X:

> This seeming paradox [is] resolved by claiming that the competitiveness and incompatibilities of the oppositional tradition do not reside in its theories but in the minds of its theorists. If opposition theorists and researchers could be shown to have logical or conceptual errors, often for the very reason that they were wedded to the idea that theories should compete rather than complement one another, their theories would be freed of their oppositional character, and could then be modified as needed for the purposes of integration. (ibid.:39–49)

Acceptance of this maneuver may justify theoretical integration, but it does not resolve the problem of contradictory arguments that get embedded and often buried in integrative theories.

Another "solution" is to advance the assumptions of one theory and appropriate just the vocabulary from others—"use the terms and ignore the claims," as Hirschi (1979:34) cleverly puts it. This tactic is the least satisfying of them all, because it does not acknowledge or perhaps even fails to recognize that the constituent parts of the integrated theory may be incompatible or may, at the very least, be viewed as incompatible by some scholars.

Yet another "solution" is to use the guiding assumptions of one theory to establish a general rule and then employ other theories with contradictory assumptions to account for empirical anomalies that the principal theory cannot handle. For example, a theorist might contend that crime is realized when that activity is chosen by an individual who has engaged in an objective cost-benefit analysis of the action. Crime is thus an outcome of rational thought. But then how does one account for instances where a rational actor would choose crime but a crime is not committed? Or, how does one account for instances where a rational actor would choose not to commit a crime but one is committed? To address such potential anomalies, a theorist might draw upon explanations that involve affect, beliefs, and/or personality traits. Inasmuch as these additional elements are nonrational, such a maneuver would generate an extremely weak argument: i.e., crime is a product of rational thought except when it is a product of nonrational influences—crime is X except when it is not-X.

Our efforts to offer a dynamic, multicontextual criminal opportunity theory reflect a general agreement with those who argue for the necessity of reconciling competing assumptions. We find it unsatisfactory to argue that crime is X and not X. We believe that it would be unsatisfactory to ignore the possibility that constituent components of our integrated theory might contain contradictory assumptions. However, we disagree with the notion that theoretical integration is not fruitful. Indeed, we believe that a careful integration of social control-disorganization and routine activities theories (one that attends to empirical compatibility as well as the reconciliation of underlying ontological assumptions) will provide an improved conceptual framework with enhanced analytical utility.

Cross-Level Integration

Despite the differing opinions regarding various issues surrounding the integrating of theories, it is generally recognized that within this broad practice fall several different, specific types of theoretical integration. First, one can attempt to integrate one microlevel theory with another microlevel theory. For example, an integrated theory that combines social bonding theory and differential association might be specified.[7] In *Crime and Human Nature,* Wilson and Herrnstein (1985) also attempt a microlevel integration of sorts, meshing ideas from economic theory, or rational choice theory, with elements from biological and psychological theories of

crime. Conversely, one can integrate several competing macrolevel theories, for example conflict theory and social disorganization theory.[8] A final
option in theoretical integration is to integrate across levels of analysis;
that is, melding microlevel theories with macrolevel theories. Some see
this as the most desirable type of theoretical integration.[9] An illustration of
cross-level theoretical integration can be found in some structural-Marxist
approaches that combine macrolevel conflict theory with microlevel elements from learning, labeling, and strain theories.[10]

In examining micro- and macrovariants of both routine activities and
social control theories simultaneously, our present efforts attempt another
cross-level integration, bridging the micro- and aggregate levels of analysis while focusing on the interplay between the individual and his or her
environment. A primary goal of this cross-level integration, then, is to tie
together pieces of two conventional theoretical traditions in criminology
that have traditionally been viewed as "competing theories" in an effort to
provide a broader, more comprehensive perspective than either one of the
traditions can provide alone. Microlevel routine activities theory and
social bonding theory rely predominantly upon individual actions and
choices, while macrostrains of routine activities theory and social control-
disorganization theory primarily emphasize society and community
dynamics. Deterrence theory emphasizes both individual and aggregate-
level effects of formal control. Our attempt to mesh these traditions under
a general criminal opportunity framework is illustrative of cross-level
integration.

Cross-level integration that incorporates elements from theories utilizing different units of analysis can be used to derive contextual-effects
models. Blalock describes research incorporating contextual-effects models as "an effort to explain individual-level dependent variables using
combinations of individual- and group-level independent variables"
(1984:353). The major theme of contextual analysis, then, is that individual
behavior is not solely a function of individual-level attributes. Rather,
broader aggregate, even global characteristics can impact upon individual
outcomes as well. Liska (1990) supports the value of employing contextual
variables to account for variation in individual-level properties (such as
victimization risk) despite the fact that variables describing characteristics
of social units often account for only a small proportion of the total variance regarding the microlevel phenomenon of interest. The idea is that
though these contextual variables explain a small proportion of variation
in any *one* phenomenon, they often do so for a great many individual-level
phenomena; thus their importance in explaining individual behavior, in
general, is quite great. According to Liska, "Durkheim, Weber, and Marx
recognized [this point] clearly, but many contemporary sociologists seem

to have forgotten it" (ibid.:298). Further, Liska emphasizes the essential use of contextual independent variables in linking micro and macro theory and levels of analysis, despite the inability of such variables to explain an overwhelming amount of variance. If we want to know, in an integrative sense, how individual attributes interact with the social setting, we must examine both types of variables together.

The need for contextual analysis is based upon the assumption that individuals are rather naturally clustered into meaningful social groups or macroentities. For example, individuals reside within neighborhoods, neighborhoods are clustered within larger census tracts, numerous census tracts make up a larger city, cities fall into certain states, states are grouped into nations, and so on. The idea is that individual-level behavior can not be taken out of these environmental contexts, because they have a substantial effect on individual characteristics.

Echoing the current surge toward theoretical and methodological integration within criminology[11] and, more generally, within the social science literature,[12] there have been several recent attempts at cross-level integration of routine activities variants and a control variant of social disorganization theory from a contextual point of view.[13] Such efforts recognize the embeddedness of individual activities, behaviors, and outcomes within a broader structural context.[14] As alluded to earlier, these integrative studies have urged the incorporation of both individual-level and community or contextual-level effects into one design. However, heretofore there has not been a systematic and consistent attempt to detail a theory that provides a solid conceptual basis from which to develop core propositions and hypotheses. A necessary step in such an endeavor is a careful consideration of some guiding assumptions.

Assumptions Guiding Contextual, Integrative Analyses

Assumptions regarding integrative, contextual-effects approaches are twofold. First, environmental-level factors, above and beyond individual attributes, aid in determining criminal acts and reactions to crime. Second, these environmental-level factors condition or contextualize relationships between individual-level characteristics (e.g., routine activities, social bonds), criminal acts, and reactions to crime. In the terms of our theory, individual attributes have differential effects on routine activities, criminal acts, and reactions to crime according to environmental context. That is, neighborhood social disorganization variables, deterrence variables, and/or macroroutine activity variables not only directly affect subsequent, criminal acts, and reactions to crime, but they interact with the microroutine-activity antecedents of these behaviors. Such integration embeds "day-to-day experiences that directly lead to deviance within the patterns of cultural and social structure" (Liska et al. 1989:9).

At present, much of the extant research attempting to merge routine activities variants and any version of social control theory is based largely on the first above-mentioned assumption regarding contextual analysis. These integrative efforts assume that inclusion of both types of variables—routine activities predictors as well as social disorganization characteristics, for instance—will increase the variation in criminal acts that is explained. Some even seem to imply that increasing explained variance is the primary reason for this integration. Thus, simply increasing the R^2 seems to largely drive the desire for theoretical integration. However, researchers such as Kennedy and Forde strive for a perhaps more comprehensive cross-level integration by "examining how social context of urban environments may influence the relationship between activities and certain types of criminal victimization" (1990:137). Similarly, Smith and Jarjoura emphasize the need for contextual analyses to observe "whether measures of individuals' routine activities and lifestyles have similar effects across different contexts" (1989:743). The inclusion of these latter intents coincides with the second above-mentioned assumption guiding contextual analysis, and thus makes for a more informative, truly integrative effort. The key assumption guiding the integrative effort involved in this book—that environmental conditions, to a certain extent, structure the effects of individual opportunity characteristics—is similar to the reasoning provided by Kennedy and Forde (1990) and Smith and Jarjoura (1989) as outlined above.[15]

Examples of this proposed relationship between environmental-level variables and the individual risk factors associated with microroutine activities theory can substantiate the need for theoretical integration on empirical grounds. Miethe and McDowall (1993) indicate that neighborhood conditions can influence the impact that individual routines have on victimization risk. For instance, individual routine activities may have a negligible effect in disorganized communities because these conditions are sufficient in themselves to account for increased victimization risk. Yet, in more prosperous areas, individual activities become a more important factor in creating the necessary conditions for a successful victimization.[16] Since social control is effective in organized communities, individual lifestyle choices in terms of microroutine activity risk factors seem to emerge as the differentiating factor, separating those likely to be targeted as victims and those likely to be avoided.

As an example, target attractiveness and guardianship measures may relate to individual victimization risk conditional on neighborhood socioeconomic status. Unattractive targets in poor neighborhoods could be chosen because of structural convenience, despite less than optimal individual-level attractiveness. So, even if guardianship were high and target attractiveness low, individuals and property might be subject to increased victimization risk because of the properties of the neighborhood. The neighborhood characteristics thus have the potential to determine the effectiveness or utility of lifestyle choices because, as Sampson and Wooldredge point out, "motivated offenders may be influenced by the criminal opportunity structure of entire areas, not just individuals and their households" (1987:373). In this way, community context can not only have direct effects on victimization, controlling for risk factors, but it can also *affect* the *effect* of such individual lifestyle characteristics or activities on victimization risk.

INTEGRATIVE COMPATIBILITY AMONG CONSTITUENT THEORIES

Given that environmental-level factors can structure and influence the effects of individual variables, integration of micro- and macroroutine activities theories and micro- and macro-social control theories seems plausible and desirable. However, previous attempts at theoretical integration within the field of criminology have been discredited due to an inattention to the compatibility of the constituent theories on philosophical grounds.[17] As mentioned earlier, much debate persists regarding the value of integrating theories that may have different domain assumptions. The cross-level integration that is proposed here, however, seeks to establish solid empirical and theoretical grounds for integration.

The emphasis of routine activities theory (both its micro- and macrovariants) on opportunity contexts suggests that it is quite suitable for integrating environmental-level constructs. The idea that opportunities for criminal acts in terms of individual or aggregate risk factors are differentially distributed across time and space is, indeed, one of the initial presuppositions directing theory on routine activities.[18] There are clear ecological foundations of the theory indicating that individual and/or societal routines within temporal and spatial structures influence the occurrence of individual criminal/victimization events and/or societal crime rates.[19] These ecological foundations make the theory quite compatible with the urban, ecological foundations of the control variant of the social disorganization perspective, for instance.

Further, the ecological distribution of individual and societal routine activities affects the operation of informal social control and thus makes routine activities theory compatible with control theories on additional grounds. The mechanisms for formal control in deterrence theory, informal control integral at the individual level in social bonding theory, and informal control at the community level in social disorganization theory all

coincide with the concept of "guardianship" in both micro- and macroroutine activities approaches.[20] Cohen and Land point out that, indeed, elements of control are vital in a criminal opportunity perspective: "If controls
over opportunities for crimes (i.e., control factors that affect suitable targets
or capable guardians) decrease, the theory predicts that illegal predatory
acts will increase" (1987:52). Conversely, related to the centrality of social
controls in both traditions, the notion of criminal opportunity, in our view,
also plays an important role in both routine activities and social control theories. The elements of control and opportunity are rather inextricably
linked in both constituent traditions. The idea that insufficient controls create opportunities for successful crime or victimization is compatible with
both theoretical perspectives.

Motivated Offenders, All?

Despite the similar ecological bases of control theory (especially social
disorganization theory) and micro- and macroversions of routine activities
theory as well as their common ground regarding control and opportunity,
these theoretical orientations are suitable for integration *if and only if* their
underlying assumptions regarding human nature and behavior are compatible. While it would be possible to simply assert that micro- and macro-
control theories as well as both macro- and microroutine activities theories
share similar if not identical domain assumptions, such an exercise would
ultimately beg the question of assumptive compatibility. Although we
believe that social control theory and routine activities theory share common guiding assumptions, even a cursory comparison of some of the
actual scholarship in those two traditions suggests that there are some
issues concerning underlying assumptions that must be resolved, especially those pertaining to the nature of criminal motivation. Given that the
unresolved debate surrounding the motivated offender assumption has
been perhaps *the* defining characteristic of modern scholarship, and given
that assumptions about motivated offenders shape every criminological
perspective, a little elaboration about its nature and importance seems
necessary.

The motivated offender assumption appears as a defining characteristic of modern scholarship precisely because crime itself has been a defining characteristic of modernity, capturing the attention of policymakers,
citizenry, and scholars. The debate surrounding the motivated offender
assumption is manifested rather insidiously by two seemingly innocent
and enduring questions in modern scholarship: What circumstances
enable or inhibit crime? and What drives some individuals to crime?
Answers to these fundamental questions have come from a wide array of
disciplinary perspectives (psychology, sociology, economics, political sci-

ence, anthropology, biology, history, and philosophy), each providing partial explanations at best. It even could be argued that these rather simple questions have given criminology its *raison d'être*, and the dissatisfaction with the incomplete explanations they have engendered has led to the remarkable expansion of that hybrid discipline. Moreover, not only do the answers to these questions reflect differing assumptions about the essences of human nature and criminal motivation, but the very manner in which the questions are posed reflects divergent assumptions about human nature and criminal motivation. At first blush, these two questions seem to be asking the same thing in different ways. However, they are not; they are quite different questions that are accompanied with answers and practical implications that contrast sharply.

The former question is associated with the classical criminology tradition, which assumes all individuals are motivated by a utilitarian principle that revolves around the pursuit of pleasure and avoidance of pain. Assuming universal and constant utilitarian motivation, crime is a function of circumstances that provide greater pleasure than pain for lawbreaking. From the classical view, crime prevention is a matter of creating contexts in which law-breaking produces more pain than pleasure for the offender.

The latter question—What drives some individuals to crime?—is identified with the positivist school of criminology, which assumes individual motivation is neither universal nor constant. Individual motives vary and they determine whether crimes are committed or not. Criminal motivations can stem from abnormal physiological traits, pathological personalities, stimulus-response-reward chains, or the frustration of socioeconomic deprivation. From the positivist tradition, crime is a matter of motivations produced either internally or in the social environment. Crime prevention viewed in this light has sought to remove those with inherent abnormal traits from the general population, or use behavior modification to reform criminals, or ameliorate socioeconomic disadvantages that generate criminal motivations.

Clearly, assumptions about motivation are important features of any theory of human behavior as well as criminological theory. Conventionally, the classical and positivist traditions are posited as competing approaches primarily because they make divergent assumptions about human nature and criminal motivations. The classical approach assumes motivation and then seeks to explain the circumstances under which individuals act upon that motivation. In contrast, the positivist position assumes crime is a product of variations in motivation and then seeks to explain the determinants of crime producing motivations. We take a rather strict, purist stance on the criminal motivation issue, agreeing with the position that theories must follow one and only one of these assumptions if they are to remain logically consistent.[21] Simply, it is impossible to assume that motivation is constant and therefore cannot explain crime, and also assume that motivation varies and is the key explanatory variable in criminological research. In the final analysis, we agree with those who argue that the most satisfactory explanation of crime does not lie in determinist, positivist notions of criminal motivation, but rather emerges from classical criminological ideas that assume pleasure/pain motivation and concentrate on variations in contexts conducive to crime.

While we embrace the classical, rational choice amotivational assumption of human behavior, it would be inappropriate to portray rational choice theory as completely unified on this issue. Rather, as Hechter and Kanazawa (1997) point out, there are both "thin" and "thick" rational choice models. The "thin" model argues that action cannot be explained by individual motivation, because motivation is universally based on maximizing pleasure while minimizing pain. In contrast, the "thick" model suggests that motivation varies and human action is only predictable if individual values and beliefs are known. However, "idiosyncratic values tend to cancel each other out" as group size increases, and consequently, "the remaining common value permits quite accurate behavioral predictions at the collective level" (ibid.:194). In criminology specifically, Opp (1997) identifies and discusses both "narrow" (i.e., thin) and "wide" (i.e., thick) rational choice models. The point here is to show that in the broader tradition of rational choice theory, a clear consensus on the precise nature of human motivation is not present.

Similarly, the key underlying assumptions of routine activities and social control theories are not necessarily unified. Conventional discussions of the underlying assumptions in routine activities and social control theories claim that they are both ultimately amotivational, thereby following the classical tradition. While we agree with this assessment, there are some instances in both theories where some ontological ambiguity occurs. To rush to declare that both traditions can be made to have complementary classical assumptions about motivation would result in a missed opportunity to identify and avoid theoretical ambiguity. In the following few paragraphs, we suggest that both traditions can be construed in a way that allows for a strong classical, amotivational stance. We then provide some telling examples of ontological incompatibility. This section concludes with our position that an integrated criminal opportunity theory that takes a strong amotivational stance can be assumptively consistent. To arrive at a logically consistent framework, conceptual elements from both routine activities and social control that stem from assumptions about differential motivations must either be discarded completely or reworked so as to be compatible with the amotivational orientation found in microroutine activities theory.

To elaborate, we will first consider the social control tradition. Control theories, also stemming from classical theory, assume a "Hobbesian" view of human nature—maximal self-gratification is the primary goal: "That man is potentially unruly is thus given in the human condition" (Kornhauser 1978:39).[22] Further, control theories assume imperfect socialization—if conditions of weak internal or external controls arise, humans may not "resist the pressure to deviate" (ibid.). Humans are active; they actively strive to satisfy their desires (ibid.). Their actions are not the products of passivity; socialization or other environmental influences do not *force* individuals into deviant pathways. Again, choices are made regarding behavior based upon costs and benefits, and criminal motivation is assumed to be universal and constant.

While social bonding and deterrence theories have typically been perceived as "pure" control theories, the social disorganization perspective outlined by Shaw and McKay (1942) is portrayed as a mixed model. It is not considered a pure control theory with classical amotivational assumptions because it incorporates notions of delinquent subcultures, which assume differential motivations to engage in crime. Still, many scholars interpret the social disorganization approach as a classical control theory,[23] given that its primary emphasis is on the weakened institutional controls resulting from the condition of social disorganization. From the perspective of the systemic model of social disorganization, one could make the classical argument that individuals choose to commit criminal acts because criminal opportunity increases as social disorganization weakens social controls.

It should be evident that one could only make this classical argument if one either ignores the fact that social disorganization theory is a mixed model or if one reconfigures its essential elements so as to reconcile them with classical amotivatonal assumptions. The latter tact has been suggested above. For instance, Shaw and McKay's identification of differences in social values can be construed in amotivational terms as indicative of variations in commitment to informal social control, rather than as motivations more or less favorable to crime. Similarly, associations with delinquent subcultures can be understood in amotivational terms as a relative lack of informal social control, rather than as contexts in which deviant motivations are valued. Whether it was Shaw and McKay's intent to make amotivational or differential motivational assumptions is not all that important. What is important is that it seems that the key constructs in social disorganization theory can be and have been understood as amotivational constructs that reflect criminal opportunity that emerges from environmental-level influences.

Compared to the variants of control theory, the assumptive terrain in the routine activities tradition is more murky. The economic approaches of

Becker (1968) and Cook (1980, 1986) claim that crime is based upon
rational choice and hedonistic-calculus assumptions, following classical
theory's perspective regarding crime and human nature. This means that
human actions are guided by the principles of pleasure and pain and that
behavior, including criminal behavior, is thus "understood as the self-
interested pursuit of pleasure or the avoidance of pain" (Gottfredson and
Hirschi 1990:5).[24] According to this philosophical position regarding
human nature, *all* individuals are seen as being capable of criminal behavior—if controls are inadequate and, thus, "pains" are not evident, individuals are free to engage in deviant behavior. It is criminal events that need
explaining rather than individual criminality.[25] Criminal motivation is
viewed as a constant rather than a variable to be explained or a factor to be
taken as given.

Let us look more closely at macroroutine activities theories. Rather ironically, even though routine activities theorists are typically viewed as having an unambiguous classical position on criminal motivation, some in the
routine activities tradition have hedged on assumptions about criminal
motivations. For example, Cohen and Felson's (1979) routine activities
theory tends to take motivation as "given," focusing on the influences of
social forces that alter large-scale patterns of routine activities in a population. Also, Clarke (1997) proposes crime-specific theories that explicitly
incorporate variations in criminal motivations. It is our position that a
number of conceptual problems would arise from these differing ontological stances within the routine activities theoretical tradition if we were to
carelessly assume that there is consensus concerning underlying assumptions within the tradition.

To further illustrate the ontological variation in the routine activities
approach, compare the strong amotivational stance posited by Becker
(1968) and Cook (1986) with Cohen and Felson's (1979) seminal article.
Cohen and Felson make what some might (mistakenly) see as a strong,
classical, amotivational assumption when they state:

> Unlike many criminological inquiries, we do not examine why individuals
> or groups are inclined criminally, but rather *we take criminal inclination as
> given* and examine the manner in which the spatio-temporal organization of
> social activities helps people translate their criminal inclination into action."
> (ibid.:589, emphasis added)

A careful reading reveals that "criminal inclinations" (i.e., motives) are
not assumed to be universal and constant, as classical criminologists posit.
Rather, motivation is treated as "given" for the sake of isolating their attention on other matters. Cohen and Felson remain strategically silent on the
motivation assumption.

In fact, it is possible to infer that Cohen and Felson actually take a positivist assumptive stance on motivation. To illustrate, earlier in the article they seem to assume differential criminal motivations:

> We further argue that the lack of any one of these elements [motivated offenders, suitable targets, and capable guardians] is sufficient to prevent the successful completion of a direct-contact predatory crime, and that the convergence in time and space of suitable targets and the absence of capable guardians may even lead to large increases in crime rates without necessarily requiring any *increase in the structural conditions that motivate individuals to engage in crime*. That is, if the *proportion of motivated offenders* or even suitable targets were to remain stable in a community, changes in routine activities could nonetheless alter the likelihood of their convergence in space and time, thereby creating more opportunities for crimes to occur. (ibid.:589, emphasis added)

Clearly, this statement claims that structural conditions can produce variations in criminal motivations. Further, by making an argument that contains a claim about "the proportion of motivated offenders," they imply that criminal motivation is not universal and constant—they suggest that motivated offenders are but a fraction of a population, not the entire population.

Cohen and Felson's support for assuming differential motivation is further illustrated in the conclusion of their classic article:

> Without denying the importance of factors motivating offenders to engage in crime, we have focused specific attention upon violations themselves and the prerequisites for their occurrence. However, the routine activity approach might in the future be applied to the analysis of offenders and their inclinations as well. (ibid.:605)

Assuming constant, universal motivation microroutine activities theory aligns with the classical utilitarian, rational choice presuppositions. Assuming differential motivations, Cohen and Felson's macroroutine activities theory stands closer to positivist, determinist orientations.

By focusing on Cohen and Felson's work, we do not mean to suggest that they are the only scholars in the macroroutine activities tradition to display nonclassical assumptions when it comes to criminal motivation. We could probably systematically explore all of the leading micro- and macropieces in this tradition to demonstrate classical or positivist derived ontological assumptions. However, that would not serve our purposes here. Rather, we merely want to show that the core of the intellectual tradition upon which our efforts are based is divided in terms of a key domain assumption—routine activities theory clearly has classical and positivist influences. We point this out because we want to avoid building ontological ambiguity or contradiction into our modified criminal opportunity approach. We desire to avoid such incertitude and contradiction because they would lead to logical inconsistencies and muddled concepts.

Perhaps the best illustration of how competing classical and positivist assumptions in micro- and macroroutine activities approaches could create conceptual problems can be found in attempts to capture variation in motivated offenders by referring to the ideas of proximity and exposure. One line of thought is to measure proximity and exposure to groups of individuals who possess characteristics associated with motivated offenders.[26] An alternative is to focus on proximity and exposure to areas with high crime rates.[27] If a strong, classical amotivational assumption is made, this line of thought is problematic. If criminal motivation is universal and constant, then, except for the occasional hermit, we all experience proximity and exposure to motivated offenders. Moreover, this tact ultimately could lead to tautological reasoning. That is, rates of criminal acts are used as proxies for criminal opportunity, which is hypothesized to be the underlying cause of criminal acts—criminal acts are indicative of criminal opportunity, and criminal opportunity explains criminal acts. These theoretical troubles can be avoided within a framework that makes a classical amotivational assumption by thinking of proximity and exposure to motivated offenders in terms of variations in the proximity and exposure to people (all of whom are motivated offenders). The central idea here is that in a conceptual framework that assumes amotivation, movements toward treating motivation as a variable generate theoretical inconsistency, logical contradiction, and conceptual confusion. For our modified opportunity theory, we integrate the insights of routine activities and social disorganization within a framework that follows the classical criminological tradition by making an amotivational assumption. In doing so, we recognize that we perhaps contradict some of the intentions of routine activity scholars such as Cohen and Felson (1979) and Clarke (1997). However, we see their more positivist statements as "unnecessary" and perhaps even "problematic" given the concepts and measures typically used in testing the theory. In line with scholars such as Cook (1986), we see classical assumptions as more clearly underlying routine activities theory, and we thus adopt that position in our integration offered here.

Profitable Integration

In summary, given the compatibility of constituent theories, contextual research relates individual-level relationships to environmental-level characteristics and patterns. The underlying assumption guiding such efforts is that individual risk for criminal acts is predicted not only by the micro- and macroconvergence of motivated offenders, suitable targets, and absence of

capable guardians, but by the level of social control-disorganization characteristic of the individual and surrounding social environment as well.
Further, this type of integration assumes that micro- and macroroutine
activities and social control-disorganization characteristics have the potential to interact; it is likely that communities are involved in structuring individual lifestyles (routines and bonds) and in structuring the impact of such
individual-level effects on criminal event risk; thus there may be environ-
ment-specific effects. In other words, the ecological context can affect the
relationships between individual-level variables and risks regarding
crime.

So, the integration of routine activities approaches with social control
theories (including the control variant of social disorganization theory)
provides a perspective in which individual risk factors impacting criminal
opportunity can be put into an environmental context—an environmental
context that, along with and in interaction with individual lifestyles, structures criminal opportunities. What emerges, then, from a successful integration of micro- and macroroutine activities perspectives with micro– and
macro–social control theories is a broader, more general, multicontextual
criminal opportunity framework in which both individual- and aggregate-
level controls and individual- and aggregate-level exposure and target suitability contribute to individual- and environmental-level opportunities for
crime and victimization, yielding a more theoretically *and* empirically
comprehensive perspective. Further, a successful integration is largely
dependent upon avoiding embedding contradictory ontological assumptions. In particular, we maintain that a strong amotivational assumption is
consistent with the classical origins of social control theories and numerous
interpretations of routine activities theory. Making such an assumption and
adhering to it is necessary to insure logical consistency in our integrated
theory. Finally, we contend that making a strong, classical amotivational
assumption is useful if one wants to focus on the circumstances that give
rise to crime rather than focusing on characteristics of the criminal.

A DYNAMIC, MULTICONTEXTUAL CRIMINAL OPPORTUNITY THEORY

The main objective of this book is to propose an alternative criminal
opportunity theory. Our theory builds upon micro- and macroapproaches
in routine activities theory, taking into account the recent developments
regarding criminal opportunity, but still extending the notion of opportunity even further. The result is what we term a dynamic, multicontextual
criminal opportunity theory. In this section, we outline the key components of our proposed theory, suggesting that criminal opportunity can be
conceptualized and operationalized through multiple dimensions and at

multiple levels of analysis. For the sake of clarity, we present the elements of the perspective in static terms.[28] Our perspective proposes two levels of analysis: individual and environmental. At each level, we propose three broad organizing constructs—motivated offenders, suitable targets, and guardianship—which necessitates borrowing from, yet reconceptualizing elements from existing criminological perspectives.

Criminal Opportunity

A task of the first order is to provide a working definition of criminal opportunity. From our view, opportunity represents the situational ability for crime to occur. Borrowing, yet modifying, the pioneering work of Cohen and Felson (1979) and Cohen et al. (1981) we maintain that *criminal opportunity* is the convergence in time and space of motivated offenders and suitable targets in the absence of capable guardians in individual- and environmental-level contexts. Table 3.1 lists the core definitions we develop in our dynamic, multicontextual criminal opportunity theory. To capture the notion of environmental-level settings being situated in time and space, we offer the concept of "bounded locales," which refers to locales bounded in particular space-time contexts. We now turn our attention to offering formal and systematic definitions of the essential concepts of criminal opportunity for both individual- and environmental-level contexts.

Individual-Level Opportunity

We offer the following as a working definition: *Individual-level context* is the set of characteristics of individuals and objects situated in locales bounded in particular space-time contexts that relate to motivated offenders, suitable targets, and capable guardians. As will become evident below, both individuals and objects possess features that make them more or less attractive targets or capable guardians. This definition also suggests that individuals and objects find themselves existing in space and time dimensions that influence the likelihood of a criminal act occurring.

Motivated Offenders. Given that we assume universal and constant criminal motivation in the human population, there are no defining characteristics that distinguish between those who are motivated and those who are not. That is, motivation is treated as a constant, not as a variable; motivated offenders are taken as a given. Thus, at the individual level, *all individuals are motivated offenders in any bounded locale*. Individuals may, however, be differentially exposed to motivated offenders (presumed to be anyone) depending upon the degree to which their activities are public vs. home-based as well as the rhythm, tempo, and timing of their activities.

Table 3.1. Definitions of Multicontextual Criminal Opportunity Concepts

Criminal opportunity	The spatiotemporal convergence of *motivated offenders* and *suitable targets* in the absence of *capable guardians* in *individual* and *environmental* contexts.
Individual-level context	The set of characteristics of individuals and objects situated in locales bounded in a particular spatio-temporal context that relate to *motivated offenders, suitable targets,* and *capable guardians.*
Motivated offenders	All individuals are motivated offenders in any bounded locale. Individuals may be differentially exposed to motivated offenders (presumed to be anyone) depending upon the degree to which their activities are public vs. home-based as well as the rhythm, tempo, and timing of their activities.
Suitable targets	The degree to which individuals and objects in a bounded locale posses qualities that relate to *vulnerability, antagonism,* and *gratifiability.*
Capable guardianship	The degree to which individuals and objects in a bounded locale possess qualities that relate to *social control* and *social ties.*
Environmental-level context	The set of ambient characteristics of locales bounded in a particular spatiotemporal context that relate to *motivated offenders, suitable targets,* and *capable guardians.*
Motivated offender concentration	The number of individuals in a bounded locale per unit of space, which can be relatively *resident* or *ephemeral.*
Aggregated target suitability	The collective degree to which individuals and objects in a bounded locale possess qualities related to *vulnerability, antagonism,* and *gratifiability.*
Aggregated capable guardianship	The collective degree to which individuals and objects in a bounded locale possess qualities related to *social control* and *social ties.*

Likewise, individuals may be differentially exposed due to spatial placement in terms of *proximity* and/or *accessibility* to others.

Suitable Targets. According to our definition of individual-level contexts, there are characteristics of individuals and objects that make them more or less suitable targets. Following Finkelhor and Asdigian (1996), we define target suitability in terms of three key dimensions: vulnerability, antagonism, and gratifiability.[29] Thus, at the individual level, *target suitability* is the degree to which individual and objects in a bounded locale possess qualities that relate to vulnerability, antagonism, and gratifiability: *target vulnerability* at the individual level is the degree to which individuals and objects in a bounded locale can be accessed, damaged, destroyed, duped, transported, and/or transferred with ease and speed; *target antagonism* at the individual level is the degree to which individuals and objects in a bounded locale engender reactions of opposition, hostility, and/or antipathy; and *target gratifiability* at the individual level is the degree to which individuals and objects in a bounded locale can provide material or corporal pleasure.

Capable Guardianship. In addition to motivated offenders and suitable targets, there are characteristics of individuals and objects that make them more or less guarded, according to our definition of individual-level contexts. A capable guardian is a person or object that provides social control. Further, capable guardianship sometimes emerges from the presence of social ties. Stating our definition of capable guardianship at the individual level formally, *capable guardianship* is the degree to which individuals and objects in a bounded locale possess qualities that relate to social ties and interpersonal control: *social ties* at the individual level are the degree to which individuals in a bounded locale possess attachments to others, manifest commitments to social institutions, and engage in conventional activities; and *interpersonal control* at the individual level is the degree to which individuals and objects in a bounded locale can be observed and impeded from experiencing a criminal act because they are proximate and exposed to agents of formal control, agents of informal control, and non-human protection devices.

Environmental-Level Opportunity

As depicted in Table 3.1, our view on criminal opportunity incorporates both individual- and environmental-level contexts. We offer the following as a definition: *Environmental-level context* is the set of ambient characteristics of locales bounded in particular space-time contexts that relate to motivated offenders, suitable targets, and capable guardians. As will become evident below, we suggest that there are aggregated features of individuals and objects in environmental contexts (e.g., neighborhoods, cities, schools, workplaces) that are related to concentrations of motivated offenders, attractive targets, and capable guardians.

Motivated Offenders. *Across space*, the number of "available" motivated offenders may vary, just because the number of people per unit of space may vary. It stands to reason that at the environmental level, as population density increases or decreases so does the density of motivated offenders and aggregate-level exposure to those offenders. To illustrate, an individual would have less contact with motivated offenders in an environment where there are one hundred people per square mile as compared to one where there are one thousand per square mile. To take this notion a step further, the density of motivated offenders is not always simply captured by the number of people who reside in a spatial unit. We know, for instance, that some areas have population densities that vary by season (e.g., tourist locations) and others that vary by time of day (e.g., business districts and entertainment areas). Assuming that a higher concentration of motivated offenders increases the likelihood of criminal events, we would conclude that areas that have low residential population density but high episodic density (e.g. downtown areas) would experience a relatively high amount of criminal acts. We therefore offer a threefold definition of motivated offender exposure at the environmental level: *motivated offender exposure* refers to the number of individuals in a bounded locale per unit of space (concentration), which can be relatively residential or ephemeral; *resident motivated offender exposure* is the number of individuals who occupy a bounded locale per unit of space more or less continuously; and *ephemeral motivated offender exposure* is the number of individuals who pass through a bounded locale per unit of space for a relatively short period of time.

Aggregate Target Suitability. Paralleling our definition of suitable targets at the individual-level context, we define target suitability at the environmental-level in terms of vulnerability, antagonism, and gratifiability.[30] At the environmental level, target suitability can be characterized in terms of the concentration of suitable targets in some specified unit of space. The more proximate and exposed to a concentration of suitable targets, the more likely an individual or object will experience a criminal event. In terms of committing a criminal act, individuals who find themselves in an environment with a relatively high concentration of suitable targets will have greater criminal opportunity. In terms of victimization, individuals and objects proximate or exposed to areas with relatively high concentrations of suitable targets will be more likely to experience a criminal event because the space they occupy is perceived to be ripe for criminal opportunity. At the environmental level, *aggregated target suitability* is the collective degree to which individuals and objects in a bounded locale possess qualities related to vulnerability, antagonism, and gratifiability: *aggregated target vulnerability* at the environmental level is the collective degree to which individuals and objects in a bounded locale can be accessed, damaged, destroyed, duped, transported, and/or transferred with ease and speed; *aggregated target antagonism* at the environmental level is the collective degree to which individuals and objects in a bounded locale engender reactions of opposition, hostility, and/or antipathy; and *aggregated target gratifiability* at the environmental level is the collective degree to which individuals and objects in a bounded locale can provide material or corporal pleasure.

Aggregate Capable Guardianship. Beyond motivated offender and suitable target concentrations, areas can be characterized in terms of the presence of capable guardians. The general idea is that areas that offer individuals and objects opportunities to be more proximate and exposed to a high concentration of capable guardians are less likely to experience criminal events. Similar to our individual-level definition, the environmental-level definition incorporates both formal and informal social control as well as animate and inanimate forms of guardianship. It also recognizes that capable guardianship might have a link to environmental social ties. At the environmental level, *aggregated capable guardianship* is the collective degree to which individuals and objects in a bounded locale possess qualities related to social ties and social control: *aggregated social ties* at the environmental level are the collective degree to which individuals and collectivities in a bounded locale engage in conventional activities and possess private, parochial, and public ties; *private social ties* are the collective degree to which individuals in a bounded locale are attached to each other on a personal level; *parochial social ties* are the collective degree to which individuals in a bounded locale participate in conventional organizations and agencies; *public social ties* are the collective degree to which collectivities in a bounded locale are linked to organizations, agencies, and institutions beyond their bounded locale;[31] and *aggregated social control* at the environmental level is the collective degree to which formal control agents, informal control agents, and nonhuman control devices in a bounded locale can observe and impede criminal acts.

Fundamental Postulates

At this point, it would be useful to summarize our theory by stating some fundamental postulates (see Table 3.2). Postulate 1 and Subpostulate 1a stem directly from current criminal opportunity theories, and in particular, the routine activities posited and refined by Cohen and colleagues.[32] However, our theory will emphasize the temporal dimensions of criminal opportunity contexts at both individual- and environmental-levels more so than have most extant applications or discussions of routine activities theory. Extant opportunity perspectives recognize the temporal dimensions of contexts with its suggestion that motivated offenders, suitable targets, and absence of capable guardianship must converge at a particular moment in time and space. What extant opportunity approaches do not consider in terms of temporality is the individual and environmental

Table 3.2.   Multicontextual Criminal Opportunity Theory Postulates

Postulate 1	Criminal behavior is accomplished in an opportunity context.
Postulate 1a	An opportunity context is the convergence of motivated offenders, suitable targets, and capable guardians in time and space.
Postulate 1b	Criminal opportunity contexts exist at the individual and environmental levels.
Postulate 1c	Environmental contexts are manifested in a variety of bounded locales (e.g., schools, neighborhoods, or cities).
Postulate 2	Individual-level criminal opportunity context is a function of the convergence of exposure to motivated offenders, of target vulnerability, target antagonism, target gratifiability, social control, and social ties.
Postulate 3	Environmental-level criminal opportunity context is a function of the convergence of resident motivated offender concentration, ephemeral motivated offender concentration, aggregated target vulnerability, aggregated target antagonism, aggregated target gratifiability, aggregated social control, and aggregated social ties.
Postulate 4	The likelihood of a criminal act occurring is the result of simultaneous direct effects at the individual and environmental levels of criminal opportunity contexts as well as individual-environmental-level interaction effects.

developmental processes that affect the convergence in time and space. Even the more recent theoretical developments of Cohen and Machalek (1988) and Vila and Cohen (1993)—which integrate temporality by suggesting an evolution of expropriative strategies based upon counterstrategies—do not address explicitly the implications of the time-varying nature of the covariates in the conceptual model. Our approach recognizes that macro- and microfactors interact with time in influencing whether criminal opportunity is present. As such, aggregate rates of criminal acts vary across time, and individual-level risks for criminal acts vary across the lifecourse. Relatedly, the individual- and environmental-level indicators of criminal opportunity are, in all probability, time-varying.

Subpostulates 1b and 1c address this potential for both individual- and environmental-level indicators of criminal opportunity. While applications of routine activities theory have traditionally been either exclusively microlevel or macrolevel, more recent developments suggest that both types of effects are important. Previous work, reviewed above,[33] shows that there are both micro– *and* macro–*simultaneous main effects* as well as *micro-macro interaction effects.* The centrality of simultaneous main effects at the individual and environmental levels as well as individual-environmental interactions effects are captured in Postulate 4. We continue this recent multilevel trend in the theory presented herein. However, our theory is more parsimonious conceptually than previous multilevel work. Most previous multilevel studies have claimed to integrate elements of routine activities and social disorganization theories, recognizing that the effects of criminal opportunity at the individual level may be conditioned by aggregate-level disorganization or informal community control. This approach, while enlightening, implicitly ignores the possibility for aggregate-level disorganization or community-level control to in fact represent environmental-level contexts of criminal opportunity. These studies have kept "opportunity" and "control" as distinctly separate theoretical constructs. We argue that this distinction is unnecessary—aggregate-level control is, in fact, an important component of multicontextual criminal opportunity. We extend this integration even further by incorporating other control theories—including social bonding and deterrence theories—into our perspective.

Furthermore, aggregate-level control, as well as other environmental components of criminal opportunity, can exist at multiple environmental levels of analysis. While most multilevel work in the routine activities tradition has focused on the neighborhood as the important macrounit, there are clearly other important environmental spatial contexts. Schools are particularly important contexts when examining adolescent crime and victimization. In adulthood, the workplace may be an important consideration. Multiple spatial contexts may impact upon criminal opportunity simultaneously or interactively such that "two-level models" are not sufficient. Instead three- or four-level nested or cross-classified models may be necessary to more fully represent the various contextual factors involved in the creating or denying of criminal opportunity.

Postulates 2 and 3 summarize the various factors at both the individual and extraindividual levels of analysis that determine criminal opportunity contexts. Previous individual-level studies of criminal opportunity have largely focused on two types of variables: lifestyle behaviors of individuals (i.e., their routine activities) and sociodemographic characteristics. The sociodemographic characteristics have been studied largely due to the absence of plentiful behavioral measures. Hence, age, sex, race, income, and marital status have been used as proxies for individual-level lifestyles or behaviors. More infrequent macrostudies have largely used one type of variable in examining criminal opportunity: aggregate-level sociodemographic characteristics. As in the individual-level studies, these group-level sociodemographic indicators have been intended as *proxies* for social behavior patterns; so female employment figures represent the moving of activities away from the home and median income represents the likelihood of consumption of valuable goods.

Our conceptualization/operationalization of criminal opportunity—discussed more fully in Chapter 4—recognizes many more factors as important in determining overall criminal opportunity, or "criminal circumstance." While individual-level sociodemographic and structural factors are important, so are behavioral patterns. Lifestyle-related routine activities are important behaviors to consider, but so too are behaviors related to the formation of social ties. Finally, all of these types of factors are characteristics of not only individuals but of the various environmental-level contexts in which individuals are embedded. Over the course of the next four chapters, we build upon our foundational postulates presented here to offer a set of systematic hypotheses aimed at explaining all manner of criminal acts as well as reactions to crime. In so doing, we establish the groundwork for a research agenda that will provide fair and rigorous tests of our dynamic, multicontextual criminal opportunity theory. Overall, we will put forward hypotheses that will test the general notion that criminal acts and reactions to crime result from simultaneous direct effects at the individual and environmental levels of criminal opportunity contexts as well as individual-environmental–level interaction effects.

NOTES

1. See the collection of essays on theory integration in Messner, Krohn, and Liska (1989).

2. For example, see Hirschi (1989).

3. For example, see Akers (1989).

4. For example, see Gottfredson and Hirschi (1990), Hirschi (1969, 1979, 1989), and Kornhauser (1978).

5. For example, see Elliot, Huizinga, and Ageton (1985), Johnson (1979), and Tittle (1995).

6. In discussing theory more generally, Alexander (1987) makes the same point. Exploring developments in twentieth-century sociological theory, Alexander (illustrates how inconsistent internal domain assumptions produce inadequate explanations. He demonstrates how these internal weaknesses become manifest when theorists are forced to modify their frameworks by accounting for various contingencies for which the base logic of the theory does not quite fit. Typically, explications of contingencies are instances where the logic of the theory is suspended and a different logic is brought in to handle the exceptions to the rule. The theory then becomes a mismatch of nonsensical parts.

7. For example, see Elliot, Ageton, and Cantor (1979), Massey and Krohn (1986), as well as Simons, Conger, and Whitbeck (1988).

8. For example, see Bursik (1988).

9. For example, see Akers (1998), Bursik (1988), and Liska et al. (1989).

10. For example, see Colvin and Pauly (1983) and Messner and Krohn (1990).

11. For example, see Colvin and Pauly (1983), Liska et al. (1989), Simcha-Fagan and Schwartz (1986), Thornberry (1987), and Wilson and Herrnstein (1985).

12. For example, see Iversen (1991) and Liska (1990).

13. See our discussion of these approaches in Chapter 2.

14. For example, see Kennedy and Forde (1990), Miethe and McDowall (1993), Petee, Kowalski, and Milner (1991), Sampson and Wooldredge (1987), Smith and Jarjoura (1989), as well as Sucoff and Upchurch (1998).

15. See also Miethe and McDowall (1993).

16. For example, see Miethe and McDowall (1993:752) and Wilcox Rountree et al. (1994).

17. For example, see Liska et al. (1989) and Hirschi (1989).

18. For example, see Messner and Tardiff (1985) as well as Sampson and Wooldredge (1987).

19. For example, see Cohen and Felson (1979) as well as Sampson and Wooldredge (1987).

20. See Bursik (1988).

21. See Hirschi (1989).

22. See also Gottfredson and Hirschi (1990).

23. See Kornhauser (1978).

24. See also Miethe and Meier (1990).

25. See Maxfield (1987a).

26. For example, see Cohen et al. (1981), Fisher et al. (1998), Miethe and Meier (1990), and Wilcox Rountree et al. (1994).

27. For example, see Fisher et al. (1998), Jargowsky and Bane (1991), Massey and Denton (1993), Massey, Krohn, and Bonati (1989), Morenoff and Sampson (1997), Sampson and Lauritsen (1990), as well as Wilcox Rountree and Land (1996a).

28. In Chapter 7 we return to the issue of temporality, concentrating on the dynamic elements of our conceptual framework.

29. It should be noted that Finkelhor and Asdigian's (1996) expansion of the notion of "suitable target" fits well with efforts in rational choice theory to expand the ideas about the motives of "self-interested" actors beyond pecuniary interests to "subjective evaluations" (Cook 1980) and "tastes" (Becker 1996).

30. See Finkelhor and Asdigian (1996).

31. As pointed out in Chapter 1, the link between social ties and social control is sometimes conditional upon characteristics such as neighborhood racial composition and neighborhood-level female-headed households.

32. For example, see Cohen and Felson (1979), Cohen et al. (1981), Cohen and Machalek (1988), and Vila and Cohen (1993).

33. For example, see Miethe and McDowall (1993), Miethe and Meier (1994), Sampson et al. (1997), Wilcox Rountree and Land (2000), and Wilcox Rountree et al. (1994).

4

Evidence and Specification of Main Effects

Having introduced the overall theory in the previous chapter, we discuss the elements of the theory in greater detail in this chapter. Specifically, we examine more fully how criminal opportunity is conceptualized and operationalized at the individual and ambient levels. To facilitate our discussion of the environmental context of criminal opportunity we consider bounded locales to consist of two fundamental types—those defined by edifices (e.g., schools, workplaces) and those defined by geographic regions (e.g., neighborhoods, cities). For the sake of brevity, we use schools and neighborhoods to illustrate our key constructs regarding each of these fundamental types of bounded locales.

Recall from the previous chapter that we defined individual-level context as the set of characteristics of individuals and objects situated in locales bounded in particular space-time contexts that relate to being motivated offenders, suitable targets, and capable guardians. Recall also that we defined environmental-level context as the set of ambient characteristics of locales bounded in particular space-time contexts that relate to motivated offenders, suitable targets, and capable guardians. The following sections elaborate upon our definitions of motivated offenders, suitable targets, and capable guardians at the individual and ambient levels (schools and neighborhoods, in particular). We also consider how (1) individual-level constitutional factors, (2) environmental-level constitutional factors, (3) environmental design, and (4) routine activities serve as mechanisms that propel the convergence of motivated offenders, suitable targets, and capable guardians at the individual and ambient levels. In doing so, we discuss specific possible operationalizations for our theoretical constructs and, where relevant, cite extant research using such measures. Our overall objective in this chapter, therefore, is to develop a working scheme of the conceptualization and operationalization of our theory when considering two possible person-context nestings: individuals nested within neighborhoods and individuals nested within schools.

CONCEPTUALIZATIONS AND MEASUREMENTS: SOME CAVEATS

Nice ✗

In presenting our conceptualizations and suggestions for possible measurements of key concepts, we must advance a few important caveats. First, note that the possible measures provided throughout this chapter are not intended to comprise an exhaustive list, but rather to serve as examples of possible measures compatible with our conceptualization of a multilevel criminal opportunity theory. The reader is advised to approach them as mere illustrations.

Second, not all sample measures provided are, in our opinion, equally strong. We do recognize that individual- and aggregate-level constitutional factors (e.g., gender, age, racial composition) are sometimes highly correlated with lifestyle and activity measures and thus can represent proxy measures. But, as will become apparent in this and subsequent chapters, these measures are often less than optimal indicators because they can serve as proxies for multiple concepts in the theory. As such, it is difficult to interpret clearly the conceptual meaning of an effect of such a measure vis-à-vis the overall theory.

A third important caveat is that the stated relationships between concepts assume all else is equal. For instance, indicating that the greater a target's gratifiability the greater the criminal opportunity assumes that guardianship and motivated offender variables remain constant. We recognize that in the real world "all else" is rarely equal. To illustrate, those who possess highly valued possessions often realize that they are at greater risk for criminal victimization and therefore take protective measures that increase guardianship. However, in theoretical discussions it is necessary to assume "all else is equal" in order to isolate a particular relationship of interest.

The final caveat concerns the treatment of contingencies presented by specific crimes. While we have stated that we intend to offer a general theory of criminal acts, we offer illustrations from routine activities research to clarify how particular characteristics of specific crimes might be handled.

In their seminal statement outlining a routine activities perspective, Cohen and Felson (1979) applied the idea of ecological interdependence between actions of offenders and behaviors of victims to understanding trends in aggregate rates of crime. In particular, they were interested in accounting for the change in U.S. crime rates from 1947 to 1974. Time series analysis of official crime rates showed that rates fluctuate according to the dispersion of activities away from the household—a measure thought to approximate the likely convergence of offenders, suitable targets, and absence of capable guardianship. Felson and Cohen (1980) elaborate on this idea, suggesting that structural characteristics such as women's labor force participation, the percentage of persons living alone, and the presence of lightweight durable goods affect rates of crime by, once again, affecting the temporal and spatial convergence of motivated offenders, attractive targets, and absence of guardianship.

The analysis of Decker, Schicor, and O'Brien (1982) has similar implications for macrolevel rates of crime, yet points out that structural changes may affect the actual direction of crime rates differentially, depending upon the crime in question. For instance, using victimization data, they find that population density is positively related to rates of auto theft, robbery, and larceny victimization but negatively correlated with rates of burglary, rape, and aggravated assault. Felson (1998:29–33) ascribes these contrasting correlations to differences in the way criminal opportunity is affected by population density uniquely for different crimes. For instance, Felson suggests that density decreases the ability of burglars to easily access homes through private rear entrances, whereas density increases the likelihood that cars will be parked in unguarded areas (e.g., public parking lots, streets), easing the chore of car thieves or those engaging in larceny from autos.

Thus, Felson delineates the need to carefully consider the crime-specific implications of "population density" in terms of the convergence of motivated offenders, suitable targets, and capable guardians in refining our hypotheses:

> High density of offenders is certainly different from high density of crime targets, high density of young thugs is certainly different from high density of little ladies, and high density of cars parked where they are easily stolen cannot be compared with high density of people who would hear a woman screaming. (ibid.:33)

While we agree with Felson that researchers need to be sensitive to particular characteristics of specific crimes, we do not believe every type of crime requires a unique set of concepts for analysis. As we stated earlier, what constitutes a "suitable target" for residential burglary is different from "suitable targets" for arson, assault, and other crimes. Similar differences across types of crime could be found for the concepts of motivated offenders and capable guardianship. These differences across types of crime require researchers to offer appropriate operationalizations of opportunity concepts; they do not require separate theories or unique sets of concepts within a theory. We believe our theory provides a flexible yet conceptually consistent guide for researchers to develop variables and measures that accurately capture the reality that they are attempting to explain.

MOTIVATED OFFENDERS

Individual-level motivation is treated as a constant, not as a variable. Thus, at the individual level, all individuals are motivated offenders in any bounded locale. However, we do recognize that individual exposure to people more generally (all being potentially motivated offenders) is variable. Some people live rather secluded or home-centered lives,[1] while others frequently engage in public activities. As such, "motivated offenders" is a variable at the individual level to the extent that it measures one's contact with people, not necessarily those noted to be "criminal" or "delinquent." Previous tests of criminal opportunity theory that have measured "exposure to motivated offenders" as "home-centeredness" versus "public activity" are thus in the spirit of the foundational amotivational assumption of our theory.[2] These studies identify a positive relationship between exposure and victimization, especially in cases of personal crime that is clearly instrumental, such as personal larceny. Thus, people who frequent bars, movies, or sporting events or people who use public transportation regularly, for instance, are more exposed to motivated offenders and are thus more likely to experience victimization. Mustaine and Tewksbury (1998) provide perhaps the most refined and comprehensive measurement of routine activities to date, examining twenty different measures of activities away from home, including specific types of activities, the time spent doing these activities, and the characteristics of the company one keeps while doing these activities. In general, they found that the type of activity outside the home was much more predictive of theft victimization than was the time spent in the activity.

Measuring actual activity is perhaps the most direct way to operationalize public exposure, but individual-level "constitutional" factors such as marital and employment status can serve as proxy measures. The Cohen et al. (1981) research, for instance, finds unmarried and unemployed people—people with presumably greater exposure due to the lower likelihood that their activities are home-based—to be at higher risk for predatory victimization. Individual-level residential location (e.g., urban versus rural residence) can also be conceived as an indicator of exposure to motivated offenders. That is, from our view, urban crime rates are higher than rural ones not because criminal propensity is greater among urban residents (an argument that would assume differential motivation) but rather because urban residence presumably translates into more frequent public activity (an argument more consistent with an amotivational assumption).

Also, the placement of individuals or objects in space affects their accessibility to people/traffic and thereby increases exposure to motivated offenders. For instance, mailboxes placed near the end of driveways, near the flow of public traffic, are much more susceptible to "bashing" or other types of vandalism than are door-side boxes. Similarly, environmental criminologists have theorized in a manner seemingly consistent with our logic regarding the conceptualization of motivated offenders. For example, the "journey to crime" research by Brantingham and Brantingham (1981) suggests that motivated offenders search for targets within an "awareness space," and so a target falling within the area bounded by the criminal's home and workplace stands a greater chance of being victimized by this particular offender than does a target in unknown territory. But home and workplace are not the only important factors; environmental criminologists have identified several other key factors in defining awareness space. Brantingham and Brantingham (1981), for instance, posit that targets near intersections and/or major traffic arteries (e.g., as opposed to targets located on cul-de-sacs or dead-end streets) are more likely to become part of a criminal's potential awareness space. Because of greater accessibility (thus exposure to offenders), such targets are more likely to be victimized. In testing these ideas, Wilcox Rountree and Land (1996a) found that living in a corner residence did not significantly affect burglary victimization risk, but Robinson and Robinson (1997) found renters living in corner apartments near college campuses specifically to be at increased risk. Wilcox Rountree and Land (1996a) show that "access routes" characterizing one's home (e.g., ground-floor windows, a rear-side alley) increased burglary victimization risk.

This same concept of "exposure to motivated offenders" in terms of "exposure to public traffic" can be extended to understanding the opportunity contexts of students or objects nested within schools. Students who participate in extracurricular activities are probably more exposed to classmates and other people than are "inactive" students. This notion coincides well with the empirical findings suggesting that involvement in extracurricular activities, though presumed to decrease delinquency,[3] may actually increase it.[4] As another example, computers placed in a ground-floor room along a row of windows at a school are accessible to outside traffic, and thus susceptible to theft. These same computers located in an interior room or a room with second- or third-floor windows are less accessible to outside traffic (unless one has a ladder), and thus potential exposure is diminished.

An overview of the conceptualization and possible operationalization of criminal opportunity provided thus far is represented by Table 4.1. It is

Table 4.1. Conceptualization and Operationalization of Criminal Opportunity, Part I

Concept	Environmental Context	Sample Measures
Individual- or object- level "motivated offender" exposure (includes indicators of proximity and accessibility since they suggest potential exposure)	Individual student or object in *school*	1. student's number of extracurricular activities 2. school property's (e.g., computers, AV equipment) proximity to ground-floor windows
	Individual resident, residence, or object in *neighborhood*	1. resident's marital status 2. resident's employment status 3. resident's number of days/nights the home is left unoccupied 4 resident's number of public activities (e.g., attending sporting events, going to bars) 5. general residential location (e.g., urban, rural) 6. specific location of residence or residential property on street (e.g., corner residence) 7. specific location of residence or residential property vis-à-vis a street or alley (e.g., proximity to street or alley) 8. type of street on which residence is located (e.g., cul-de-sac/dead-end street, busy through street)

worth noting that measures that tap involvement in crime/delinquency, often used as a measure of exposure in previous studies[5] under the assumption that offenders are immersed in a criminal subculture, are less pertinent to the concept of motivated offenders within our theoretical framework. This is so because they seem to reject our assumption that those with a criminal past are really no more or less motivated than those with a "clean record." Within a criminal opportunity framework, these measures of involvement in crime or number of criminal peers are perhaps best conceived as representing ineffective guardianship, since people involved in deviance are unlikely to rely upon police, principals, teachers, or other agents of social control. Conceived in this way, such measures fit within the theoretical framework without violating any of its underlying assumptions.

In terms of conceptualizing motivated offender at the environmental level, the number of motivated offenders may vary across contextual units because the number of people per unit of space may vary. In Chapter 3, we offered a threefold definition of motivated offender exposure at the environmental level: motivated offender exposure is the number of individuals in a bounded locale per unit of space, which can be relatively resident or ephemeral; resident motivated offender exposure refers to the number of individuals who occupy a bounded locale per unit of space more or less continuously; and ephemeral motivated offender exposure is the number of individuals who pass through a bounded locale per unit of space for a relatively short period of time. While exposure is thus largely a function of density or concentration of people, we also recognize that it is also a function of differential proximity and accessibility. Thus, variation in environmental design and juxtaposition can also serve to differentiate contexts in terms of aggregate-level motivated offender exposure.

To illustrate these concepts, in a school context, resident motivated offender concentration could be measured in terms of school enrollment. For instance, Gottfredson and Gottfredson's (1985) seminal work, *Victimization in Schools,* reported that larger total enrollment directly affected teacher victimization rates across a national sample of junior high schools, even while controlling for student and community characteristics.[6]

In a neighborhood context, resident motivated offender concentration can perhaps be most directly measured in terms of population density. There is a long history of examining the effect of population density on community crime rates or victimization likelihood in the macrocriminology literature. The literature largely supports the notion that community density, size, or degree of urbanism increase crime/victimization rates.[7]

Other measures of offender concentration are possible. In their comprehensive application of routine activities theory to victimization on college campuses—a setting representing something in between the neighborhood and school contexts used as examples throughout this chapter—Fisher et al. (1998) examine the effects of exposure in several unique ways. Specifically, they included the size of the dorm and percentage of students living on/off campus as additional measures of proximity (potential exposure), consistent with the conceptualization of exposure used here. Of these measures, only percentage of students living on campus was significant.

At first blush, ephemeral motivated offender concentration would not seem germane to criminal acts in school contexts, because locales defined by buildings seem to be inherently limited to populations that are resident.

Yet, schools (or even workplaces) that allow a high degree of nonresident traffic in the buildings or on their grounds would increase opportunities for criminal acts. In a school context, ephemeral motivated offender concentration could be measured, therefore, in terms of daily/weekly/monthly average number of visitors.

For neighborhood contexts, ephemeral motivated offender concentration can be captured in terms of the nonresident traffic that flows through an area. In the literature, this notion has been captured by studies that examine nonresidential land use patterns. Jane Jacobs (1961, 1968), for example, illustrates how nonresidential land use promotes regular street use and thus a dense "ephemeral" traffic.[8] While Jacobs's (1961, 1968) perspective was that this traffic density is accompanied by increased surveillance potential, most other work in the environmental criminology literature has suggested that nonresidential land use attracts crime because informal social control is impaired.[9] The guardianship potential associated with mixed land use will be discussed further below. For the purposes of the present discussion, it is worth noting that regardless of whether land use helps or hinders guardianship, it may be related to criminal opportunity for population density reasons. If mixed land use increases ephemeral traffic/density, then the supply of motivated offenders (i.e., anyone) is higher than in purely residential areas. In support of this perspective, empirical work shows that crime/victimization risk tends to be higher in areas with busy places,[10] including, more specifically, fast-food restaurants,[11] bars/taverns,[12] and public high schools.[13]

Along these same lines, the land use characterizing the neighborhoods in which schools are located would seemingly have implications for the opportunity contexts of students, especially en route to and from school. If students encounter many people due to a dense, public traffic area surrounding the school, criminal opportunity is enhanced. Aggregate-level accessibility of people and objects in schools and neighborhoods is also related to potential exposure to motivated offenders. For instance, compared to inner-city schools or residential areas that have main streets and a system of alleys, neighborhoods and schools that are removed from main traffic lines make the houses, schools, and the valuables they contain less accessible to ephemeral motivated offenders. Thus, building upon the example started above, while individual- (or object-) level exposure to motivated offenders is exemplified by a computer located in a classroom with ground-floor windows, the inner-city versus residential or rural location of the school itself serves as an environmental-level indicator of exposure to ephemeral motivated offenders. Not only are the accessibility features of the computer itself important, so are the accessibility features of the school context in which the computer is embedded. The design of the school in combination with school policy regarding class change might also affect aggregate-level exposure in terms of accessibility to ephemeral and resident motivated offenders. For instance, schools with students who are contained in one or two classrooms per day represent less exposed/accessible contexts than do schools where frequent classroom and even building changes are common among students throughout the day.

The notion of aggregate accessibility—indicating potential exposure to motivated offenders—also applies to neighborhoods. While there is variation in accessibility among individuals and objects within neighborhoods, communities themselves also vary along these lines. For instance, neighborhoods located close to densely populated and frequently visited central city areas are more accessible in comparison to remote locations. As such, urbanism, or proximity to central city, serves as a possible measure of aggregate-level exposure to motivated offenders. Table 4.2 provides a summary of our ideas regarding conceptualization and operationalization of the aggregate-level motivated offender portion of overall criminal opportunity.

SUITABLE TARGETS

In defining suitable targets at the individual level, we followed Finkelhor and Asdigian (1996) and discussed target suitability in terms of three key dimensions: vulnerability, antagonism, and gratifiability. That is, at the individual level, target suitability is the degree to which individual and objects in a bounded locale possess qualities that relate to vulnerability, antagonism, and gratifiability. Target vulnerability at the individual level is the degree to which individuals and objects in a bounded locale can be damaged, destroyed, duped, transported, and/or transferred with ease and speed; target antagonism at the individual level is the degree to which individuals and objects in a bounded locale engender reactions of opposition, hostility, and/or antipathy; and target gratifiability at the individual level is the degree to which individuals and objects in a bounded locale can provide material or corporal pleasure. Target suitability is largely a function of constitutional characteristics, but routine activities or environmental design issues can impact target suitability, especially at the environmental level.[14]

Finkelhor and Asdigian's (1996) notion of target vulnerability suggests that women, children, the elderly, those who are mentally challenged, and those under the influence of drugs or alcohol would be relatively more vulnerable targets. Likewise, objects that are lighter and more easily moved or transported are more vulnerable targets (Felson 1998). These examples hold for individuals and objects in both school and neighborhood contexts. It should be clear that the sociodemographic measures

Table 4.2. Conceptualization and Operationalization of Criminal Opportunity, Part II

Concept	Environmental Context	Sample Measures
Aggregate-level "motivated offender" exposure (includes resident and ephemeral concentration and accessibility)	*School* context	1. student enrollment or density (e.g., number of students per unit space) 2. number of visitors per unit time 3. general location of school (e.g., urban/rural) 4. specific location of school on street (e.g., on street corner) 5. specific location of school vis-à- vis a street or alley (e.g., close to street or alley) 6. type of street on which school is located (e.g., cul-de-sac, busy through street) 7. number of classroom changes/day
	Neighborhood context	1. population size or density 2. number of businesses or other nonresidential land uses 3. location of the neighborhood vis-à-vis central city

offered here, including gender and age, are proxy measures of vulnerabilities related to strength and size, for instance. However, since social scientists rarely collect precise measures of strength and size, these sociodemographic correlates may be reasonable yet clearly imperfect approximations. Their effects should be interpreted with caution; these proxy measures can sometimes be invalid indicators of strength and size. In addition, such measures are not only proxies for strength and size (vulnerability) but other concepts related to criminal opportunity, such as home-centeredness. For instance, it is conceivable that, in the absence of a precise measure of home-centered versus public activity, a researcher might use a constitutional measure such as marital status or age as a proxy measure. If age can help indicate both exposure to motivated offenders and target vulnerability, it is difficult to disentangle the precise meaning of the effect of this measure in relation to the theoretical constructs. Because of this difficulty, we advocate measuring strength and size in as precise a fashion as possible, yet we recognize that social and demographic indicators can be potential (albeit somewhat ambiguous) proxies when more concrete measures are unavailable.

For target antagonism, Finkelhor and Asdigian (1996) argue that individuals or objects can possess some qualities or attributes that increase the likelihood of experiencing a criminal act because those characteristics give rise to anger, jealousy, or destructive impulses in certain offenders. Some might infer that this definition of target antagonism implies that motivations (e.g., disruptive impulses) to commit criminal acts vary among individuals. Obviously, this would not be compatible with our assumption of a universal and constant motivation to offend. However, target antagonism does not necessarily imply a differential motivation assumption. That is, we can assume that all individuals are motivated to commit criminal acts in their pursuit of maximizing pleasure and minimizing pain, while at the same time acknowledging that targets (both individuals and objects) variably possess characteristics that are associated with "pleasure" from another's vantage point (e.g., monetary reward, confrontation of a despised out-group). While the monetary reward offered by a target does not fit within Finkelhor and Asdigian's definition of target antagonism, attributes associated with out-groups certainly do. Individual characteristics that are likely to be associated with the confronting of an out-group can be based on both ascribed statuses related to such things as bigotry and hatred (e.g., ethnic/racial characteristics, sexual orientation) and achieved statuses considered noxious (e.g., antisocial personality, low self-control). Object characteristics that might be linked with such reactions could be symbols (e.g., crosses, churches/synagogues) of ascribed and achieved status antagonisms. Again, using sociodemographic measures as proxies for target antagonism has some important limitations. For instance, assuming race as an indicator of target antagonism assumes that it represents something undesirable to others. This perception would, of course, vary across contexts. In certain segments of our society, racial and ethnic minorities are perceived as out-groups, while in other segments they are treated with inclusion. This perception also varies across individuals within any one segment of society. So, we caution that using sociodemographic variables as measures of target antagonism is, again, likely to yield an analysis laden with measurement error. More precise measures of social desirability, including behavioral dimensions of desirability such as self control, are optimal.

Target gratifiability is yet another dimension pertaining to target suitability. Considering target gratifiability, targets can be perceived to have attributes that could provide material or corporal pleasure. The monetary value associated with persons and objects is the most obvious measure of the degree of material pleasure a person/object can bring. Most previous studies, using a variety of measures, indicate that property victimization risk increases with target attractiveness. Attractive targets—as indicated by incomes or SES,[15] housing value,[16] or amount of portable, valuable household goods (e.g., VCRs, camcorders, stereos),[17] or amount of money spent on nonessential items[18]—are generally found to be at an increased risk for experiencing criminal victimization, especially property victimization. In contrast, corporal pleasure is relevant to sex offenses. We do not mean to suggest here that sex offenses are committed out of a desire for sexual gratification. Rather, we merely suggest that the domination and physical abuse associated with sex offenses require a body, sometimes of a particular sex and age, depending upon the type of sex offender (e.g., pedophile versus adult rapist). While sex and age can be indicators of target gratifiability for certain crimes, we again emphasize the difficulty in interpreting the effects of such sociodemographic variables, since these same characteristics can be used as indicators of other concepts.[19] See Table 4.3 for a summary of the conceptualization and operationalization of the individual-level target suitability component of criminal opportunity.

At the environmental level, aggregate target vulnerability can be understood to mean that areas vary in the number of individuals and objects that are susceptible to criminal events because they possess characteristics that make them relatively easy to overpower, dupe, transport, and exchange. To illustrate further, the elderly are commonly perceived (sometimes erroneously, to the chagrin of would-be cons) to be easily duped. So it would follow from our definition that a retirement community might be perceived to possess a high concentration of vulnerable targets, thus making elderly in that area more susceptible to confidence scams.

While aggregated individual-level characteristics including the percentage of elderly, percentage of women/men, percentage of low IQ, average drug/alcohol use, average strength, etc. are potential indicators of environmental-level target vulnerability,[20] so too are aspects of environmental design. For instance, indicators of territoriality and/or symbolic or real barriers characterizing a neighborhood or school can suggest to potential offenders that the property is not easily damaged, destroyed, transported, etc., regardless of the aggregate composition of the individuals within the environment. So, neighborhoods with clearly marked entranceways, gates, sidewalks, and landscaping send a message to would-be intruders that the people and property contained within are not easily obtained for purposes of violent or property victimization. Likewise, schools with designated marquees, locked entrances, inaccessible roofs, and no evidence of entrapment areas (e.g., interior or exterior hiding places created by landscaping, the layout of the building, placement/design of lockers, bathrooms, stairwells) do not appear vulnerable. As such, the criminal opportunity characterizing students within these schools may be relatively low, even though

Table 4.3. Conceptualization and Operationalization of Criminal Opportunity, Part III

Concept	Environmental Context	Sample Measures
Individual- or object-level target vulnerability	Individual student or object in *school* and Individual resident, residence, or object in *neighborhood*	1. student's/resident's gender 2. student's/resident's age 3. student's/resident's weight 4. student's/resident's mental capacity 5. student's/resident's substance use 6. school property's/ residential property's portability
Individual- or object-level target antagonism	Individual student or object in *school* and Individual resident, residence, or object in *neighborhood*	1. student's/resident's race/ethnicity 2. student's/resident's sexual orientation 3. student's/resident's personality (e.g., anti-social, low self-control)
Individual- or object-level target gratifiability	Individual student or object in *school* and Individual resident, residence, or object in *neighborhood*	1. student's/resident's socioeconomic status 2. student's/resident's gender 3. student's/resident's age 4. student's/resident's number of portable, valuable goods owned/carried

characteristics of individual students in such schools might suggest vulnerability.

For aggregate target antagonism, areas can vary in the number of individuals and objects that are susceptible to criminal events because they possess characteristics that give rise to anger, jealousy, or destructive impulses. For example, environmental contexts that manifest a relatively high degree of ethnic/racial heterogeneity might present greater opportunities for crimes associated with bigotry.[21] To illuminate further, areas identified with a large number of symbols from out-groups (e.g., ethnic enclaves, churches, synagogues, temples, or offices for political activists) might be perceived as locations for criminal opportunity.

Aggregate target gratifiability is the third environmental-level dimension of target suitability. Areas can have a greater or lesser concentration

Table 4.4.   Conceptualization and Operationalization of Criminal Opportunity, Part IV

Concept	Environmental Context	Sample Measures
Aggregate-level target vulnerability	*School* and *Neighborhood* context	1. gender composition 2. age composition 3. average weight/strength 4. average mental capacity (or proportion low IQ) 5. average substance use among students/residents 6. signs of territoriality (e.g., obvious or architecturally distinct entranceways, marquees, gates, sidewalks, landscaping)
Aggregate-level target antagonism	*School* and *Neighborhood* context	1. ethnic/racial heterogeneity 2. number of symbolic targets (e.g., race, religion-specific churches, synagogues) in surrounding area
Aggregate-level target gratifiability	*School* and *Neighborhood* context	1. Average socioeconomic status 2. gender composition 3. age composition

of targets considered to be valuable in terms of the material, corporal, emotional, and psychological pleasure. To illustrate, relatively affluent neighborhoods with a high concentration of valuable, lightweight goods (e.g., jewelry, personal computers, stereos, and televisions) are perceived as being areas rich in criminal opportunity. Therefore, the likelihood of criminal events (burglary, in particular) occurring in those areas is enhanced. All-male prep schools may be perceived as a gratifiable target for a pedophile targeting young boys, given the high (sole) concentration of individuals with characteristics considered valuable or necessary for the commission of his crime. Table 4.4 summarizes the conceptualization and operationalization of aggregate-level target suitability as yet another component of overall criminal opportunity.

CAPABLE GUARDIANSHIP

Along with motivated offenders and suitable targets, our general opportunity theory of crime holds that there are characteristics of individuals and objects that make them more or less proximate and/or exposed to capable guardians in individual-level contexts. In the previous chapter we defined capable guardianship as the degree to which individuals and objects in a bounded locale possess qualities that relate to social ties and interpersonal control. As will be illustrated below, guardianship in the form of social ties, interpersonal control, and social control (at the aggregate level) largely emerge from routine activities and environmental design.

An elaboration of our notion of social ties is in order. Effective control is partly a matter of social bonds.[22] The degree to which individuals are bonded to conventional others, social institutions, and activities are indicators of the degree to which individuals are objects of concern among available, interested, and capable guardians.[23] Hirschi noted the psychological control that was created when an individual feared disappointing a loved one or jeopardizing an important commitment or activity (e.g., a job, a college education); this control is thus effective even outside the physical presence of the loved one, the boss, the college admission committee, etc. While Hirschi did not explicitly link such ties or "bonds" to the notion of "criminal opportunity," we argue that an implicit connection exists. As stated in previous chapters, ineffective control or guardianship—in the form of ties/bonds or supervision/intervention—is indeed a necessary component of a criminal opportunity context. If such bonds or controls are present, control theorists posit that crime is unlikely. We agree, but also stipulate that crime can still be unlikely in the presence of weak control if a suitable target or a potential offender is unavailable.

For a student in a school context, social ties consist primarily of the individual's ties to teachers and peers and commitment to education, grades, etc. With Hirschi's social bonding theory serving as theoretical rationale, there is an extensive empirical literature in criminology pointing to the importance of school-related attachments and commitments—operationalized in terms of GPA or school performance/failure, perceived importance of school activities, truancy, and dropout—as important elements in controlling adolescent substance use and other delinquency.[24] Likewise, applied research has revealed promising support for delinquency-prevention programs aimed at increasing bonding to school.[25]

For an individual in a community context, social ties consist of friendships, kinships, or networks with neighbors as well as ties to social institutions including family, work, or church. Again, much bonding-theory-related empirical support exists regarding the importance of such individual-level ties. For instance, there is general support for Hirschi's notion that children with strong feelings of attachment to parents are less likely to initiate delinquency. More specifically, studies have shown that parent-child communication and affect decrease antisocial behavior.[26] In contrast, parental rejection tends to be associated with increased levels of adolescent delinquency.[27] Similarly, parental management styles presumably related to poor parent-child communication and affect have been associated with increased probabilities of delinquency.[28] Specifically, studies show that inconsistent discipline[29] and hostile parenting[30] are positively related to adolescent delinquency. Other findings indicate that marital discord and family conflict—presumed to diminish the likelihood of effective parent-child communication, parental supervision, etc.—are positively related to adolescent problem-behavior.[31]

Religious ties, while not addressed as explicitly by Hirschi, have been incorporated into subsequent studies of social bonding theory. In most instances, attachment, commitment, involvement, and belief with regard to religion have been associated with lower levels of delinquency.[32] Ties to conventional institutions other than education, family, or religion are less numerous, though limited empirical evidence does suggest that salient ties to institutions such as work and the military also have important controlling effects on crime.[33]

Interpersonal control, our second component of guardianship, is based on the notion that individuals and objects vary in the degree to which they can be observed and monitored. For instance, individuals with neighbors who spend a large amount of time away from home are provided less surveillance. Objects too can be considered as having qualities pertaining to surveillance. For instance, objects located in/near windows or in open view have more ability to be guarded by people in surrounding areas than do objects that are placed in out-of-the way locations. In addition to an observational or surveillance component, social control, at its core, is a matter of preventing or impeding criminal acts. The location of individuals and objects vis-à-vis agents of formal and informal control influence the likelihood of a criminal act being committed by or against those individuals and objects—those more proximate and exposed to such agents are less likely to experience a criminal act for guardianship reasons.

Likewise, the possession of inanimate protection devices designed to impede criminal acts (e.g., mace spray or a alarm system) are forms of social control. In recognizing the ever-expanding private efforts taken by many to protect themselves, some studies attempt to tap the number of safety precautions employed to avoid victimization as a way to measure a nonsocial dimension of guardianship.[34] Generally, people who lock their doors, mark their property, have a watchdog, have a security system, are members of a community watch program, etc., are at lower risk for experiencing any type of criminal victimization. It should be noted that while weapon carrying is often included in scales tapping general "safety precautions"[35] and these scales are often negatively related to victimization, other work has shown that, when isolated, the effect of weapon carrying on victimization is positive.[36] As such, we do not suggest there that weapons necessarily serve as a measure of individual-level guardianship; they may, in fact, provide a measure of weak control.

While most examples of guardianship given thus far have emerged from people's routine activities, environmental design can also be the mechanism by which guardianship either emerges or is absent. For instance, above, we discussed the environmental-design-related issue of "accessibility" as a determinant of the motivated offender component of criminal opportunity—those places, objects, persons, etc., that could be accessed were thus exposed to more traffic (e.g., potential offenders). The ability to flee the scene of a crime and/or escape detection is often thought of as related to accessibility, but we argue that these are different issues. While accessibility determines the degree of "motivated offender exposure," ability to flee or escape detection determines the degree of effective/ineffective guardianship. A target can have both high accessibility and low surveillance potential (e.g., computers along ground-floor windows of the back side of a school building), making criminal opportunity all the more pronounced, but a target can also have high accessibility and high surveillance potential (e.g., computers along ground-floor windows of the front side of a school building) or low accessibility and low surveillance potential (e.g., computers stored in third-floor interior rooms). Also, it should be noted that some "design" features characterizing objects or persons may, at the same time, diminish accessibility yet impede surveillance. Privacy fencing offers a good example. A home surrounded by an eight-foot privacy fence is less accessible to neighborhood traffic, thus seemingly diminishing criminal opportunity. However, traffic that is able to overcome this relative inaccessibility will have fewer surveillance obstacles, since neighbors will be unlikely to detect home invasions taking place on the other side of a privacy fence.[37] The privacy fence closes the property to both potential offenders and potential guardians. Perhaps a better solution would be to build a symbolic barrier—such as an attractive row of low hedges—around the property. The symbolic barrier serves to diminish public traffic, yet does not fully impede the view of would-be guardians. Refer to Table 4.5 for an overview of the conceptualization and possible operationalization of individual-level guardianship as the fifth component of criminal opportunity.

Our general opportunity theory of crime also incorporates a conceptualization of guardianship at the aggregate level, which we defined as the collective degree to which individuals and objects in a bounded locale possess qualities related to social ties and social control. So, similar to the individual level, capable guardianship at the environmental level also consists of social ties. Areas vary in terms of the degree to which individuals and collectives (e.g., community centers, social clubs, labor unions, business organizations, and philanthropic groups) within the areas possess

Table 4.5.   Conceptualization and Operationalization of Criminal Opportunity,
          Part V

Concept	Environmental Context	Sample Measures
Individual- level social ties	Individual student or object in *school*	1. student's attachment to teachers in school 2. student's commitment to school
	Individual resident, residence, or object in *neighborhood*	1. resident's attachment to parents —level of parent-child communication —level of parental rejection —level of inconsistent/erratic discipline —marital discord 2. resident's ties to other friendship/kinship networks 3. resident's ties to conventional institutions (e.g., church, work, military)
Individual- or object-level interpersonal control	Individual student or object in *school*	1. supervision provided to student by school staff (e.g., hall monitors, security officers) 2. placement of school property vis-à-vis the "view of others" (e.g., near windows on front side of building)
	Individual resident, residence, or object in *neighborhood*	1. supervision provided by neighbors 2. placement of residence and residential property vis-à-vis "view of others" (e.g., near windows on front-side of residence; behind privacy fence obstructing surveillance)
		1. resident's number of safety precautions (e.g., installing alarms, locking doors)

attachments to others, manifest commitments to social institutions, and engage in conventional activities. In an environmental context, attachments can be understood in terms of aggregate private, parochial, and public control—the extent to which people/groups in the environment are tied to one another, to other local organizations, and to external agencies and organizations respectively.[38] Another important environmental-level social tie is culture. Culture can be viewed as representing the aggregate commitments and involvements of individuals/groups within the larger environmental context. Finally, areas can vary in terms of the degree of social control or aggregate-level surveillance that they provide. At the environmental level, aggregated social control is the collective degree to which formal control agents, informal control agents, and inanimate control devices in a bounded locale can observe and impede criminal acts.

In school contexts, social ties at the environmental level consist of the overall attachment among faculty, between faculty and principals, between faculty and students, and between school personnel and extraschool agents, such as school board members, community business leaders, parents, and local politicians. Schools with strong attachments presumably have a strong collective, internal stake in conformity as well as having support from external resources for effectively guarding against crime. Evaluation research finds support for prevention programs aimed at strengthening school climate in terms of teacher and student morale, alienation, and "smooth" administration.[39] In addition, in school contexts, the aggregate commitments and activities of students and teachers help define school culture.[40] So, schools with a large proportion of students striving to gain admission to college, with a large proportion of teachers with demanding academic standards, and with an extensive college preparatory curriculum are said to be "academically oriented" and are thought to provide limited opportunities for delinquent activity.[41] Other schools may experience the emergence of a "jock culture," a "drug culture," or a "violent culture," depending upon the alternative aggregate commitments and activities of their students, teachers, and principals. These latter two school cultures present less guardianship against crime.[42]

School-level guardianship is also influenced by aggregate-level or edifice-level formal control, informal control, and control by inanimate devices. Schools with police/security officers are characterized by guardianship in the form of formal social control. Schools with faculty hall monitors, clearly stated behavior codes and disciplinary practices, and peer "snitch lines" (e.g., phone lines that can be used to anonymously report misbehavior) display guardianship in the form of informal social control. Schools with security cameras, on the other hand, utilize social control on the part of inanimate objects. The environmental design of the school can also influence school-level guardianship. For instance, schools designed with wide, straight hallways offer greater surveillance potential per guardian than do schools with hallways laid out in a hexagonal or octagonal fashion (which were popular architecturally in the 1960s and 1970s). In the latter example, the hallways "bend" such that it is easy for students to escape supervision unless guardians are placed at every point in the hexagon or octagon. Locker bays that are built into the walls of long, straight hallways seem particularly optimal for surveillance purposes. One individual positioned at each end of the hallway can see what occurs in the entire set of lockers. In contrast, lockers that are designed in a bay fashion (e.g., a set of four of five rows of free-standing lockers) require that a supervisor be positioned at the end of each row in order for the entire area to be fully guarded, thus requiring four to five monitors as opposed to one or two monitors. The architectural design of bathroom entrances and stalls within schools can also help or hinder school-level control. For instance, maze entry systems into bathrooms allow audio- and olfactory-based surveillance without sacrificing the privacy of those inside. Teachers and other guardians can more easily hear cries of distress, smell smoke, etc., when such entranceways are used instead of traditional closed, double-door bathroom entrances. Furthermore, bathroom stalls that allow for surveillance above and below the partitions provide greater opportunity for social control and thus diminished criminal opportunity.

In neighborhood contexts, social ties consist of friendship and kinship networks among neighbors (private control), citizen participation in local organizations (parochial control), and neighborhood ties to extracommunity agencies such as police and garbage service. Contemporary research in the tradition of social disorganization theory has supported the idea that friendship ties do reduce local crime rates;[43] less empirical work has tested the effects of parochial and public control on neighborhood rates of crime.

Beyond friendship and kinship ties and neighbor networks, another community-level tie is integral in the emergence of criminal opportunity: "collective commitments and involvements"—a notion closely resembling "culture." The process of attenuation of "middle-class" culture can be linked to weakened community-level guardianship. The structurally rooted social disorganization existing in some communities may be accompanied by an attenuation of mainstream values. Ethnographic evidence suggests that many people in particularly disadvantaged and isolated communities may perceive middle-class expectations as unviable given the current structural constraints.[44] Exacerbating the problem is often the absence of positive adult role models.[45] Hence, adaptive—often deviant—strategies are employed as techniques for "getting by" within specific situational contexts. In this light, Sampson (1992, 1997) suggests that the structure of communities helps form "cognitive landscapes" for formation of normative expectations within the specific local setting. In settings in which following mainstream codes of conduct seems untenable, "deviant" behavior, including unwed teenage motherhood, young male joblessness, and adolescent drug use and violence, can become accepted as ways of life and thus easily transmitted culturally among members within a community.[46] If this process occurs, guardianship against crime is less likely, and criminal opportunity is enhanced.

Beyond aggregate ties, including collective commitments and involvements (culture), guardianship is also provided by aggregate social control. For instance, neighborhoods with relatively few street lights provide low surveillance potential. Neighborhoods with a greater concentration of home security systems per hundred households possess a greater potential to thwart criminal events. Neighborhoods with more police on patrol per city block or more neighborhood watch participants per city block have a higher concentration of social control agents who could impede criminal acts.

Much research has been conducted on the effects of "informal social control" on neighborhood crime rates. Previously, many of these studies would use aggregate-level "constitutional" variables as proxy measures of community-level informal social control. Social disorganization scholars, for instance, have suggested that factors such as community-level poverty rates, community-level ethnic heterogeneity, community-level mobility rates, and community-level family disruption (e.g., percentage of divorced, percentage of female-headed households) are related to higher rates of community crime because such characteristics impede the formation of communitywide values, social ties, and informal control practices. Thus, while we discussed earlier the ways in which some of these "constitutional" factors might represent aggregate-level target vulnerability, antagonism, or gratifiability, there is theoretical rationale for expecting such characteristics to also measure aspects of aggregate level social control.

While using "constitutional" proxy measures of community informal social control has been a standard practice for many years in the social disorganization literature, there are also extant studies that more directly measure this concept. Historically, studies that do measure informal social control operationalize this process in terms of neighborhood-level supervision and/or intervention (e.g., watching neighbor's property, calling police). Several, however, have been hampered by extremely small sample sizes.[47] More recent studies, with larger sample sizes, shed greater light on the role of processes of informal social control within the community-level social disorganization model, but complete consensus and generalizability regarding this role does not necessarily emerge. The work of Sampson and colleagues has indicated strong support for the effects of measures of informal social control (e.g., supervision of youth groups, intervention in disorderly conduct, social cohesion) on violence and other forms of mis-behavior.[48] However, in a multisample examination of neighborhood effects on adolescent development, Elliot, Wilson, Huizinga, Sampson, Elliott, and Rankin (1996) found informal control to decrease problem behavior (including delinquency, drug use, and arrests) for adolescents in Chicago, but the effect was nonsignificant among Denver youth. Thus, the empirical generalizability of the effects of informal social control remains to be seen.

Environmental design in terms of street layout and land use can also affect community-level social control. While we have already discussed the implications for mixed land use on motivated offender exposure, research suggests that nonresidential land use diminishes resident-based social control since residents of such areas are less likely to use their front yards and to be capable of distinguishing neighbors from outsiders.[49] Presence of vacant lots and buildings, buildings with few doors and windows, and institutional land can also impede resident-based surveillance and increase crime in or near such spaces.[50] Table 4.6 summarizes what we have written here as a conceptualization and possible operationalization of the aggregate-level guardianship dimension of criminal opportunity.

CONCLUSION: TOWARD A SPECIFICATION OF MAIN EFFECTS

Based upon the conceptualization and operationalization of criminal opportunity provided above (and summarized in Tables 4.1 through 4.6), we can arrive at various general propositions. We also provide some examples of specific hypotheses regarding the main effects of individual- and aggregate-level motivated offender exposure/concentration, individual- and aggregate-level target suitability, and individual- and aggregate-level guardianship. The specific hypotheses offered are intended as illustrations of how to move from our broad propositions to hypotheses that could be tested empirically. They are not presented as an exhaustive list, nor do they represent our conception of the research agenda for our theory. The propositions and example hypotheses provided below reflect our interest in both offending and victimization, and thus revolve around "criminal acts"—actions that involve force, fraud, and/or activities prohibited by law.

> Proposition 4.1: All else being equal, individual- or object-level "motivated-offender" exposure is positively related to criminal acts.
>
> Sample Hypothesis 4.1a: All else being equal, as a student's number of school-related extracurricular activities increases, criminal acts increase.
>
> Sample Hypothesis 4.1b: All else being equal, residential properties located on through streets experience a greater number of criminal acts than do residential properties located on dead-end streets.

Table 4.6. Conceptualization and Operationalization of Criminal Opportunity, Part VI

Concept	Environmental Context	Sample Measures
Aggregate-level social ties (conventional attachments, commitments, and involvements)	*School* context	1. private control (e.g., ties among faculty, ties between faculty and principal, ties between faculty and students) 2. parochial control (e.g., level of organizational participation among students, parents, teachers) 3. public control (e.g., ties between school personnel and extracommunity agencies) 4. proportion of students who are "college track" 5. number of college-preparatory courses offered 6. academic standards
	Neighborhood context	1. private control (e.g., ties among neighbors) 2. parochial control (e.g., residential participation in local organizations) 3. public control (e.g., ties between residents and extra-community agencies) 4. proportion of young female residents who are single teenage mothers 5. proportion of young male residents who are jobless
Aggregate-level guardianship	*School* context	1. presence of hall monitors, security officers, etc. 2. presence of security cameras 3. presence of clearly posted behavioral codes 4. hallway layout (e.g., straight, wide hallways with unobstructed view) 5. locker construction (e.g., built into wall or protruding from wall) 6. bathroom entry (e.g., maze entry, door held open, etc.)
	Neighborhood context	1. presence/frequency of police patrol 2. supervision/intervention provided by neighbors 3. social structural indicators of weak informal social control (e.g., proportion residents in poverty, ethnic heterogeneity, residential mobility, family disruption) 4. physical structural indicators of weak informal control (e.g., mixed land use)

Proposition 4.2: All else being equal, aggregate-level "motivated-offender" exposure is positively related to criminal acts.

Sample Hypothesis 4.2a: All else being equal, as school-level student enrollment increases, criminal acts increase.

Sample Hypothesis 4.2b: All else being equal, as neighborhood-level nonresidential land use increases, so do criminal acts.

Proposition 4.3: All else being equal, individual- or object-level target vulnerability is positively related to criminal acts.

Sample Hypothesis 4.3: All else being equal, as individual-level (student- or resident-level) substance use increases, criminal acts increase.

Proposition 4.4: All else being equal, individual- or object-level target antagonism is positively related to criminal acts.

Sample Hypothesis 4.4: All else being equal, as individual-level (student- or resident-level) self-control decreases, criminal acts increase.

Proposition 4.5: All else being equal, individual- or object-level target gratifiability is positively related to criminal acts.

Sample Hypothesis 4.5: All else being equal, as individual-level (student- or resident-level) number of portable, valuable goods increases, criminal acts increase (regarding property crime specifically).

Proposition 4.6: All else being equal, aggregate-level target vulnerability is positively related to criminal acts.

Sample Hypothesis 4.6: All else being equal, as school- or neighborhood-level signs of territoriality (e.g., marquees, sidewalks, landscaping) increase (indicating low vulnerability), criminal acts decrease.

Proposition 4.7: All else being equal, aggregate-level target antagonism is positively related to criminal acts.

Sample Hypothesis 4.7: All else being equal, as school- or neighborhood-level ethnic heterogeneity increases, criminal acts increase.

Proposition 4.8: All else being equal, aggregate-level target vulnerability is positively related to criminal acts.

Sample Hypothesis 4.8: All else being equal, as school- or neighborhood-level average SES increases, so do criminal acts (regarding property crime specifically).

Proposition 4.9: All else being equal, individual-level social ties are negatively related to criminal acts.

Sample Hypothesis 4.9a: All else being equal, as student-level attachment to teachers increases, criminal acts decrease.

Sample Hypothesis 4.9b: All else being equal, as resident-level parental rejection increases (indicating weak social ties), criminal acts increase.

Proposition 4.10: All else being equal, individual- or object-level interpersonal control is negatively related to criminal acts.

Sample Hypothesis 4.10a: All else being equal, as student's level of teacher-provided supervision increases, criminal acts decrease.

Sample Hypothesis 4.10b: All else being equal, as resident's number of safety precautions (e.g., locking doors, installing alarm system) increases, criminal acts decrease.

Proposition 4.11: All else being equal, aggregate-level social ties are negatively related to criminal acts.

Sample Hypothesis 4.11a: All else being equal, as school-level ties among faculty increase, criminal acts decrease.

Sample Hypothesis 4.11b: All else being equal, as neighborhood-level proportion of young jobless males (indicative of nonconventional commitments or attenuated culture) increases, criminal acts increase.

Proposition 4.12: All else being equal, aggregate-level guardianship (social control) is negatively related to criminal acts.

Sample Hypothesis 4.12a: All else being equal, schools in which bathroom doors are held open or are of the maze-entry type are associated with fewer criminal acts than schools in which bathroom doors are shut during the day.

Sample Hypothesis 4.12b: All else being equal, as neighborhood-level residential mobility (indicating low guardianship) increases, criminal acts increase.

In closing, we have provided in this chapter a schematic of the conceptualization and sample operationalization of a multilevel criminal opportunity theory. From this process emerged a series of propositions (along with some specific sample hypotheses) describing the expected main effects of each of the major concepts within the theory. It is clear from these propositions that we expect both individual and ecological (e.g., school, neighborhood) indicators of motivated offender exposure, target suitability, and guardianship to affect criminal opportunity. However, an assumption that these simultaneous effects of individual- and contextual-level indicators are entirely independent of one another would be naive. Instead, we presume that these indicators interact, with contextual indicators perhaps moderating or conditioning the effects of the individual-level indicators. Such contextual interactions are the subject of the following chapter.

NOTES

1. See Cohen and Felson's (1979) original articulation of routine activities theory.
2. For example, see Cohen and Felson (1979), Cohen et al. (1981), Fisher et al. (1998), Kennedy and Forde (1990), Miethe and McDowall (1993), Mustaine and Tewksbury (1998), Sampson and Lauritsen (1990), as well as Wilcox Rountree et al. (1994).

3. See Hirschi (1969).

4. See Polakowski (1994).

5. For example, see Fisher et al. (1998), Jensen and Brownfield (1986), Lauritsen, Sampson, and Laub (1991), and Mustaine and Tewksbury (1998).

6. See also Bryk and Driscoll (1988). However, see Hellman and Beaton (1986) for null effects of school size.

7. For example, see Bailey (1984), Bellair and Roscigno (2000), Blau and Blau (1982), Crutchfield (1989), Crutchfield et al. (1982), Crutchfield and Pitchford (1997), Krivo and Peterson (1996), Land, McCall, and Cohen (1990), Laub (1983), Parker and Pruitt (2000), Patterson (1991), Sampson (1983, 1985), Shihadeh and Flynn (1996), and Smith and Jarjoura (1988).

8. Compare broadly with Stark (1987) as well as Taylor and Covington (1988).

9. For example, see Roncek (1981), Taylor (1987, 1988), Taylor and Brower (1985), Taylor, Gottfredson, and Brower (1981, 1984), and Taylor, Koons, Kurtz, Greene, and Perkins (1995).

10. For example, see Miethe and McDowall (1993), Sherman, Gartin, and Buerger (1989), Wilcox Rountree et al. (1994), as well as Wilcox Rountree, Quisenberry, Cabrera, and Jones (2000).

11. See Brantingham and Brantingham (1982).

12. For example, see Roncek and Bell (1981), Roncek and Maier (1991), and Roncek and Pravatiner (1989).

13. For example, see Roncek and Faggiani (1985) and Roncek and LoBosco (1983).

14. For example, see Hough (1987), Messner and Blau (1987), and Singer (1981).

15. For example, see Cohen et al. (1981), Miethe and McDowall (1993), Miethe and Meier (1994), and Sampson and Wooldredge (1987).

16. See Massey et al. (1989).

17. For example, see Miethe and McDowall (1993), Miethe and Meier (1994), Wilcox Rountree and Land (1996a), and Wilcox Rountree et al. (1994).

18. See Fisher et al. (1998).

19. For example, see our discussion of target vulnerability.

20. See our earlier discussion of the problems with using sociodemographic measures as proxies for vulnerability.

21. But again, see our earlier discussions of the measurement error associated with sociodemographic proxy measures.

22. See Hirschi (1969).

23. It should be noted that we have excluded Hirschi's (1969) conception of belief from our definition of social control. We have done so because differential belief about rule-breaking and law-abiding behaviors seems to suggest differential motivation to offend, which could arise from socialization or subcultural influences. It should also be noted that although we have not discussed Hirschi's bonding perspective specifically, its compatibility with criminal opportunity theory is widely accepted. Indeed, Hirschi (1989) has gone so far as to state that his social control perspective and the routine activities approach are part of the same theory.

24. For example, see Albrecht, Amey, and Miller (1996), Gottfredson (1986), Inciardi, Horowitz, and Pottieger (1993), Jarjoura (1993), Jenkins (1997), Jessor (1976), and Krohn and Massey (1980).

25. For example, see Hawkins, Arthur, and Catalano (1995), Hawkins, Catalano, Morrison, O'Donnell, Abbott, and Day (1992), Hawkins, Doueck, and Lischner (1988), Hawkins, Von Cleve, and Catalano (1991), and O'Donnell, Hawkins, Catalano, Abbott, and Day (1995). See Gottfredson (2001) for an extensive review of this literature.

26. For example, see Akers and Cochran (1985), Jessor and Jessor (1977), Kandel, Kessler, and Margulies (1978), Kandel, Simcha-Fagan, and Davies (1986), Patterson and Dishion (1985), and Patterson, Reid, and Dishion (1995).

27. For example, see Elliot et al. (1985), Kaplan, Martin, Johnson, and Robbins (1986), and Kaplan, Martin, and Robbins (1984).

28. For example, see DeMarsh and Kumpfer (1986), Johnson and Pandina (1991), McCord (1991), and Zucker (1989).

29. See Kandel and Andrews (1987).

30. See Norem-Hebeisen, Johnson, Anderson, and Johnson (1984).

31. For example, see Larzelere and Patterson (1990), Loeber and Stouthammer-Loeber (1986), Needle, Su, and Doherty (1990), Rankin and Kern (1994), as well as Simcha-Fagan, Gersten, and Langer (1986).

32. For example, see Albrecht et al. (1996), Burkett and White (1974), Cochran and Akers (1989), Johnson, Marcos, and Bahr (1987), and Marcos, Bahr, and Johnson (1986).

33. For example, see Laub and Sampson (1993), Sampson and Laub (1993, 1996), and Uggen (2000).

34. For example, see Braga and Clarke (1994), Buck, Hakim, and Rengert (1993), Clarke (1992), Fisher et al. (1998), Massey et al. (1989), Miethe and McDowall (1993), Miethe and Meier (1990), and Mustaine and Tewksbury (1998).

35. For example, see Miethe and McDowall (1993), Miethe and Meier (1994), and Wilcox Rountree et al. (1994).

36. See Wilcox (2002).

37. See Brown and Altman (1981); but compare with Wilcox Rountree and Land (1996a).

38. For example, see Bursik and Grasmick (1993), Hunter (1985), Sampson (1988, 1991), and Wilcox Rountree and Warner (1999).

39. For example, see Gottfredson (1986, 1987) and Gottfredson, Gottfredson, and Hybl (1993).

40. See Anderson (1982).

41. For example, see Gottfredson (1987), Malvin, Moskowitz, Schaeffer, and Schaps (1984). See Gottfredson (2001) for a extensive review.

42. For example, see Felson, Liska, South, and McNulty (1994), Lefkowitz (1998), Malvin et al. (1984), and Wilcox Rountree and Clayton (1999).

43. For example, Bellair (1997, 2000), Patterson (1991), Patillo (1998), Sampson and Groves (1989), and Warner and Wilcox Rountree (1997).

44. For example, see Anderson (1990), Dash (1996), Furstenberg, Cook, Eccles, and Eccles (1999), Horowitz (1987), Suttles (1968), and Wilson (1996).

45. See Jencks and Mayer (1990).

46. See Sucoff and Upchurch (1998) and Warner and Rountree (2000).

47. For example, see Greenberg, Rohe, and Williams (1982), Hackler, Ho, and Urquart-Ross (1974), and Macoby, Johnson, and Church (1958).

48. For example, see Sampson (1987), Sampson and Groves (1989), Sampson et al. (1997), and Sampson and Raudenbush (1999).

49. For example, see Appleyard (1981), Baum, Davis, and Aiello (1978), Brown and Altman (1981), Greenberg et al. (1982), and Taylor et al. (1995).

50. See Ley and Cybriwsky (1974).

5

Evidence and Specification of Moderating Effects

Consider the following findings from recent research:

- Urbanness of school location alters the effect of school attachment on student likelihood of carrying a weapon to school. School attachment's negative effect on weapon carrying is tempered in less urban as opposed to more urban school settings.[1]
- Urbanness of school location also conditions the effect of previous arrest on the likelihood of in-school weapon carrying. In a comparison across three Kentucky counties, the effect of previous arrest was positive in an urban county and negative in two more rural counties.[2]
- Neighborhood-level incivilities temper the negative effect of safety precautions on burglary victimization likelihood. In disorderly communities, safety precautions are not as effective in reducing burglary victimization risk.[3]
- Neighborhood-level public activity tempers the positive effect of living alone on burglary victimization likelihood. Living alone matters less in terms of predicting burglary risk in busy areas.[4]
- Neighborhood social disorganization conditions the effects of living alone on assault victimization likelihood. The positive effect of living alone on assault likelihood is increased (i.e., *exacerbated*) by area-level social disorganization.[5]
- Neighborhood social disorganization (e.g., low SES, high public activity) alters the effect of individual-level income on likelihood of experiencing assault victimization. Income's negative effect on assault

likelihood is strongest in the most *organized* areas; in disorganized areas, individual income has a minimal effect.[6]

- Neighborhood-level ethnic heterogeneity reduces (i.e., *tempers*) the positive effect of race (nonwhite) on violent victimization likelihood. Being nonwhite increases risk of violent victimization in ethnically homogeneous communities specifically.[7]

Each of the empirical findings summarized above suggests that the "main" effects of some individual-level indicators of criminal opportunity vary substantially across environmental contexts, and that characteristics indicative of ambient-level opportunity can help explain this variation. Figure 5.1 represents a visual display of this notion. Ambient criminal opportunity can condition or moderate the main effects of indicators of individual-level criminal opportunity. The dashed arrows in Figure 5.1 (from aggregate-level opportunity) depict this potential conditioning or moderation. These arrows represent the altering of the effects on criminal acts of individual-level motivated offender exposure, target suitability, and guardianship.

The unearthing of such cross-level interaction effects through sophisticated multilevel modeling procedures has, frankly, been received with varying levels of enthusiasm among scholars within the field of criminology. On the one hand, such effects offer promise for advancement of the field in that they further refine what we know about crime and its predictors. This is helpful from a policy standpoint because it suggests that individual-level crime reduction efforts may be more or less effective in particular environmental contexts. On the other hand, we are hard-pressed to really understand these interaction effects from a theoretical standpoint since little criminological theory to date explicitly addresses these sorts of conditioning influences. Researchers who discover such findings really have little a priori theoretical grounds for exploring micro-macro interactions in the first place. As a result, such exploration often gets termed "data-drudging" or "a fishing expedition." When theoretical explanations for individual-context interactions are offered, they are necessarily post hoc and incomplete, and so we are in a state in criminology where the methods lie ahead of the theory, so to speak. We have the methodological and statistical tools available for exploring person-environment interactions,[8] yet we do not have strong theory for justifying or explaining such effects. In this vein, our multicontextual criminal opportunity theory is uniquely situated to provide a theoretical framework for such justification and explanation purposes. The remainder of this chapter discusses the very notion of micro-macro interactions more fully within the context of our conceptual model and delineates general theoretical propositions regarding such interactions.

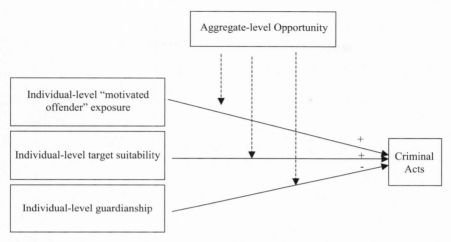

Figure 5.1.   Moderating effects of aggregate-level opportunity on the relationship between individual- or object-level opportunity factors and criminal
acts.

STATISTICAL INTERACTION EFFECTS

We begin by offering some general background information regarding statistical interaction effects using, as an example, how ambient opportunity
might interact with individual-level motivated offender exposure. Simply
put, aggregate-level indicators of criminal opportunity can either temper
or exacerbate the proposed overall positive main effect of motivated
offender exposure.[9] These possibilities are illustrated in Figure 5.2. If a particular aggregate-level characteristic makes the positive main effect more
strongly positive, then the effect is exacerbated. If, on the other hand, an
ambient-level characteristic diminishes the main effect, then the effect is
said to be tempered. To exemplify, the effect of individual-level motivated
offender exposure might be tempered in certain contexts to the extent that
it, in fact, becomes virtually null or even reverses direction (i.e., becomes
negative).

There are, then, three possibilities regarding the interaction of aggregate-level opportunity with individual-level motivated offender exposure: (1) it can have no significant interaction, (2) it can have a significant
positive interaction, or (3) it can have a significant negative interaction.
Again, these possibilities have implications in terms of how they alter the
main effect (or the slope) of individual-level motivated offender exposure
on criminal acts. These possibilities are displayed in another form in

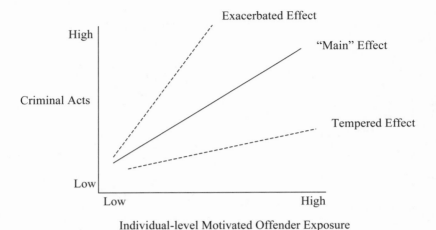

Figure 5.2. Hypothetical main and moderating effects regarding the relationship between individual-level motivated offender exposure and criminal
acts.

Figure 5.3. If an aggregate-level characteristic does not interact with individual-level motivated offender exposure, then the individual-level slope
will not change, regardless of the level of that particular aggregate-level
characteristic within the environment. The slope will stay constant; the
change in the slope is zero (as indicated by the horizontal line in Figure
5.3). When there is no interaction—when the change in the slope is zero—
the main effect (see solid line in Figure 5.2) applies across contexts.

A positive interaction effect, in this case (given that the main effect is
presumed positive), suggests that the slope increases as levels of the aggregate-level indicator of opportunity in question increase. Thus, the main
effect is not constant across contexts, but increases as ambient opportunity
increases. The positive effect is thus exacerbated; in high-opportunity contexts the slope would be steeper, or more strongly positive. If the main
effect is positive (as is presumed here) and the interaction effect is negative, however, then the positive effect is declining as ambient opportunity
increases, and the main effect is said to be tempered. Again, Figures 5.2
and 5.3 depict hypothetical interaction scenarios using the posited positive
main effect of individual-level motivated offender exposure as an example. It should be noted that, since the effect of individual-level target suitability on criminal acts is also presumed to be positive,[10] hypothetical
scenarios for cross-level interactions with individual-level target suitability would be the same as those depicted in Figures 5.2 and 5.3.

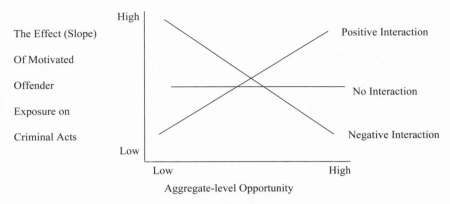

Figure 5.3.   Hypothetical contextual (interaction) effects: The effect of aggregate-level opportunity on the relationship between individual-level motivated offender exposure and criminal acts.

However, rather than having a positive main effect, an individual-level
"main" effect in question might be negative. For instance, the relationship
between guardianship and criminal acts is presumed to be negative, i.e., as
guardianship increases, criminal acts decrease. For individual-level variables with a negative main effect, a positive interaction with ambient
opportunity would temper the negative main effect, thereby making it less
negative (i.e., the slope would still reflect a negative relationship but it
would not be as steep), or even reverse the negative main effect, making it
positive. For individual-level variables with a negative main effect, a negative interaction with ambient opportunity would exacerbate the negative
main effect, thereby making it more negative (i.e., the slope would reflect
a negative relationship and it would be steeper). Using the effect of individual-level guardianship on criminal acts as an example, Figures 5.4 and
5.5 depict hypothetical interaction-effect scenarios when the main effect in
question is negative as opposed to positive.

At this point, the reader is cautioned to avoid confusing correlation of
environmental- and individual-level factors with cross-level interaction
effects. For instance, this is a statement of a positive correlation between
environmental- and individual-level concepts: individual-level guardianship measures tend to be greater in environmental contexts where aggregate guardianship is greater, and conversely, individual-level guardianship
measures tend to be fewer in environmental contexts where aggregate
guardianship is less. This is a simple correlation between environmental-
and individual-level concepts. In contrast, the following is a statement of a

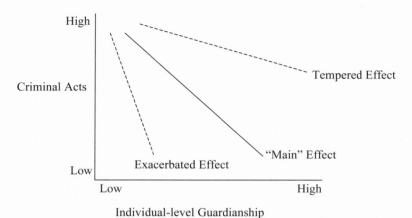

Figure 5.4. Hypothetical main and moderating effects regarding the relationship between individual-level guardianship and criminal acts.

more complex, cross-level interaction effect: the effect individual-level
guardianship measures have on the likelihood of victimization (i.e., a criminal act) is more pronounced in environments with relatively high aggregate levels of guardianship. To illustrate this hypothetical cross-level
interaction in practical terms, consider the effect of installing a home alarm
system in two different neighborhoods. The cross-level interaction effect
suggested here would imply that installing a home alarm system in a neighborhood that possesses a high level of community guardianship reduces
one's burglary risk substantially more than does installing the same home
alarm system in a neighborhood that has a low level of community
guardianship. Potential burglars might well reason that if they set off a
home alarm in a neighborhood with a high level of community guardianship, they have a pretty good chance of being detected and caught due to
police response, attention of neighbors, and so on. On the other hand, in an
ecological context with a relatively low level of community guardianship,
potential burglars might well reason that their chances of being detected
and caught are low, even if they were to set off a home alarm. In short,
detecting a cross-level interaction effect means that some environmental-
level variable is affecting the effect some individual-level variable has on
criminal acts.

AMBIENT OPPORTUNITY AND ITS MODERATING EFFECTS

Based upon the discussion thus far, it is clear that we expect ambient
opportunity to exert not only main effects on criminal acts (as discussed in

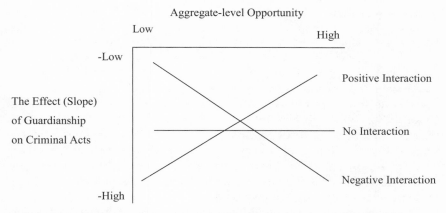

Figure 5.5. Hypothetical contextual (interaction) effects: The effect of aggregate-level opportunity on the relationship (presumed negative) between
   individual-level guardianship and criminal acts.

Chapter 4), but to also moderate or condition, either positively or negatively, the effects on criminal acts of individual-level indicators of criminal
opportunity. But when can a particular context be defined as exhibiting
"contextual opportunity?" What are the conditions that define whether
contexts exacerbate or temper main effects? As we have outlined in previous chapters, contextual or ambient opportunity is conceptualized in
terms of aggregate-level motivated offender exposure, aggregate-level target suitability, and aggregate-level guardianship. Thus, there are three
unique dimensions of ambient criminal opportunity. We offer theoretical
propositions regarding the effects that each of these dimensions should
have on each of the individual-level relationships depicted in Figure 5.1:
(1) the relationship between criminal acts and individual-level motivated
offender exposure, (2) the relationship between criminal acts and individual-level target suitability, and (3) the relationship between criminal acts
and individual-level guardianship.

As such, we are approaching the examination of cross-level interaction
effects using a 3 × 3 matrix of sorts—with each of the three overarching
dimensions of individual-level opportunity interacting with each of the
three overarching dimensions of aggregate-level opportunity. In previous
chapters, we have delineated subconcepts within each of the three indi-
vidual- and aggregate-level domains of opportunity (e.g., target vulnerability, target antagonism, and target gratifiability are subconcepts related
to the overarching dimension of target suitability at both individual and
aggregate levels; social ties and social control are subconcepts related to
aggregate-level guardianship). However, we do not expect differences

across subconcepts within any one overarching concept or dimension in terms of cross-level interactions. Thus, for example, we expect individual-level target vulnerability, target antagonism, and target gratifiability to all interact similarly with any one particular aggregate-level concept. Similarly, we expect aggregate-level subdimensions of one underlying aggregate-level opportunity dimension—such as social ties and social control—to interact similarly with any one individual-level opportunity concept. So, while the conceptualization scheme outlined in Chapter 4 could yield a 6 × 6 matrix of possible cross-level interactions (we defined a total of 6 individual-level concepts and 6 aggregate-level concepts), in order to simplify an already-complex presentation and to avoid redundancy given expected similarities among subconcepts linked to common overarching dimensions, we discuss micro-macro interactions in terms of the three overarching individual-level dimensions vis-à-vis the three overarching aggregate-level dimensions of criminal opportunity.

GROUNDING THEORETICAL PRINCIPLES AND LOGIC

To develop specific propositions about the moderating effects that ecological opportunity concepts have on individual-level opportunity constructs, we must ground our expectations in our theoretical framework. In puzzling out possible cross-level interaction effects, we must provide some clear, underlying logic to the relationships we eventually posit. In other words, *why* should we suspect that variations in ecological contexts will affect the effects of individual-level opportunity on criminal acts? Given the paucity of multilevel research that has discovered cross-level interaction effects, our expectations are primarily derived deductively, rather than emerging inductively from hard empirical evidence. Underlying our expectations is the principal logic of criminal opportunity—criminal acts are socially produced in contexts that possess a sufficient supply of criminal opportunity, which is a function of individual- and environmental-level motivated offenders, suitable targets, and lack of capable guardians.

In developing our rationale for cross-level interactions, we refer to the grounding orientations found in criminal opportunity theory. According to Cook, "criminal opportunity theory employs the economic theory of markets to describe and predict how criminals and victims interact" (1986:1).[11] A cornerstone of an economic theory of markets is the utilitarian assumption that individuals maximize their utility, seeking pleasure and avoiding pain. As we suggested earlier, this premise is expressed in criminal opportunity theory's assumption about offender motivation. Following Becker, we have suggested further that opportunity theory's classical assumption about criminal motivation "provides a solid foundation for making predictions" and it "prevents the analyst from succumbing to the temptation of simply postulating" (post hoc) a shift in the quality or quantity of motivation "to 'explain' all apparent contradictions to his[/her] predictions" (1976:5).

Here, the motivational assumption is important because it is key to understanding "market forces" inherent in aggregate criminal opportunity structures. Using an economic markets perspective, we can advance that market demand for criminal acts is a reflection of the aggregated supply of individuals who desire criminal acts (i.e., those who are motivated to offend). Because each individual is assumed to have the same motivation to offend, that is, the same desire for criminal acts, the aggregated supply of motivated offenders can simply be conceptualized as a function of the number of individuals in a space-time context and/or the accessibility offered to those individuals. This brings us to our *supply of aggregate motivated offenders axiom*: demand for criminal acts will increase as the supply of aggregate motivated offenders increases, *ceteris paribus*.[12] We do not posit a direct, one-to-one correspondence between the supply of motivated offenders and the manifestation of criminal acts. That is, we would not expect every unit increase in the supply of motivated offenders to yield a corresponding increase in criminal acts. The supply of motivated offenders will increase the aggregate demand for criminal acts, but, as is true for other economic markets, a portion of that aggregate demand will go unsatisfied. All we mean to suggest here is that an increase in the supply of motivated offenders will correspond to an increased aggregate demand for criminal acts, which will only be partially satisfied in the occurrence of actual criminal acts.[13]

This axiom implies some important aggregate marketplace principles. To illustrate, consider an environment where the only change that occurs over a period of time is an increase in the supply of motivated offenders, which amounts to an increase in the aggregate demand for criminal acts. The supply of motivated offenders axiom maintains that there will be movement toward satisfying the increased aggregate demand for criminal acts; that is, criminal acts will increase. But how? What are the mechanisms that produce such an effect? We have stated that nothing other than the supply of motivated offenders has changed in this hypothetical ecological context. The activities that expose individuals to motivated offenders has remained the same. Targets have not increased to meet the increased demand. Guardianship has not decreased so as to make "successful" criminal acts more facile. Therefore, an answer to how the supply of motivated offenders is linked to the occurrence of actual criminal acts cannot be fashioned from those factors.

The keys to understanding the link between the supply of motivated offenders and the occurrence of criminal acts are three aggregate principles that pertain to *market exposure*, *market value*, and *market cost*. First, increases in the supply of motivated offenders, by definition, creates a market that has greater exposure to motivated offenders, all else being equal. Second, increases in the supply of motivated offenders will increase the market value of targets in that environment, all else being equal. Simply put, increases in the supply of motivated offenders correspond to increases in aggregate demand for criminal acts, which requires a supply of suitable targets to be satisfied. When the aggregate demand for targets increases relative to their aggregate supply, market forces suggest that the value of targets will be enhanced. Third, increases in the supply of motivated offenders will decrease the market costs of criminal acts, all else being equal. It seems reasonable to suggest that most of the costs of criminal acts relate to effort, detection, and apprehension—all of which involve avoiding guardianship or minimizing its effectiveness. One way of viewing market costs of criminal acts is to think of it in terms of the supply of aggregate motivated offenders relative to the supply of aggregate capable guardianship. When the supply of motivated offenders increases relative to the supply of guardianship (e.g., an increased supply of aggregate motivated offenders relative to a constant supply of aggregate guardianship), the market cost of criminal acts is diminished.

In addition to the supply of aggregate motivated offenders axiom, the economic perspective of criminal opportunity suggests two other important aggregate, marketplace axioms. From our economic perspective, we can advance a *supply of aggregate suitable targets axiom*: as the supply of aggregate suitable targets increases, the market value of targets is diminished, *ceteris paribus*. This follows the logic of aggregate market forces, which suggests that when the supply of a good increases relative to its demand, the market value of that good decreases.[14] We also posit a *supply of aggregate capable guardians axiom*: as the supply of aggregate capable guardians increases, the market cost of criminal acts increases, *ceteris paribus*. When the supply of motivated offenders decreases relative to the supply of guardianship (e.g., a constant supply of aggregate motivated offenders relative to an increased supply of aggregate guardianship), the market cost of criminal acts increases.

With these three guiding axioms and associated principles, we further develop our theoretical rationale for cross-level interactions by returning to the propositions of individual-level main effects advanced in Chapter 4.

Concerning motivated offenders, we posited that individual- or object-level motivated offender exposure is positively related to criminal acts, all else being equal. What possible interaction effects might we expect to find with aggregate-level motivated offender exposure, aggregate-level target suitability, and aggregate-level guardianship?

The supply of motivated offenders axiom suggests a particular cross-level interaction between aggregate-level motivated offender exposure and individual-level exposure. Namely, increases in the supply of motivated offenders will increase potential victims' market exposure to motivated offenders, all else being equal. Stated in terms of moderating effects, as the supply of aggregate motivated offenders increases, the positive effect of individual- or object-level motivated offender exposure on criminal acts is increased. Thus, we suspect that aggregate supplies of motivated offenders will have an exacerbating effect on the positive effect between criminal acts and individual- or object-level motivated offender exposure. To illustrate, consider the exposure associated with walking alone at night. Holding all else constant, we could say that this individual exposure in and of itself has some measurable, positive effect on experiencing a criminal act. For the sake of illustration, let us call this the baseline individual exposure effect. Now imagine that same act of exposure in environmental contexts with varying supplies of aggregate motivated offenders—say we have data on one hundred neighborhoods ranging in resident density from twenty to one thousand people per square mile. Our theory would lead us to predict that increases in the supply of aggregate motivated offenders will make the positive effect of the individual exposure baseline more strongly positive.

Still considering the positive effect that individual- or object-level motivated offender exposure has on criminal acts, we explore the possibility of an interaction effect with aggregate-level target suitability. The supply of aggregate suitable targets axiom is a useful place to begin considering this cross-level interaction. Recall that as the supply of suitable targets increases, the market value of suitable targets diminishes, *ceteris paribus*. Increases in the supply of suitable targets makes "attractive" targets appear less "attractive." Logic suggests that as aggregate supplies of suitable targets increase, therefore diminishing the relative value of any one target, individual distinctions in terms of exposure will be all the more important. Thus, we suspect that aggregate supplies of suitable targets would have an exacerbating effect on the positive effect individual- or object-level motivated offender exposure has on criminal acts.

We now turn to the possibility of a cross-level effect between aggregate-level guardianship and individual- or object-level motivated offender exposure. Recall that as the supply of capable guardians increases, the market cost of criminal acts increases, *ceteris paribus*. It seems logical that as the supplies of aggregate guardianship increase, the positive effect individual-level motivated offender exposure has on criminal acts would diminish. But why? The reason is that the supply of aggregate guardianship serves as a deterrent. As the market cost of a criminal act increases, individual exposure matters less. Therefore, the positive effect individual-level exposure to motivated offenders has on criminal acts would decrease as the supply of aggregate guardianship increases. Thus, we suspect that aggregate supplies of guardianship would have a tempering effect.

Pertaining to suitable targets, we posited that individual- or object-level target suitability is positively related to criminal acts, all else being equal. In the following paragraphs, we consider possible interaction effects individual-level target suitability might have with supplies of aggregate-level motivated offender exposure, aggregate-level target suitability, and aggregate-level guardianship.

The supply of motivated offenders axiom suggests a particular cross-level interaction between aggregate-level motivated offender exposure and individual-level target suitability. Namely, this axiom suggests that increases in the supply of motivated offenders increase the market demand for criminal acts, which will enhance the market value of suitable targets in that environment, all else being equal (i.e., the demand for suitable targets is greater than the supply). In terms of interaction effects, as the aggregate supply of motivated offenders increases, the positive effect of individual-level target suitability is increased. Thus, we suspect that aggregate supplies of motivated offenders will have an exacerbating effect on the overall positive "main" effect that individual-level target suitability has on criminal acts.

Further considering the positive effect that individual-level target suitability has on criminal acts, we explore the possibility of an interaction effect with the supply of aggregate suitable targets. The supply of suitable targets axiom is instructive here. Specifically, as the supply of suitable targets increases, the market value of targets is diminished, *ceteris paribus*. Following the supply of aggregate suitable targets axiom, we argue that aggregated supplies of suitable targets would temper the positive effect individual- or object-level target suitability has on criminal acts.

Next we explore the possibility of a cross-level effect between aggregate-level guardianship and individual-level target suitability. Here, the supply of aggregate capable guardians axiom is illuminating. As the supply of capable guardians increases, the market cost of criminal acts increases, all else being equal. It seems logical that as the supplies of aggregate guardianship increase, the positive effect individual-level target suitability has on criminal acts would diminish. Why? Again, the reason is that the supply of aggregate guardianship functions as a deterrent. As the market cost of criminal acts increases, individual target suitability matters less. Therefore, the positive effect individual-level target suitability has on criminal acts would decrease as the supply of aggregate guardianship increases. This suggests that aggregate supplies of guardianship would have a tempering effect.

Finally, we take up the possibility of interaction effects surrounding individual-level guardianship. In Chapter 4, we stated that individual-level guardianship is negatively related to criminal acts, all else being equal. This proposition reflects opportunity theory's contention that guardianship acts as a deterrent to criminal acts. Below, we explore possible interaction effects between individual-level guardianship and aggregate-level motivated offender exposure, aggregate-level target suitability, and aggregate-level guardianship.

Once again the supply of aggregate motivated offenders axiom suggests a particular cross-level interaction between aggregate-level motivated offender exposure and individual-level guardianship. Specifically, increases in the supply of aggregate motivated offenders will decrease the relative market costs of criminal acts. In regard to interaction effects, as the aggregate supply of motivated offenders increases, the negative effect of individual-level guardianship is diminished. Thus, we suspect that aggregate supplies of motivated offenders will have a tempering effect on the negative effect individual-level guardianship has on criminal acts. Recall that a negative "main" effect is tempered via a positive interaction effect, as illustrated in Figures 5.4. and 5.5.

Now we will address the possibility of a moderating effect between aggregate-level target suitability and the negative effect individual-level guardianship has on criminal acts. Again we refer to the supply of suitable targets axiom—as the supply of aggregate suitable targets increases, the value of any one target is diminished, *ceteris paribus*. It would seem that as supplies of aggregate suitable targets increase, therefore diminishing the relative value of any one target, individual distinctions in terms of guardianship will be all the more important. This suggests that individual guardianship measure will be more effective at deterring criminal acts in contexts with a relatively high supply of suitable targets. The negative effect of individual-level guardianship will become more strongly negative as the supply of aggregate suitable targets increases. Thus, we argue that aggregate supplies of suitable targets would have an exacerbating effect (but a negative interaction term) on the negative effect individual-level guardianship has on criminal acts.

Finally, we explore the possibility of a cross-level effect between aggregate-level guardianship and individual-level guardianship. We find it necessary to refer to the supply of aggregate capable guardians axiom again—as the supply of aggregate capable guardians increases, the market costs associated with criminal acts increases, *ceteris paribus*. We contend that as the supplies of aggregate guardianship increase, the effect individual-level guardianship has on criminal acts becomes greater. Again this is due to the fact that the supply of aggregate guardianship functions as an overarching deterrent. As market costs of a criminal act increase in an ecological context, individual guardianship matters more. Therefore, the negative effect individual-level guardianship has on criminal acts would increase as the supply of aggregate guardianship increases. This suggests that supplies of aggregate guardianship would have an exacerbating effect

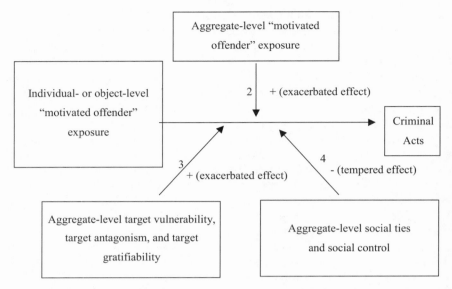

Figure 5.6. Moderating effects of aggregate-level opportunity on the relationship between individual-level motivated offender exposure and criminal
acts.

(but a negative interaction term) on the negative effect individual-level
guardianship has on criminal acts.

KEY PROPOSITIONS

Having examined the guiding principles of opportunity theory and the
underlying logic of possible cross-level interactions, we are ready to state
our propositions more formally in this section. We begin by looking more
closely at the contextual moderating effects on the relationship between
individual-level motivated offender exposure and criminal acts. Figure 5.6
displays the conceptual model regarding the presumed positive main
effect of individual-level motivated offender exposure on criminal acts
(arrow 1) and potential moderating effects of different dimensions of
aggregate-level opportunity (arrows 2, 3, and 4). The following propositions help define more fully the precise nature of the moderating effects:

Proposition 5.1: All else being equal, aggregate-level supply of motivated offenders exacerbates the positive effect of individual-level motivated

offender exposure. A large supply of offenders makes individual-level exposure seemingly all the more risky. Arrow 2 in Figure 5.6 thus depicts a positive interaction effect.

Proposition 5.2: All else being equal, aggregate-level supply of suitable targets exacerbates the positive effect of individual-level motivated offender exposure. With a high supply of suitable targets in a particular context, the value of any one target is diminished, and individual distinctions in terms of exposure become all the more important. The effect depicted by arrow 3 in Figure 5.6 is thus positive.

Proposition 5.3: All else being equal, aggregate-level supply of guardianship tempers the positive effect of individual-level motivated offender exposure on criminal acts. This is due to the deterrent effect of aggregate guardianship. The effect represented by arrow 4 in Figure 5.6 is, therefore, negative.

Next, let us consider the positive main effect of individual-level target attractiveness on criminal acts and the possible ways in which different aspects of ambient opportunity might alter this main effect. Figure 5.7 is a conceptual model of these main and moderating effects. In order to guide understanding of the moderating effects here, we offer the following propositions:

Proposition 5.4: All else being equal, aggregate supply of motivated offenders exacerbates this positive effect. A large supply of offenders increases demand for targets, making individual features of suitability all the more important. Arrow 2 in Figure 5.7 thus represents a positive interaction effect.

Proposition 5.5: All else being equal, aggregate supply of suitable targets tempers this positive effect. With a large supply of targets in the context, the value associated with any one target is diminished. As such, the direction of the interaction effect depicted by arrow 3 in Figure 5.7 is negative.

Proposition 5.6: All else being equal, aggregate supply of guardianship tempers this positive effect. The interaction effect represented by arrow 4 in Figure 5.7 is negative.

Lastly, we consider the presumed negative relationship between individual-level guardianship and criminal acts. Figure 5.8 represents a conceptual model of this main effect and the potential moderating influences. Fuller understanding of arrows 2, 3, and 4 in this figure can be gleaned from the following propositions:

Proposition 5.7: All else being equal, aggregate-level supply of motivated offenders tempers this negative relationship. With a high supply of offenders, demand for crime targets (persons or objects) is great, and costs associated with individual targets matter less. A tempering of a negative main effect, however, would suggest a *positive* interaction effect. Arrow 2 in Figure 5.8 is thus posited to be a positive effect.

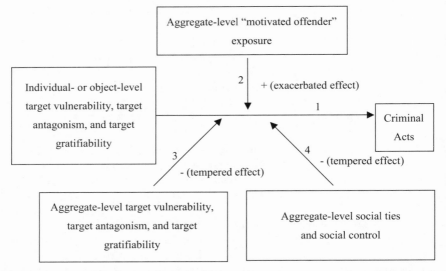

Figure 5.7. Moderating effects of aggregate-level opportunity on the relationship between individual-level target suitability and criminal acts.

Proposition 5.8: All else being equal, aggregate-level supply of suitable targets exacerbates this negative relationship. A high supply of suitable targets diminishes the value of any one target, and renders "costly" targets all the more avoidable. Exacerbation of a negative main effect occurs through a negative interaction effect. Thus, the interaction effect represented by arrow 3 in Figure 5.8 is negative.

Proposition 5.9: All else being equal, aggregate-level supply of guardianship exacerbates this negative relationship. This is due to the deterrent effect of aggregate guardianship. As such, individual guardianship effects are enhanced. The interaction effect depicted by arrow 4 in Figure 5.8 is negative.

FINDING MODERATING EFFECTS IN AMBIENT OPPORTUNITY CONTEXTS: EIGHT IDEAL TYPES

Each of the nine propositions stated above provides theoretical rationale for expected moderating effects of one particular concept related to ambient opportunity, while holding all else constant—while controlling for levels of other, possibly confounding effects. These propositions are thus compatible with the way we typically go about estimating interaction effects within multivariate statistical models of crime. When we include an interaction effect between an indicator of individual-level guardianship

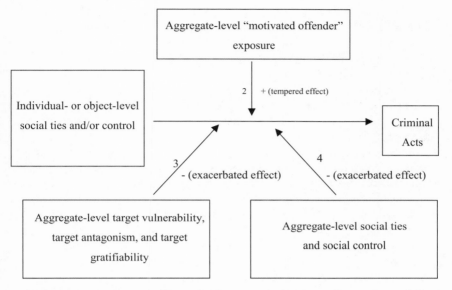

Figure 5.8.   Moderating effects of aggregate-level opportunity on the relationship between individual-level guardianship and criminal acts.

and an indicator of aggregate-level guardianship, for instance, we typically "control" for aggregate-level motivated offender exposure and aggregate-level target suitability. That is, we hold the other dimensions of ambient opportunity constant while examining the possible interaction between one dimension and an individual-level indicator. However, we recognize that contexts exhibit important differences in the extent to which they produce criminal opportunity in an overall, or combined, sense across all three contextual dimensions. It is possible for contexts to exhibit substantial criminal opportunity along one dimension, two dimensions, or all three dimensions. These distinct possibilities have important implications regarding overall ambient criminal opportunity as well as the ways in which individual-level relationships might be altered by context. Also, these distinct possibilities can be helpful in determining how best to detect moderating effects.

We posit a scheme that takes into account the different types of "criminal opportunity" that might exist at the ambient level, depending upon the simultaneous, *additive* influence of each of the three dimensions of environmental opportunity. More specifically, we propose that environmental contexts can be characterized overall as a function of the additive effects of the three dimensions of ambient opportunity: the supply of motivated offenders (SoM), the supply of suitable targets (SoT), and the supply of capable guardians (SoG). Based upon the varying combinations of these three dimensions, we can identify eight ideal types of environmental opportunity contexts and provide a rough characterization of the volume of criminal acts in such contexts.

At this point, a brief consideration of the nature and uses of ideal types might prove helpful. Weber (1949) is credited with developing the notion of ideal type in sociology. For Weber, an ideal type is a heuristic device, a "conceptual pattern," that "brings together certain relationships and events of historical life into a complex, which is conceived as an internally consistent system" (ibid.:90). As heuristic devices, ideal types are tools to explicate and develop theoretical understandings of real world phenomena. Little provides a cogent description of the relationship between the theoretical development of ideal types and the analysis of concrete social phenomena:

> The theoretical construct [i.e., ideal type] functions as an organizing device in terms of which the social scientist attempts to analyze and explain concrete social phenomena. The social scientist works back and forth between the abstract theoretical concept and the concrete social phenomena, shedding light on the concrete phenomena by showing how its various elements hang together. But social scientists rarely deduce conclusions about social phenomena based on the abstract logic of the theoretical construct without considering the concrete particularity of the event in question. (1991:226)

Ideal types are not depictions of particular real world events or situations per se. Rather, they are theoretical tools. Ideal types are characterizations of the abstract, essential elements of social processes and structures. From our view, the essential elements of ambient criminal opportunity pertain to motivated offenders, targets, and guardianship. We offer eight ideal types of criminal opportunity in bounded locales to shed light on how various combinations of the ambient dimensions of criminal opportunity might come together as "ambient opportunity." These ideal types are merely a means to organize and put forward our theoretical framework. As theoretical tools, our ideal types are necessarily hypothetical and abstract. Ultimately, our main purpose in offering these ideal types is to shed light upon the essential features of the social production of criminal acts in various ecological contexts of criminal opportunity.

Context 1: High SoM + High SoT + Low SoG

This is a condition where the supplies of motivated offenders and suitable targets are high and the supply of guardians is low. This provides the greatest environmental opportunity for criminal acts to occur. It should be noted that the manifestation of this kind of context in the real world would appear to be unlikely. Essentially, this ideal type of context represents a bounded locale that would exhibit a high degree of social disorganization, as the low supply of capable guardians would indicate. But, at the same time, this ideal type suggests that this kind of bounded locale would possess a high supply of suitable targets. Given that highly disorganized locales are typically associated with relatively low supplies of suitable targets, the hypothetical relationships depicted for this ideal type should be read as useful illustrations of the logic of our theory, not as portrayals of real world situations.

Context 2: High SoM + High SoT + High SoG

This is a condition where the supplies of motivated offenders, suitable targets, and capable guardians are all high. This suggests an environment where the potential for criminal acts is high, but offset by guardianship. Hypothetically, this ideal type might best approximate gentrified central-city locales. It is possible to imagine a location in a traditional urban downtown where relatively affluent residents have apartments, condominiums, and parking garages filled with desirable material goods. Such an area might be proximate to a relatively dense resident population (e.g., either in the downtown area proper or in nearby disadvantaged, inner-city enclaves), and might be exposed to ephemeral motivated offenders (e.g., as individuals frequent commercial or entertainment establishments in the downtown area). In such a context, downtown residents and business owners could invest (socially and materially) in collective (e.g., neighborhood watch, street patrols, hired security) and individual (e.g., alarm systems, locks, guard dogs) protective measures that would enhance guardianship. Perhaps those who would find owning a business or living "downtown" alluring might also perceive such a location as relatively high risk for criminal victimization, and they might therefore regard investments in protective measures as necessary, normal, and acceptable costs.

Context 3: High SoM + Low SoT + Low SoG

This is a condition where the supply of motivated offenders is high, while the supplies of suitable targets and guardians are low. This provides a favorable environment for criminal acts to occur. Hypothetically, this ideal type might best be exemplified by neighborhoods of the urban underclass.[15] Such a location might be densely populated and comprised of relatively poor residents. Social and material targets might be in low supply or considered relatively unattractive. Further, such an area might be characterized by a high degree of social disorganization, which impedes residents' abilities to make collective and individual investments, both socially and materially, in guardianship.

Context 4: High SoM + Low SoT + High SoG

This is a condition where the supply of motivated offenders is high, the supply of suitable targets is low, and the supply of guardians is high. This provides an environment that is relatively unfavorable for criminal acts to occur, given high demand in a context of low supply and high social control. Hypothetically, this ideal type might be best illustrated by relatively densely populated urban neighborhoods consisting of individuals whose incomes keep them above poverty, but who are yet engaged in a "pay-check-to-paycheck," "just getting by" existence. Residents in such a location might not possess the material resources, either collectively or individually, to invest in things that would enhance target suitability. However, it also possible to imagine that such a location might possess enough social capital (e.g., well-established social ties) to maintain a relatively high degree of guardianship.

Context 5: Low SoM + High SoT + Low SoG

This is a condition where the supply of motivated offenders is low, the supply of suitable targets is high, and the supply of guardians is low. This provides an environment that is relatively favorable for modest criminal activity—low demand in a context of high supply and low social control. Hypothetically, this ideal type might be best approximated by sparsely populated rural areas or small towns. In such a context, perhaps walking alone at night is not all that risky, because the chances of encountering someone on the journey would be slight. Perhaps leaving the keys in the car parked in the drive and the house unlocked while out is not perceived as risky because passersby are uncommon. In such a context, minimal individual and collective guardianship measures might be seen as sufficient.

Context 6: Low SoM + High SoT + High SoG

This is a condition where the supply of motivated offenders is low, the supply of suitable targets is high, and the supply of guardians is high. This provides an environment that is relatively unfavorable for criminal activity—even though the supply of targets is high, low demand and high guardianship suggest low criminal activity. Hypothetically, this ideal type might best approximate sparsely populated, gated communities. In such a situation, the supply of social and material targets might be quite attractive, but collective guardianship measures would prove to be extremely effective in preventing criminal acts.

Context 7: Low SoM + Low SoT + Low SoG

This is a condition where the supplies of motivated offenders, suitable targets, and capable guardians are all low. This provides a mixed environment—not many people for offending or victimization, few targets, but, because of low guardianship, deterrence is relatively low. This is a context of low market exposure, value, and cost. Hypothetically, this ideal type might be best approximated by sparsely populated, impoverished rural areas or small towns. Similar to Context 5, perhaps the dangers of walking alone at night are minimal, because the chances of encountering someone would be slight. Also similar to Context 5, minimal individual and collective guardianship measures in this environment might be seen as sufficient. In this context, the attractive targets that would be available might be more valued because they are relatively rare. For instance, a modest CD collection might appear to be a highly prized possession in such a relatively barren context.

Context 8: Low SoM + Low SoT + High SoG

This is a condition where the supplies of motivated offenders and suitable targets are low, but the supply of capable guardians is high. This provides the theoretically most unfavorable environment for criminal acts—low demand and a low supply of targets, plus relatively high market cost. Context 8 is similar to Context 1 above in that the manifestation of this kind of context in the real world is probably unlikely. Essentially, this ideal type of context represents a bounded locale that would exhibit a high degree of social *organization,* as the high supply of capable guardians would suggest. However, at the same time, this ideal type suggests that this kind of bounded locale would have relatively few people and material resources to provide such guardianship. Certain types of isolated communities (e.g., communes) with a fervent commit to internal policing might approximate this ideal type in the real world. As with Context 1, the hypothetical relationships presented for this ideal type should be viewed as illustrative of the logic of our theory, not as a picture of real world circumstances.

These ideal types suggest a range in the levels of criminal acts across contexts. To facilitate our examination of the level of criminal acts across contexts, let us begin by eliminating Contexts 1 and 8. It is prudent to do this because both of these contexts are unlikely to be found in the real world. Contexts 2 through 7 can be arranged in descending order of criminal activity as follows:

- Context 3: High SoM + Low SoT + Low SoG, e.g., urban underclass neighborhoods
- Context 4: High SoM + Low SoT + High SoG, e.g., urban working poor neighborhoods
- Context 2: High SoM + High SoT + High SoG, e.g., gentrified central-city locales
- Context 5: Low SoM + High SoT + Low SoG, e.g., sparsely populated middle-class rural towns
- Context 6: Low SoM + High SoT + High SoG, e.g., gated communities
- Context 7: Low SoM + Low SoT + Low SoG, e.g., sparsely populated impoverished rural towns

Given our theoretical understandings, Context 3 has the greatest ambient criminal opportunity and would exhibit the greatest number of criminal acts. It represents an ecological context where there is a critical mass of people (i.e., for offending and victimizing), and it is relatively socially disorganized. Contexts 5 through 7 have the least ambient criminal opportunity and would manifest the fewest number of criminal acts. This is so because each of these contexts lacks a critical mass of people, and without a critical mass differential social organization and the supply of suitable targets are rather moot points. Finally, Contexts 4 and 2 would have moderate ambient criminal opportunity, and would probably exhibit a greater volume of criminal acts than Contexts 5–7, but less than Context 3. These contexts have sufficient supplies of motivated offenders and suitable targets, but the opportunity provided by these dimensions is counterbalanced by social organization.

A close inspection of these ambient contexts suggests why ecological moderating effects might be difficult to detect and what researchers might do to increase their chances of finding cross-level effects. We began our chapter with a listing of such effects that have been found previously, but this list was a short one. Indeed, most studies that do examine potential moderating effects of context on individual-level opportunity-crime relationships come up rather empty-handed. While these studies typically show that the mean levels of crime (i.e., the intercepts in our statistical models) vary significantly across ecological contexts, the individual-level effects on crime (i.e., the slope coefficients in our statistical models) tend to be stable across contexts, revealing non-significant micro-macro interaction effects.

Crime is largely considered an urban phenomena and the bulk of empirical studies in criminology focuses on environments captured in Contexts 2–4, which are more urban and crime prone. We characterized each of these contexts as having a high supply of motivated offenders. This suggests that there is relatively little variation across these contexts on this dimension. Relatively little variation reduces the chances of detecting interaction effects. Moreover, given the central importance of the motivated offender dimension, as suggested by the supply of aggregate motivated offender axiom and its related principles, it would be desirable to capture a wider range of motivated offender supplies than Contexts 2–4 would afford. Additionally, while there is more variation on the dimensions of aggregate suitable targets and guardianship among Contexts 2–4, the range would appear to be compacted toward the low end for target suitability and skewed toward the upper end for guardianship. It seems that such distributions would also make interaction effects more difficult to detect.

This conceptual exercise suggests that in order to increase the chances of capturing the posited interaction effects for each of the three dimensions of ambient opportunity, researchers might construct studies that include middle-class and impoverished rural communities as well as inner-city neighborhoods of the urban underclass and gentrified urban enclaves. The desirability of such empirical designs seems obvious; their practicality is another matter.

COMPATIBILITY WITH EXTANT RESEARCH

While the list of examples of moderating effects found in previous research introduced at the beginning of this chapter was a short one, and the brevity of this list may be due to the methodological reasons outlined above, it was also noted that most of these findings had been discovered with little a priori theory to justify or explain them. Throughout the rest of the chapter, we have proposed and applied theoretical propositions regarding expected moderating effects of the three dimensions of ambient opportunity. We now return to extant findings regarding micro-macro interaction effects, and discuss the compatibility of such findings in light of the theoretical propositions offered here.

- Urbanness of school location alters the effect of school attachment on student likelihood of carrying a weapon to school. School attachment's negative effect on weapon carrying is tempered in less urban as opposed to more urban school settings.[16]

If we presume that school attachment is an indicator of individual-level guardianship and urbanness an indicator of aggregate-level motivated offender exposure, we can invoke Proposition 5.7, which would suggest that urbanness would temper the negative relationship between school attachment (guardianship) and criminal acts. As such, this empirical finding is *not* consistent with our theoretical proposition.

- Urbanness of school location also conditions the effect of previous arrest on the likelihood of in-school weapon carrying. In a comparison across three Kentucky counties, the effect of previous arrest was positive in an urban county and negative in two more rural counties.[17]

Presuming that previous arrest is an indicator of individual-level guardianship (*low* guardianship more precisely, since those with a record are less likely to rely upon formal controls, etc.) and, again, that urbanness is an indicator of aggregate-level motivated offender exposure, then we can again invoke Proposition 5.7. Since Proposition 5.7 states that an aggregate-level motivated offender concentration/access *tempers* the *negative* relationship between guardianship and crime, the converse is that aggregate-level motivated offender concentration/access (indicated by urbanness) would *exacerbate* the *positive* relationship between *low* guardianship and crime. As such, the empirical finding above is consistent with the theoretical propositions provided here.

- Neighborhood-level incivilities temper the negative effect of safety precautions on burglary victimization likelihood. In disorderly communities, safety precautions are not as effective in reducing burglary victimization risk.[18]

If safety precautions were viewed as a measure of individual-level guardianship, and neighborhood incivilities were perceived as a measure of aggregate-level *weak or ineffective* guardianship, then Proposition 5.9 is relevant. Proposition 5.9 suggests that aggregate guardianship exacerbates the negative relationship between individual guardianship and crime. A converse would suggest that *low* aggregate guardianship (e.g., incivilities) would *temper* the negative relationship between individual guardianship and criminal acts. Proposition 5.9 is thus supported by this empirical finding.

- Neighborhood-level public activity tempers the positive effect of living alone on burglary victimization likelihood. Living alone matters less in terms of predicting burglary risk in busy areas.[19]

Regarding the crime of burglary, living alone is typically perceived as an indicator of individual-level weak guardianship. Public activity can be perceived as an indicator of aggregate-level motivated offender concentration/access. Invoking a converse to Proposition 5.7, we would expect that public activity (aggregate motivated offender concentration/access) would *exacerbate* the *positive* effect of *weak* guardianship on criminal acts. Proposition 5.7 is thus *not* supported by this particular research finding.

- Neighborhood social disorganization conditions the effects of living alone on assault victimization likelihood. The positive effect of living alone on assault likelihood is increased (i.e., exacerbated) by area-level social disorganization.[20]

Regarding violent crime, living alone, similar to marital status, can be viewed as a measure of individual-level motivated offender exposure. While social disorganization can be viewed in multiple ways, we will consider it here as both a proxy for aggregate-level motivated offender exposure and aggregate-level *weak* guardianship. If disorganization is a presumed indicator of aggregate-level supply of motivated offenders, we invoke a converse of Proposition 5.1 and expect that social disorganization would exacerbate the positive effect of living alone (exposure) on criminal acts. If disorganization is a presumed indicator of aggregate-level weak guardianship, then a converse of Proposition 5.3 applies. According to this proposition, we would expect that disorganization (weak guardianship) would exacerbate the positive effect of living alone (exposure) on criminal acts. In both scenarios, the theoretical propositions are supported by the empirical findings.

- Neighborhood social disorganization (e.g., low SES, high public activity) alters the effect of individual-level income on likelihood of experiencing assault victimization. Income's negative effect on assault likelihood is strongest in the most organized areas; in disorganized areas, individual income has a minimal effect.[21]

Precisely what individual-level income indicates in terms of opportunity for assault is somewhat ambiguous. Since assault is not a property crime, income is not really an indicator of target suitability in this instance. However, it is possible to perceive of income as a proxy for individual-level motivated offender exposure since higher SES individuals probably have greater resources which insulate them from the public (e.g., they have cars rather than having to walk or take public transportation). If individual-level income is thus seen as a proxy for individual-level exposure and social disorganization is presumed to be an indicator of aggregate-level motivated offender exposure, then we can invoke a converse of Proposition 5.1. This proposition would posit that social disorganization would temper the negative effect of income (individual-level *low* exposure) on assault victimization. Alternatively, if social disorganization is presumed to be a proxy for aggregate-level weak guardianship, then we can invoke a converse of Proposition 5.3, which would suggest that disorganization—or *weak* guardianship—would temper the negative effect of income, or *low* exposure. Both of these propositions, then, are consistent with the empirical literature in this instance.

- Neighborhood-level ethnic heterogeneity reduces (i.e., tempers) the positive effect of race (nonwhite) on violent victimization likelihood. Being nonwhite increases risk of violent victimization in ethnically homogeneous communities specifically.[22]

Like the above example regarding individual-level income, interpreting this finding within the framework of our theoretical propositions for moderating effects is difficult since it is particularly difficult to classify individual-level race as a proxy for a certain criminal opportunity concept. In fact, arguments can be made that individual-level race serves as a proxy for any three of the overarching individual-level concepts in criminal opportunity theory. Likewise, aggregate-level racial/ethnic heterogeneity could be presumed to be a proxy for any three of the overarching contextual concepts in the expanded criminal opportunity theory offered here. Keeping in mind this predicament, let us assume for illustrative purposes only that individual-level race is a measure of target suitability (e.g., in the form of target antagonism). If we make this assumption along with an assumption that neighborhood ethnic heterogeneity measures aggregate-level "motivated-offender" exposure, then we can invoke Proposition 5.4 and posit that neighborhood ethnic heterogeneity should exacerbate the positive effect of being nonwhite (individual-level race measured as a dichotomy). This proposition would thus *not* be supported by the finding cited above. If we still presume nonwhite as a proxy for target antagonism but assume that neighborhood ethnic heterogeneity is an indicator of aggregate-level supply of suitable targets, then we invoke Proposition 5.5 and suggest that ethnic heterogeneity should temper the positive effect of nonwhite. The hypothesis emerging from this proposition would, therefore, be consistent with the finding. Finally, if we continue to presume that nonwhite is a measure of target antagonism but neighborhood ethnic heterogeneity is an indicator of aggregate-level weak guardianship, then Proposition 5.6 is relevant. This proposition would suggest that neighborhood heterogeneity should exacerbate the positive effect of individual-level nonwhite, and would be inconsistent with the research finding.

CONCLUSION

Overall, when examining the extant research, few interactions have been found between individual- and aggregate-level indicators of criminal opportunity. In part, this is because methodological and statistical advances allowing for estimation of such cross-level effects are relatively recent (these methods will be discussed in Chapter 8). As such, few studies to date actually estimate such potential moderation. Despite the paucity of micro-macro interactions found within the literature, the previous section points to the fact that many of those that have been unearthed appear consistent with the theoretical propositions offered within this chapter. Thus, while previous research has often "stumbled" upon these findings, with little theoretical rationale guiding their exploration or interpretation, we conclude that the propositions offered here as part of a multilevel criminal opportunity theory might prove fruitful for continued exploration of such person-environment interaction effects.

While our propositions appear fairly consistent with many of the interaction effects found previously, we note that several obstacles can hinder the applicability of the framework offered here. First, the samples employed in much criminological research are sufficiently homogeneous to disallow a comprehensive test of micro-macro interactions. Homogeneous samples offer less than optimal variation in theoretical concepts, thus diminishing the likelihood of cross-concept interactions. Second, the measures employed in extant studies often represent ambiguous operationalizations of theoretical concepts (e.g., sociodemographic variables serving as proxies for target suitability, exposure). Without refinement in measurement, future work will be hard-pressed to posit specific micro-macro interactions, even with theoretical schemes such as the one offered here available for a priori theorizing.

It should also be noted that a limitation of the theoretical scheme offered here regarding main and moderating effects is that it has, thus far, been presented as a static model. In other words, a temporal dimension of criminal opportunity has not yet been considered. This is a serious limitation in that individuals are not only nested within environments, but they and their environments are dynamic. The main and moderating effects that are the focus of Chapters 4 and 5 thus need to be embedded within a longitudinal perspective. Such is the focus of Chapter 7.

Before considering the temporal dimensions of our theoretical framework, Chapter 6 recognizes that multicontextual criminal opportunity can affect not only criminal offending and victimization but also reactions to crime/victimization, including cognitive risk perception, emotionally based fear of crime, and risk- or fear-related precautionary behavior. We extend the theoretical ideas addressed in Chapters 3 through 5 to show how criminal opportunity can be useful in understanding these various reactions to crime. More specifically, we explore the linkages between various types of crime, victimization, and reactions to crime. This orientation builds on contemporary research that has suggested that the criminal opportunity model is not only applicable to various kinds of criminal acts but to reactions to crime as well (e.g., perceived risk, fear, and constrained behavior). We thus seek to provide an explicit demonstration of the interrelationships between crime, victimization, and reactions to crime within the conceptual framework of our criminal opportunity theory.

NOTES

1. See Wilcox Rountree (2000).
2. See Wilcox Rountree (2000).
3. See Miethe and McDowall (1993), Miethe and Meier (1994), Wilcox Rountree et al. (1994).
4. See Miethe and McDowall (1993).
5. See Miethe and Meier (1994).
6. See Miethe and Meier (1994).
7. See Wilcox Rountree et al. (1994).
8. See Chapter 8.
9. See Chapter 4 for discussion of proposed main effects.
10. See Chapter 4.
11. For an economic approach to human behavior generally, see Becker (1976). For economic approaches to crime specifically, see Becker (1968), Ehrlich (1973), Becker and Landes (1974), Heineke (1978), Cook (1980), Pyle (1983), and Eide, Asssness, and Skjerpen (1994).[[reference list has only Eide and Skjerpen (1994)]]
12. As an axiom, the supply of aggregate motivated offenders axiom is taken as a self-evident truth upon which we build our theory. Nonetheless, we believe that it is amendable to empirical investigation and have also formulated it as a proposition (see Proposition 4.2).
13. We could take the economic analogy one step further by suggesting that not all criminal acts are "realized" (i.e., completed successfully), just as not all financial investments are realized in profit. Things such as attempted murder and attempted robbery are criminal acts even though they are not "realized."
14. Ironically, this suggests that attractive targets are actually less attractive in ecological contexts characterized by relatively high supplies of suitable targets. In practical terms this could mean that an extremely valuable jewel collection in a neighborhood that has numerous such collections is less attractive a target than the small diamond on the wedding ring of a family heirloom in a neighborhood that is highly impoverished.

15. See Wilson (1987).

16. See Wilcox Rountree (2000).

17. See Wilcox Rountree (2000).

18. See Miethe and McDowall (1993), Miethe and Meier (1994), and Wilcox Rountree et al. (1994).

19. See Miethe and McDowall (1993).

20. See Miethe and Meier (1994).

21. See Miethe and Meier (1994).

22. See Wilcox Rountree et al. (1994).

6

Implications for Reactions to Crime

Consider the following findings from recent research:[1]

- Crime risk perception is enhanced by the following individual- and neighborhood-level characteristics, considered simultaneously: safety precautions, access routes to and from one's house, previous victimization, neighborhood incivilities, and neighborhood crime.
- Crime risk perception is diminished, simultaneously, by the following individual- and neighborhood-level characteristics: age, male gender, nonwhite race, neighborhood social integration, and neighborhood-level SES.
- Fear of burglary is enhanced by the following individual- and neighborhood-level characteristics, considered simultaneously: number of expensive household goods owned, number of safety precautions, burglary victimization, risk perception, and neighborhood burglary.
- Fear of burglary is diminished by the following individual- and neighborhood-level characteristics, considered jointly: age, family income, and neighborhood violent crime.
- Fear of violence is enhanced, simultaneously, by the following individual- and neighborhood-level characteristics: nonwhite race, number of dangerous public activities, number of carried valuables, number of safety precautions, violent victimization, risk perception, and neighborhood violent crime.
- Fear of violence is lowered by the following individual-level characteristics, net of neighborhood-level characteristics: age, male gender, and family income.

- Precautionary behavior is enhanced by the following individual- and neighborhood-level characteristics, considered simultaneously: earlier precautionary behavior, family income, burglary victimization, neighborhood social integration, neighborhood SES, and neighborhood burglary.
- Precautionary behavior is lowered by the following individual-level characteristics, net of neighborhood-level characteristics: age and living alone.
- Neighborhood incivilities exacerbates the negative effect of race (nonwhite) on risk perception. Nonwhite residents feel less crime risk in comparison to white residents, especially in disorderly communities.
- Neighborhood incivilities exacerbates the positive effect of number of nights one's home is left unoccupied on crime risk perception.
- Neighborhood-level percentage nonwhite tempers the negative effect of gender (male) on fear of violence. Men are less fearful of violence (in comparison to women) in communities with few nonwhites specifically.

Such findings hint that some of the same multilevel processes affecting the occurrence of criminal acts may also affect cognitive, emotional, and behavioral reactions to criminal acts, including risk/safety perception, fear of crime, and constrained behavior. These reactions seem to be influenced simultaneously by individual- and environmental-level measures of criminal opportunity. In addition, environmental opportunity appears to condition the effects of certain individual-level opportunity variables. In the remainder of this chapter, we propose that the multilevel criminal opportunity theory proposed thus far is, indeed, applicable in understanding not only criminal acts, but individual responses to actual or potential criminal acts.

Cook (1986) was one of the first to note that an important omission from most conceptualizations of criminal opportunity theory is the idea that individual-level opportunity factors, in particular, are often influenced by an individual's concern about crime. He proposed a notion of a conceptual feedback loop in which elements of individual-level criminal opportunity (e.g., motivated offender exposure, target suitability, guardianship) affect the likelihood of experiencing criminal acts, but these criminal acts or even the perceived likely occurrence or fear of these criminal acts, in turn, influence future indicators of criminal opportunity. While Cook did not articulate his notion of feedback loop precisely this way, the assumption seems to be that, in response to criminal opportunity, an individual will: (1) develop a certain level of perceived risk, or perceived likelihood of experiencing crime/victimization; (2) develop a certain level of fear, or emotionally based worry or anxiety about experiencing crime; and (3) develop a behavioral strategy in adjusting accordingly levels of exposure, target suitability, and/or guardianship in order to diminish future experiences with criminal acts. As such, criminal opportunity can be viewed as affecting not only criminal acts themselves, but perceptions, feelings, and behaviors that are commonly termed reactions to crime. Similarly, ambient or environment-level opportunity might moderate or condition the effects of individual-level opportunity on these reactions.

RATIONALITY AND THE FEAR OF CRIME

Consistent with underlying assumptions addressed thus far, the perspective that multilevel opportunity influences reactions to crime, both in terms of main and moderating effects, is rooted in a rational choice framework and assumes that individuals react to cues—indicative of criminal opportunity—from both individual experiences and social environments. These cues provide information about the likelihood of criminal acts, and thus influence cognitive, emotional, and behavioral reactions such as risk perception, fear of crime, and constrained or precautionary behavior. While many would accept the feasibility of cognitive risk perception and precautionary behavior as being rationally based, greater argument might arise regarding the presumed rationality of fear of crime, and thus this issue should be addressed before we proceed much further with this theoretical application.

Some have concluded that individuals are not rational in their fears. Fear is, after all, presumed to be an emotionally based reaction,[2] with physiological indicators such as increased heart rate, sweaty palms and raised hair. It is often presumed that when things involve emotions, they cannot involve rational calculation.

But, the fact that fear is emotionally derived does not necessarily negate the idea that it can be rational. While a rapidly beating heart, sweaty palms, and raised hair may be the work of emotions (in combination with physiology), these responses themselves may certainly emerge from cognitive processing. Why might some individuals become fearful of attack, as manifested in an increased heart rate and the hair on the back of the neck standing upright? Likely, they have perceived cues in the proximal environment that lead them to believe that an attack is probable. Hence, emotional fear would seem to emerge most directly from cognitive perceptions of risk. Indeed, empirical evidence supports the fact that cognitive risk perception is a very powerful predictor of emotional fear.[3] As such, rational calculation seems inherently compatible with rather than inherently contradictory to emotional fear, though the two are clearly distinct constructs, theoretically and empirically.

PROPOSITIONS REGARDING MAIN EFFECTS

Based upon the above discussion, we posit propositions regarding the main effects of concepts related to criminal opportunity on reactions to crime. As can be seen, these propositions mirror the propositions offered in Chapter 4 regarding the main effects of criminal opportunity concepts on criminal acts. In fact, we think the relationships between criminal opportunity and reactions to crime emerge because of the relationships between dimensions of criminal opportunity and criminal acts. Rational individuals often assess correctly the likelihood of experiencing criminal acts based upon the opportunity presented by things such as lifestyle, routines, and social and physical environment. As such, not only does criminal opportunity heighten the likelihood of crime, it heightens perceptions of risk, fear, and perhaps even subsequent avoidance behavior. The following six propositions state generally, then, the expected relationships:

> Proposition 6.1: All else being equal, individual- or object-level exposure is positively related to risk perception, fear of crime, and constrained behavior.
>
> Proposition 6.2: All else equal, aggregate-level motivated offender exposure is positively related to risk perception, fear of crime, and constrained behavior.
>
> Proposition 6.3: All else equal, individual- or object-level target vulnerability, target antagonism, or target gratifiability is positively related to risk perception, fear of crime, and constrained behavior.
>
> Proposition 6.4: All else equal, aggregate-level target vulnerability, target antagonism, or target gratifiability is positively related to risk perception, fear of crime, and constrained behavior.
>
> Proposition 6.5: All else being equal, individual-level social ties or interpersonal control is negatively related to risk perception, fear of crime, and constrained behavior.
>
> Proposition 6.6: All else equal, aggregate-level social ties or social control is negatively related to risk perception, fear of crime, and constrained behavior.

Figure 6.1 summarizes the main effects posited by Propositions 6.1 through 6.6. In general, if a concept is positively related to criminal acts, we think that it will also be positively related to reactions such as risk perception, fear, and precautionary behavior. Conversely, if a concept is negatively related to criminal acts (e.g., individual- and aggregate-level

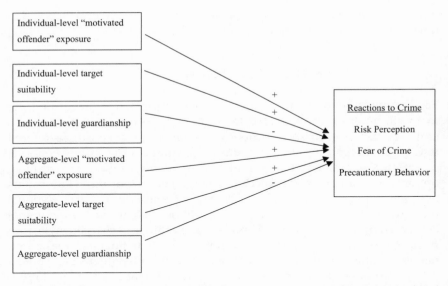

Figure 6.1. Main effects of individual- and environmental-level opportunity
    to reactions to crime.

guardianship), then we propose that it will also be inversely related to risk,
fear, and constrained behavior.

PROPOSITIONS REGARDING MODERATING EFFECTS

Just as ambient opportunity can condition the relationships between individual-level opportunity and criminal acts, so too can it condition the relationships between individual-level opportunity and reactions to crime.
Again, the propositions we offer regarding the moderating effects of ambient opportunity in relation to reactions mirror those put forth in relation to
criminal acts in Chapter 5. The propositions are based upon the same
axioms: (1) criminal acts will increase as the supply of aggregate motivated offenders increases; (2) the market value of targets is diminished as
the supply of aggregate suitable targets increases; and (3) as the supply of
aggregate guardianship increases, the market cost of criminal acts
increases. Furthermore, we assume that risk perception, fear, and precautionary behavior are rational calculations and thus vary with criminal
opportunity in a manner similar to criminal acts. We begin with propositions regarding the moderating effects of aggregate-level opportunity on

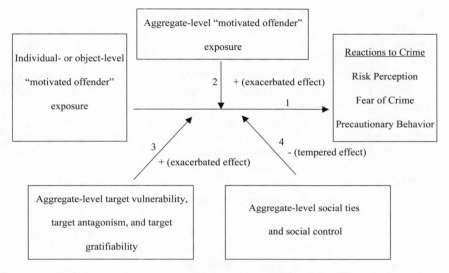

Figure 6.2. Moderating effects of aggregate-level opportunity on the relation-ship between individual-level motivated offender exposure and reactions to crime.

the relationship between individual-level motivated offender exposure and reactions to crime.

Proposition 6.7: All else being equal, aggregate-level motivated offender exposure exacerbates the positive effect of individual-level exposure on risk perception, fear, or constrained behavior.

Proposition 6.8: All else being equal, aggregate-level supply of suitable targets exacerbates the positive effect of individual-level exposure on risk perception, fear, or constrained behavior.

Proposition 6.9: All else being equal, aggregate-level guardianship tempers the positive effect of individual-level exposure on risk perception, fear, or constrained behavior.

Figure 6.2 summarizes these propositions regarding the moderating effects of aggregate-level opportunity on the relationship between individual-level exposure on reactions to crime. Since aggregate-level motivated offender exposure suggests increased demand for criminal acts, it should heighten the positive effect of individual-level exposure on risk perception, fear, and precautionary behavior. A large supply of offenders makes individual-level exposure seemingly all the more risky, and vulnerability-related reactions should become even stronger. Similarly, the relationship between individual-level exposure and such reactions should be exacerbated in the presence of a high aggregate-level supply of suitable targets. With a high supply of suitable targets in a particular context, the value of any one target is diminished, and individual distinctions in terms of exposure become all the more important in terms of determining opportunity. As such, exposed targets are likely to feel all the more at-risk or fearful in such contexts. In contrast, the relationship between individual-level exposure and reactions should be tempered by aggregate-level guardianship. Since aggregate-level guardianship serves as a deterrent, increasing costs associated with crime, individuals and objects in such contexts feel diminished vulnerability, and the relationship between individual-level risk factors and risk perception, fear, and the need for precaution may therefore weaken.

> Proposition 6.10: All else being equal, aggregate-level motivated offender exposure exacerbates the positive effect of individual-level target suitability on risk perception, fear of crime, or constrained behavior.

> Proposition 6.11: All else being equal, aggregate-level target suitability tempers the positive effect of individual-level target suitability on risk perception, fear of crime, or constrained behavior.

> Proposition 6.12: All else being equal, aggregate-level guardianship tempers the positive effect of individual-level target suitability on risk perception, fear of crime, or constrained behavior.

Propositions 6.10 through 6.12 are summarized in Figure 6.3. In contexts with an increased demand for crime due to high concentrations of people (offenders) or high accessibility, individual-level target suitability matters more and makes one all the more vulnerable. As such, the presumed positive relationships between individual-level target suitability and opportunity-related crime reactions are enhanced in such contexts. In contrast, in a context in which there is a bountiful supply of suitable targets, individual-level target suitability matters less—it does not serve as a distinguishing feature to the extent that it does in less bountiful contexts. With opportunity somewhat diminished by the context, individual-level target suitability generates perceived risk, fear, and constrained behavior to a lesser degree—the relationship is tempered. Similarly, individual-level target suitability matters less in contexts with high aggregate guardianship. The high cost associated with crime in such contexts reduces the attractiveness of suitable targets, therefore likely reducing the probability that target suitability will generate vulnerability and fear.

> Proposition 6.13: All else being equal, aggregate-level motivated offender exposure tempers the negative relationship between individual-level guardianship and risk perception, fear of crime, or constrained behavior.

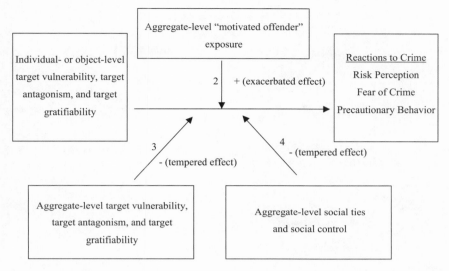

Figure 6.3. Moderating effects of aggregate-level opportunity on the relation-ship between individual-level target suitability and reactions to crime.

Proposition 6.14: All else being equal, aggregate-level target suitability exacerbates the negative effect of individual-level guardianship on risk per-ception, fear of crime, or constrained behavior.

Proposition 6.15: All else being equal, aggregate-level guardianship exacer-bates the negative effect of individual-level guardianship on risk perception, fear of crime, or constrained behavior.

These final three propositions—all dealing with the moderating effects of aggregate-level opportunity on the relationship between individual-level guardianship and reactions to crime—are summarized in Figure 6.4. In contexts characterized by a high supply of offenders, demand for crime targets (persons or objects) is great, and costs associated with individual targets matter less in determining the likelihood of criminal acts occurring. Likewise, costs associated with individual-level guardianship should mat-ter less in determining levels of perceived risk, fear, and reactionary, pre-cautionary behavior in high-demand contexts. In contrast, contexts with a high supply of attractive targets diminish the value of any one target, and thus render "costly" targets all-the-more avoidable. Hence, individual guardianship matters more in terms of lowering the likelihood for crimi-nal acts and opportunity-related reactions like risk perception, fear and precautionary behavior. These negative relationships are exacerbated in

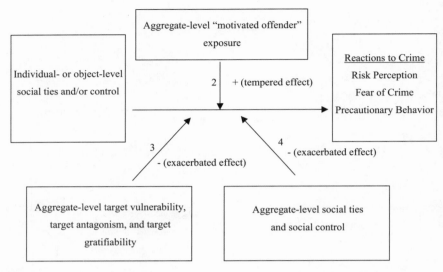

Figure 6.4.   Moderating effects of aggregate-level opportunity on the relationship between individual-level guardianship and reactions to crime.

high-target-supply contexts. These relationships are also exacerbated in
high-cost contexts. Highly guarded environments serve as a deterrent, and
make individual-level guardianship measures all the more effective in preventing criminal acts. With the likelihood of crime more strongly reduced
by individual guardianship in such contexts, levels of perceived risk and
fear are also more strongly reduced.

COMPATIBILITY WITH EXTANT RESEARCH

The propositions outlined above, again, are based upon the notion that
criminal acts are not the only outcomes of individual and environmental
opportunity indicators. Rather, opportunity also influences perceived likelihood of experiencing crime/victimization, emotionally based worry or
anxiety about experiencing crime, and behavioral adjustments (termed
"precautionary behavior" throughout this chapter) intended to diminish
future levels of exposure, target suitability, and/or guardianship. We are
aware of no study to date that has explicitly tested these ideas while using
such theoretical propositions a priori. However, a few studies have examined the main and moderating effects of indicators of criminal opportunity

and can thus help in evaluating the merit of our theoretical propositions. Findings from these studies were listed at the beginning of this chapter. We will now revisit these findings and discuss each set of findings in conjunction with Propositions 6.1 through 6.15.

- Crime risk perception is enhanced by the following individual- and neighborhood-level characteristics, considered simultaneously: safety precautions, access routes to and from one's house, previous victimization, neighborhood incivilities, and neighborhood crime.

In general, Propositions 6.1 through 6.6 offered in this chapter are supported by such findings. Most specifically, Propositions 6.1 and 6.6 are supported in that indicators of criminal opportunity in the form of individual-level exposure (e.g., access routes) and aggregate-level *weak* guardianship (e.g., neighborhood incivilities) are positively related to risk perception. One obvious exception to the support is the finding regarding the positive effect of individual-level safety precautions on risk perception. Invoking Proposition 6.5, we would expect that this indicator of interpersonal control would be *negatively* related to risk perception. We attribute this contradiction to problems of temporal order. While safety precautions can be an indicator of criminal opportunity in the form of guardianship, they can also be influenced by criminal opportunity and resulting levels of perceived risk and fear—as part of the feedback loop initially proposed by Cook (1986) and serving as the basis for this very chapter. Without longitudinal data, it is therefore difficult to disentangle the cause versus effect when examining the relationship between precautionary behavior and risk perception.

- Crime risk perception is diminished, simultaneously, by the following individual- and neighborhood-level characteristics: age, male gender, nonwhite race, neighborhood social integration, neighborhood-level SES.

Some of the findings here are supportive of Propositions 6.1 through 6.6, though there is considerable ambiguity introduced by the specific measures used here, in terms of how they fit into the operationalization scheme of criminal opportunity theory. The negative effect of neighborhood social integration is clearly in support of Proposition 6.6, suggesting that aggregate-level social ties is negatively related to risk perception. If male gender and age are perceived as proxies for physical strength (excluding the elderly), then these findings are also in support of the converse of Proposition 6.3, indicating that *low* target vulnerability should be negatively related to risk perception. As indicated in the previous chapter, race can serve as a proxy for multiple dimensions of criminal opportunity, with conflicting hypotheses sometimes emerging depending upon which concept race is measuring. Neighborhood-level SES is similar in that it might indicate aggregate target gratifiability, aggregate guardianship, or even low aggregate-level motivated offender concentration/accessibility. Due to the difficulty in pigeonholing such measures neatly into particular opportunity constructs, further discussion (beyond that introduced for example purposes in the previous chapter) of the compatibility of the findings regarding such measures is less than fruitful.

- Fear of burglary is enhanced by the following individual- and neighborhood-level characteristics, considered simultaneously: number of expensive household goods owned, number of safety precautions, burglary victimization, risk perception, and neighborhood burglary.

In general, indicators of criminal opportunity, including measures of target suitability (expensive household goods) as well as actual measures of victimization and area crime do appear to increase fear of burglary, as Propositions 6.1 through 6.6 would suggest. A discrepancy in the empirical findings and the propositions offered here again surrounds the measure of "safety precautions." If presumed to be a measure of guardianship, then Proposition 6.5 would predict a negative effect. Instead, research shows a positive effect. We suspect problems with temporal ordering is the reason for this contradiction.

- Fear of burglary is diminished, simultaneously, by the following individual- and neighborhood-level characteristics, considered jointly: age, family income, and neighborhood violent crime.

These findings somewhat contradict the propositions offered in this chapter (Propositions 6.1 through 6.6 regarding main effects, in particular). For instance, family income is often viewed as a measure of target vulnerability regarding property crime. Invoking Proposition 6.3 would yield a hypothesis that family income would thus increase rather than diminish fear of burglary. The finding regarding the negative effect of neighborhood-level violent crime appears contradictory at first blush, but when one considers the fact that neighborhoods with high rates of violence and high rates of burglary can be very different, then a high violent crime rate (often found in low SES communities, for instance) may say very little about opportunity for burglary. In fact, it might suggest little opportunity for burglary (e.g., low aggregate-level target suitability)—in which case, the finding revealed here would be consistent with the theoretical propositions we offer in this chapter.

- Fear of violence is enhanced, simultaneously, by the following indi-
  vidual- and neighborhood-level characteristics: nonwhite race, number of dangerous public activities, number of carried valuables,
  number of safety precautions, violent victimization, risk perception,
  and neighborhood violent crime.

Most of these findings for fear of violence seem consistent with Propositions 6.1 through 6.6 regarding expected main effects of individual and
ambient opportunity. For instance, indicators of individual-level exposure
(dangerous public activities), individual-level target antagonism (nonwhite), and individual-level target gratifiability (carried valuables) have
been shown to be positively related to fear of violence, as Propositions 6.1
and 6.3, most specifically, would predict. The positive effect of safety precautions, once again, contradicts Proposition 6.5 offered here, though we
suspect an inability to clearly specify temporal order (in the research cited
above) as the reason for the contradiction.

- Fear of violence is lowered by the following individual-level characteristics, net of neighborhood-level characteristics: age, male gender,
  and family income.

As discussed in Chapter 5, family income is perhaps viewed best as an
indicator of low individual-level exposure when considering violent
crime. If we assume that family income is a proxy for low exposure when
violent crime is in question, then the finding shown here is, indeed, consistent with Proposition 6.1. Employing a converse of 6.1, we would suspect that low exposure would be negatively related to fear. Also, to the
extent that age and male gender are proxies for low individual-level target
vulnerability, then the negative effects for these variables emerging in
extant research are indeed consistent with a converse of Proposition 6.3.

- Precautionary behavior is enhanced by the following individual- and
  neighborhood-level characteristics, considered simultaneously: earlier precautionary behavior, family income, burglary victimization,
  neighborhood social integration, neighborhood SES, and neighborhood burglary.

While many of the findings here are clearly consistent with the idea that
criminal opportunity can lead to precautionary behavior, other findings
are less clearly compatible with such a notion. For instance, invoking
Proposition 6.6, neighborhood social integration (aggregate guardianship)
should be negatively not positively related to precautions. The positive
effects of family income and neighborhood SES are more difficult to assess,

largely due to the ambiguity in what these variables are actually measuring in terms of opportunity concept. If one argues that they represent individual- and aggregate-level target gratifiability (e.g., considering property crime), then these findings would be consistent with Propositions 6.3 and 6.4. However, if one were to argue that they represented proxies of low exposure (e.g., considering violent crime), then these findings would contradict Propositions 6.1 and 6.2.

- Precautionary behavior is lowered by the following individual-level characteristics, net of neighborhood-level characteristics: age and living alone.

Excluding the elderly, vulnerability typically decreases with age. As such, we would expect age to be negatively related to precautionary behavior, invoking Proposition 6.3. The finding for living alone, in contrast, appears to contradict our theoretical propositions. If living alone is a proxy for low guardianship, we would expect a positive relationship between living alone and precautionary behavior (Proposition 6.5). Likewise, if living alone is a proxy for exposure (as an indicator of marital status), we would also expect a positive effect on precautionary behavior (invoking Proposition 6.1).

- Neighborhood incivilities exacerbate the negative effect of race (nonwhite) on risk perception. Nonwhite residents feel less crime risk in comparison to white residents in disorderly communities, especially.

Presuming neighborhood incivilities as a proxy for weak aggregate-level guardianship and nonwhite as a proxy for individual-level target antagonism, Proposition 6.12 is relevant. According to this proposition, aggregate-level guardianship tempers the effect of target suitability on risk perception. A converse, however, would suggest that *weak* aggregate-level guardianship *exacerbates* the effect of target suitability. As such, we conclude that this empirical finding is compatible with the theoretical propositions regarding moderating effects offered here.

- Neighborhood incivilities exacerbate the positive effect of number of nights one's home is left unoccupied on crime risk perception.

Again, we presume that neighborhood incivilities is a proxy for weak aggregate-level guardianship. The number of nights one's home is left unoccupied is presumed to be a measure of individual-level exposure to motivated offenders. As such, Proposition 6.9 is applied. According to Proposition 6.9, we would expect aggregate-level guardianship to temper the effect of individual-level exposure on risk perception. The converse of this proposition thus seems supported here; it is expected that *weak* aggregate guardianship would *exacerbate* the effects of individual-level exposure.

- Neighborhood-level percentage nonwhite tempers the negative effect of gender (male) on fear of violence. Men are less fearful of violence (in comparison to women) in communities with few nonwhites specifically.

Assessing the applicability of this cross-level interaction is difficult due to the ambiguity in what "neighborhood-level percentage nonwhite" represents in terms of aggregate-level opportunity concepts. As discussed in the previous chapter, this could seemingly be a proxy for all three aggregate-level opportunity concepts. Assuming that male gender is a proxy for low target vulnerability, if we presume that percentage nonwhite is a proxy for aggregate-level motivated offender exposure, then Proposition 6.10 is relevant. According to a converse of this proposition, we would expect that aggregate-level exposure (percentage nonwhite) would *temper* the effect of *low* vulnerability on fear. As such Proposition 6.10 appears compatible with this research finding. If we assume that percentage nonwhite instead represents aggregate-level target antagonism, then Proposition 6.11 is relevant. Invoking a converse of this proposition, we would anticipate that aggregate-level target antagonism (percentage nonwhite) would *exacerbate* the effect of *low* individual-level target vulnerability (male) on fear. As such, this finding is not consistent with Proposition 6.11. Finally, we could presume that percentage nonwhite represents a proxy for weak aggregate-level social ties and/or social control, and invoke Proposition 6.12. Employing a converse of 6.12, we would expect that *weak* aggregate-level guardianship would *temper* the effect of *low* target vulnerability on fear. Hence, Proposition 6.12 would be supported by this empirical finding.

In sum, as in Chapter 5, we suggest that many extant findings are compatible with our theoretical propositions. This exercise in comparing our theoretical propositions to previous findings is difficult to do, since the research efforts offering these findings were not designed explicitly to test such theoretical propositions. As such, measures employed often do not offer a precise conceptualization and operationalization of a multilevel criminal opportunity theory. Nonetheless, we find it worthwhile to illustrate how less ambiguous measures of criminal opportunity (according to our conceptualization and operationalization) do often reveal findings consistent with the predictions offered by the integrated framework provided here. This exercise has also raised the issue of the importance of time. We noted that lack of compatibility between theoretical propositions and extant findings regarding the precautions (guardianship)-reactions relationships was probably related to problems of causal order. In fact, as implied in this chapter, precautionary behavior can be both an indicator and a result of criminal opportunity. Since guardianship as measured by safety precautions is probably reciprocally related to risk and fear, cross-sectional modeling of the relationship is likely to be somewhat misinformative. We turn, in Chapter 7, to this issue of temporal order more fully, explicitly incorporating a dynamic component into our framework.

NOTES

1. All of the listed findings come from recent analyses of Seattle survey data (Wilcox Rountree and Land 1996a, 1996b; Wilcox Rountree 1998).

2. For example, see Ferraro and LaGrange (1987), Ferraro (1995), and Warr (1990).

3. For example, see Ferraro (1995), Warr and Stafford (1983).

7

A Dynamic Perspective

Borrowing heavily from routine activities theory, we have posited an opportunity theory that emphasizes that an adequate explanation of criminal acts must examine spatial and temporal contexts. We have elaborated and expanded an opportunity approach that understands criminal acts and the responses to crime in ecological terms, emphasizing the necessity to build the theory in a manner that revolves around the reality that individuals experience criminal acts within space-time environments. We have thus far focused on theorizing about the main and interaction effects associated with individuals acting in particular spatial contexts. For the purposes of clarity we have not yet incorporated temporal dimensions into our theory. That is, we have presented our opportunity theory in rather static terms so as to establish what we believe to be its foundational propositions. Having done this, we now turn to a more explicit consideration of the temporal dimensions of criminal acts to which we referred at the outset.

Our discussion of the temporal dimensions of our theory is presented in two parts. First, we provide a general discussion of how the notions of rhythm, tempo, and timing can be incorporated into the framework we have thus far presented. Such an incorporation necessitates neither additional concepts nor unique propositions. Rather, we suggest that issues pertaining to rhythm, tempo, and timing can be integrated into the concepts we have thus far presented. Second, we consider how our multicontextual opportunity theory of crime can be used to analyze criminal acts across the life course.

RHYTHM, TEMPO, AND TIMING

In their original formulation of routine activities theory, Cohen and Felson (1979) borrowed temporal concepts from Hawley's (1950) human ecology theory. This conceptual integration represented an elegant and significant advance for criminological theory. As Cohen and Felson stated:

> While criminologists traditionally have concentrated on the *spatial* analysis of crime rates within metropolitan communities, they seldom have considered the *temporal* interdependence of these acts. In his classic theory of human ecology, Amos Hawley (1950) treats the community not simply as a unit of territory but rather as an organization of symbiotic and commensalistic relationships as human activities are performed over both space and time. (1979:589, emphasis in the original)

Indeed, the importance of temporal dimensions is suggested in the very name Cohen and Felson (1979) gave to their theory—*routine* activities. The notion of routine activities implies that the elements of criminal opportunity appear in particular time-space contexts because of the customary movements of individuals through time and space.

Cohen and Felson use the temporal nature of human ecology to argue that "since World War II, the United States has experienced a major shift of routine activities" (ibid.:593), which has contributed to a significant increase in direct-contact predatory crime. For Cohen and Felson this shift in routine activities captures the spatial and temporal interdependence of human ecology nicely. According to Cohen and Felson, since World War II, the spatial and temporal interdependence of human ecology in the United States has been one in which the *time spent at home* has decreased, while the *time spent away from home* has increased. The fact that individuals are spending more time pursuing work- and leisure-related activities has made the convergence of "criminogenic circumstances" (i.e., the convergence of motivated offenders, suitable targets, and lack of capable guardians) more prevalent in post-World War II U.S. society (ibid.:590).

Without a doubt, Cohen and Felson's adroit incorporation of temporal organization as a central component of their ecological understanding of crime contributed greatly to routine activities becoming one of criminology's more robust and enduring theoretical frameworks. Oddly enough, the exploration of the temporality inherent in the routine activities approach has not received explicit theoretical attention since Cohen and Felson's original formulation. We believe that it would be useful to explicitly link the ideas of rhythm, tempo, and timing with the basic concepts of our multilevel criminal opportunity theory.

Cohen and Felson define rhythm as "the regular periodicity with which events occur, as with the rhythm of travel activity" (ibid.:590). Rhythm is the relative regularity of activities, which suggests the predictability of activities. As such, rhythm is not a matter of how often activities occur in a given time period, but rather pertains to patterns of activity across time. To illustrate, say an individual attends church services the first Sunday of each month. Say another attends every Sunday, and yet another attends every Tuesday and Sunday. Although the tempo (i.e., the frequency within a common time frame) of activities is different for each of these hypothetical individuals, they all attend church service with a steady, regular rhythm. Assuming that these patterns never vary, a would-be burglar who knew of the habits of these individuals would be able to accurately predict when each one would be away from home. To illustrate further, say another individual attends church services four times in a month, but in a completely random fashion. Even though this person with random attendance has the same frequency of attendance as that of our second hypothetical individual, her attendance does not possess a discernible rhythm. Rhythmic activities mean that individuals' movements are more or less predictable, which could thus make them more susceptible to (say) a burglar or stalker who is aware of their habitual movements.

While rhythm is a relevant concept for understanding routine activities at an individual level, Hawley (1950), as well as Cohen and Felson (1979), employed the concept to depict the rhythms of places. Human ecology suggests that the movement of people in bounded locales has patterned regularity. For instance, neighborhoods with a high percentage of families with school-aged children have a fairly predictable routine on school days, with children (and sometimes parents) making their way to bus stops or to schools themselves. Neighborhoods free from chronic unemployment have predictable movements (primarily Monday through Friday) as individuals make their way to their places of employment. Business districts have movements into and out of the area during business hours, and have sparse off-hours activity. Places that provide entertainment have greater movement during evening and weekends, and sparse activity during regular working hours. If the entertainment area caters to a lunch crowd and also provides evening diversions, it might be characterized by a Monday through Friday rhythm where there is a rest from activity from 2:00 A.M. to 10:00 A.M., then by increased activity from 10:00 A.M. until 2:00 P.M., followed by a rest between 2:00 P.M. and 5:00 P.M., and then picking up again from 5:00 P.M. until 2:00 A.M. Rhythm is discernible not only daily or weekly but also across broader spans of time. For example, resort communities are characterized by "peak-season" and "off-season" rhythms. Rhythm is also found in the micropatterns within a day. For instance, schools are characterized by the rhythm of the beginning of the day, passing periods, lunch, and dismissal.

The concept of rhythm is thus relevant at both the individual and environmental levels. The ecological foundations of our theory suggest that criminal opportunities ebb and flow with the hourly, daily, weekly, monthly, and seasonal rhythms of individuals and places. However, this temporal ebbing and flowing of criminal opportunity does not occur completely randomly. Rather, to a large degree, movements in space across time have a discernible and even predictable rhythm—that is, there are micro and macro, individual and environmental, predictable, routine activities.

A second temporal dimension is tempo. Of the three temporal dimensions identified by Cohen and Felson (1979) tempo is the most straightforward. Cohen and Felson clearly define tempo as "the number of events per unit of time" (ibid.:590). At the individual level, tempo refers to how often individuals engage in particular actions, calling specific attention to public vs. home-based activities (e.g., how often one dines out per week). At the environmental level, tempo can refer to the aggregate tempo of the individuals in a bounded locale (e.g., the average times per week residents in a neighborhood dine out). It can also refer to the frequency of activities of the collectivity (e.g., how often a neighborhood association meets).

The third temporal dimension is timing. For Cohen and Felson timing is "the coordination among different activities which are more or less interdependent" (ibid.). Timing is a matter of when an activity begins and when it ends in relationship to when another activity begins and ends. The interdependent nature of timing can be such that there is complete overlap of the activities (i.e., the exact same endings and beginnings). With complete overlap we could say that the timing is "in unison." Timing of activities can be such that there is only partial overlap. Similarly, timing of activities can possess no overlap at all. Complete or partial overlap may be related to increased criminal opportunity (e.g., some overlap between the activities of targets and motivated offenders) or reduced criminal opportunity (e.g., some overlap between activities between targets and capable guardians). Similarly, the lack of overlap in the timing of activities may be related to increased criminal opportunity (e.g., no overlap between targets and capable guardians) or reduced criminal opportunity (e.g., no overlap between targets and motivated offenders). This suggests that the degree of overlap (i.e., no overlap to unison) in and of itself does not determine the degree of criminal opportunity. Moreover, this also suggests that the duration of the overlap is important for understanding criminal opportunity. Timing involves the temporal overlap between individual-level activities as well as between individual- and environmental-level activities.

Even though we recognize the importance of the temporality of activities, we do not suggest that separate time-based concepts need be added to the core set of motivated offenders, suitable targets, and lack of capable guardians. Rather, we maintain that to capture the convergence of motivated offenders, suitable targets, and lack of capable guardians (i.e., criminal opportunity contexts) it is necessary to answer three basic questions about the temporal dimensions of activities found in particular bounded locales: How regular (rhythm)? How often (tempo)? When (timing)?

To develop the most complete picture of criminal opportunity in bounded locales, these questions would need to be asked about individual and collective activities that are identified as relevant to the emergence of criminogenic circumstances. The enumeration of specific "relevant" individual and collective activities depends upon the type of bounded locale in question. For instance, activities that are relevant for residents in neighborhoods (e.g., work schedules, neighborhood patrols) would be different from those that would pertain to students in middle schools (e.g., transitions to and from class rooms, extracurricular events). There seem to be two rather obvious guiding principles in the identification of "relevant" activities for bounded locales. One would be a focus on movements of people (individually and collectively) *across* time and space. These activities would capture activities of transition. In the broadest terms, these activities would represent home-based to public-venue, public-venue to home-based, and public-venue to public-venue movements. A second principle would be to focus on activities (individual and collective) *within* time and space. This suggests that it is important to ascertain the "beginnings," "endings," and durations of activities that occur within a space (i.e., within a bounded locale).

We noted above that the temporality inherent in the routine activities perspective has not received explicit theoretical attention since Cohen and Felson's (1979) original formulation. This is not an uncommon fate for theoretical contributions that resonate with the scholarly community as profoundly astute and valid—"definitive statements," by definition, do not require rumination or elaboration. Another possible reason for this lack of theoretical attention might be derived from the practical difficulties associated with investigating the temporality of activities empirically.

More specifically, while ascertaining the tempo ("how often") of activities is rather straightforward and easily accomplished, matters of rhythm and timing are more complex and challenging to measure precisely. Investigators can easily ask and expect fairly accurate responses to questions such as: During a typical week, how often do you walk alone in your neighborhood? In contrast, collecting data on the regularity of individual and collective activities (i.e., rhythm) could be quite daunting. To get the most precise data on the rhythm of activities, a researcher might want to have year-long, hourly diaries for all the activities of individuals and collectives in a bounded locale. While this would reveal hourly, daily, weekly, and seasonal rhythms with great precision, it would require an incredible expenditure of resources (i.e., time, money, and investigator mental health). Similarly, diarylike data collection would provide the means for a researcher to discover critical temporal overlaps (i.e., timing) among and between individual and collective activities; but such efforts would require a considerable investment of resources.

These practical difficulties with examining temporality are neither insurmountable nor unusual. Research is hardly ever conducted under ideal circumstances or in an ideal manner. Indeed, the craft of research seems to revolve around the mastery of managing modifications. For instance, in trying to tap both tempo and timing, a researcher might ask: During a typical week, how often do you walk alone in your neighborhood at night? While the management of modifications is less than ideal, it represents reasonable attempts to gather some accurate data on things deemed important. Modifications are carried out with the hope that some data will prove to be better than no data at all. Sometimes this hope is fulfilled; sometimes it is not. Regardless, the point here is that a fair and accurate investigation of criminal opportunity theory requires some attention to issues pertaining to rhythm, tempo, and timing. Such attention will give rise to creative and efficient (albeit imperfect) ways to understand individual and collective activities in terms of rhythm, tempo, and timing.

DEVELOPMENTAL, LIFE COURSE CRIMINOLOGY

Aside from the temporal dimensions in routine activities theory, the temporality of crime has received considerable attention in theory and research that can be broadly conceived of as developmental or life course criminology. Over the past several decades, criminologists have discussed the need for longitudinal analyses that account for the onset, continuity, and change in crime and delinquency.[1] In essence, a developmental or life course perspective points out that human beings' behaviors are age-dependent, changing as individuals move from infancy to childhood to adolescence to young adult to mature adult. Most move through these developmental sequences in socially appropriate manners that are "on time." Others manifest age-inappropriate behaviors either because a life transition occurs "too early" (e.g., childhood drug use) or "too late" (e.g., being relatively uninvolved in the paid labor market well into mature adulthood). Taken as a whole, developmental criminology theories suggest that criminality has multiple origins, including genetic influences, neuropsychological deficits, antisocial personality traits, maladaptive parental socialization, and early problems in school. Such theories argue that as individuals age, factors that had previously insulated them from or exposed them to crime may have little to no effect later in life (e.g., parental bonds and delinquent siblings, respectively). This view suggests that the criminally involved are more likely to persist in their criminality if their life transitions are impeded or disrupted (e.g., chronic adult unemployment, perhaps due to early educational failure). Conversely, the criminally involved are more likely to desist from crime if there are "successful," normative life transitions (e.g., joining the military, finding a good job, getting married).

Building on the insights of developmental or life course criminologists, we suggest that onset, continuity, and change regarding criminal events as well as reactions to crime can be understood within a common sociogenic perspective. This section extends the theoretical framework offered in previous chapters in order to understand continuity versus change in criminal acts and reactions to crime. According to the perspective offered here, continuity versus change in criminal acts and reactions to crime can be understood as resulting from continuity versus change in structured opportunity both at the individual and ecological levels. More specifically, the two traditions integrated previously—including routine activities theories and social control-disorganization theories—can be used to understand criminal acts longitudinally, with an explicit emphasis on the structure of opportunities at multiple levels of analysis. Before attending to these issues, it is first necessary to situate our efforts in the context of the time and crime debate that has captured the attention of criminologists.

Time and Crime

Current perspectives regarding the stability versus change in crime over time are varied, but can broadly be viewed as falling into three camps: purely static, purely dynamic, and mixed-model, static-dynamic camps. The "static" camp, most prominently represented by Gottfredson and Hirschi (1990), essentially argues that the relationship between age and crime is constant (i.e., individuals, regardless of other demographic characteristics—such as sex, race, and social class—commit less crime as they age), and therefore age as such is not useful in explaining crime. The "dynamic" camp disagrees with the assertion that the relationship between age and crime is constant. The dynamic camp therefore advocates the development of theoretical frameworks and empirical methods that take age as a key to explaining crime. The mixed-model, static-dynamic camp suggests that *for some*, the relationship between age and crime is constant; these individuals are persistent offenders across the life course. The mixed-model perspective also argues that *for some* the relationship between age and crime is dynamic, with offending being limited to the adolescence stage in the life course.

Considering offending (i.e., criminal acts *committed*), the "static" view claims that crime experienced by any one individual is relatively stable. Hirschi and Gottfredson, for instance, have argued for the stability of the aggregate age-crime curve across time and space.[2] According to these scholars, the time(age)-crime relationship depicts an increase in offending rates into the mid-teen years followed by a sharp and continued decline thereafter. They suggest that this aggregate curve looks the same, regardless of the type of crime in question, for all demographic groups, irrespective of social or cultural conditions. Furthermore, they suggest that the causes of crime are the same regardless of life course positioning. Though there is an aggregate decline in crime with time(age) after a peak in midadolescence, Gottfredson and Hirschi do recognize that criminal propensity, as an individual-level characteristic, remains relatively stable—adult criminals are likely to have been juvenile delinquents as well. Their explanation for this individual stability is that there is a propensity towards crime in the form of low self-control. According to Gottfredson and Hirschi, low self-control emerges from poor early childhood socialization, and subsequent attempts at resocialization by other institutions for the most part fail. It is invariant low self-control, *in combination with criminal opportunity*, that is the cause of crime at all stages of the life course. Given these various assumptions of invariance, they reject the need for longitudinal or life-course studies on crime.

In contrast, a dynamic view is offered by other criminologists who challenge the static assumptions of invariance and argue for longitudinal or life-course examinations.[3] First, the notion that the aggregate age-crime curve is invariant has been challenged by research suggesting that aggregate onset, peak and desistance patterns are different across different types of crime.[4] Some of this work on offending trajectories has also emphasized the idea that theoretical explanations should be age-graded, considering factors associated with crime that vary according to age and can thus account for individual-level age variation in offending patterns. Sampson and Laub's age-graded theory,[5] which suggests that desistance from crime over time is a function of the formation of salient adult social bonds, serves as an example of such an age-graded explanation. Another example of an age-graded criminological theory is Blumstein, Farrington, and their colleagues' developmental perspective,[6] which maintains a variety of factors, insulate youths from criminal careers (e.g., shyness and conforming families) and—similar to Sampson and Laub's view—a sundry of influences promote desistance among offenders (e.g., employment and marriage). In sum, by emphasizing chronicity or persistence and desistance patterns—found through examining variation in *individual* rather than *aggregate* age-crime curves—this body of work clearly argues for a longitudinal, developmental, "criminal careers" paradigm.

The mixed-model, static-dynamic perspective is the third view on the relationship between age and crime. This view suggests that there are distinct types of offenders even within any one category of crime, each with different onset, peak, and desistance patterns. For instance, Moffitt and her colleagues make the distinction between two developmental trajectories for offending: "life-course persistent" and "adolescence-limited." The life-course persistent engage in antisocial behavior throughout their lifetimes, while the "adolescence-limited" age out of criminal activity as they reach adulthood.[7] Following a similar line of inquiry, Land, Nagin, and their colleagues identify additional latent classes of criminal career trajectories over the life-course.[8] Similar to the purely dynamic approach, the mixed-model, static-dynamic view focuses on persistence and desistance patterns, and thus suggests the need for longitudinal, developmental research.

It is important to note that these three points of view share a common orientation. Namely, they approach the issue of time and crime from the vantage point of the *offender*. So, they question whether individual offending patterns are stable or variant over the individual life-course. As such, crime as experienced by victims is ignored, as are reactions to crime, including risk perception, fear, and constrained behavior, which were discussed in Chapter 6. This emphasis on the offender serves as the basis of a point of departure for our theory. As we have stated, our interest is in criminal acts, which include offending and victimization, and can be extended to reactions to crime. We think the issue of time and crime can and should incorporate all of these elements of criminal acts, and our theory seeks to do just that. Our efforts here that argue for a *dynamic* criminal opportunity theory of criminal acts are somewhat hampered in that the extant work drawn upon exclusively focuses on continuity and change in individual offending, rather than exploring continuity and change in criminal acts more generally.

An Overview of Developmental or Life-Course Perspectives

According to Sampson and Laub, life-course theories "focus on the duration, timing, and ordering of major life events and their consequences for later development" (1993:8).." Proponents of life-course perspectives maintain that developmental explanations have a number of strengths that have emerged as correctives for shortcomings found in static, nondevelopmental frameworks. For instance, Thornberry argues:[9]

> Nondevelopmental theories suffer from a number of limitations. They fail to identify and explain different dimensions of delinquent careers, to define and explain subtypes of offenders based on developmental considerations, to study systematically the precursors and consequences of delinquency,

and to utilize changes in development over the life-course to help explain changing patterns of crime and delinquency. A developmental approach argues that each of these limitations, and their combination, retards the construction of a fuller and more complete explanation for criminal behavior. (1997:5)

These core interests generate some common, guiding questions in developmental criminology. Why do some begin criminal careers and others do not? For those who have embarked on criminal careers, why do some continue and some desist? For those involved in criminal careers, why do some escalate the severity of their offending (e.g., transition from shoplifting to burglary), while others decrease the severity of their offending, and still others maintain a stable level of severity? For those who have left criminal careers, what causes them to reenter criminal careers? Even though there are several different developmental or life-course approaches in criminology, they all attend to these issues pertaining to the dynamics of crime.

Another common aspect of developmental criminology is an emphasis on "two central concepts that underlie the analysis of life-course dynamics" (Sampson and Laub 1993:8)—*trajectory* and *transition*. Sampson and Laub explain:

> A trajectory is a pathway or line of development over the life span, such as work life, marriage, parenthood, self-esteem, or criminal behavior. Trajectories refer to long-term patterns of behavior and are marked by a sequence of transitions. Transitions are marked by life events (such as first job or first marriage) that are embedded in trajectories that evolve over shorter time spans. . . . Some transitions are age-graded and some are not; hence, what is often assumed to be important are the normative timing and sequencing of role transitions. . . . The interlocking nature of trajectories and transitions may generate turning points or a change in the life course. Adaptation to life events is crucial because the same event or transition followed by different adaptations can lead to different trajectories. The long-term view embodied by the life-course focus on trajectories implies a strong connection between childhood events and experiences in adulthood. However, the simultaneous shorter-term view also implies that transitions or turning points can modify life trajectories—they can "redirect paths." Social institutions and triggering life events that may modify trajectories include school, work, the military, marriage, and parenthood. (ibid.:8–9)

The dynamic interplay between trajectories and transitions is a key element in developmental explanations of criminal activity.

While it is possible to identify common concerns and concepts shared by developmental perspectives, a variety of life-course approaches exist in criminology. For instance, the initial interest in infusing criminology with a developmental perspective is often traced to the pioneering work of

Loeber and LeBlanc.[10] Offering a distinctive psychological orientation, Loeber, LeBlanc, and their colleagues have focused attention on the onset, persistence, desistence, and escalation of antisocial behavior. Using data from the Pittsburgh Youth Study, Loeber, LeBlanc, and their colleagues argue that some begin criminal careers early in life, while others begin later.[11] Their research reveals that the early onset (prior to age thirteen) of delinquency is associated with such things as deviant peers, familial maladies, and depression, whereas later onset is correlated with relatively low educational motivation. This line of inquiry has also revealed that there are multiple paths to criminal careers. Loeber et al. (1993) suggest three distinct beginnings to criminal careers: authority conflict, and covert and overt pathways. The authority conflict pathway entails resistance, active defiance, and avoidance of authority; the covert pathway originates with relatively petty chicanery (duplicity, minor theft), which can escalate to more serious forms of criminality (auto theft, drug dealing); and the overt pathway entails early bullying leading to more extreme forms of violence (assault, robbery). Each of these pathways can result in sustained criminal careers. However, those who pursue two or more of these pathways are more likely to become persistent offenders. Research has also shown that even though sustained criminal careers can be identified by early onset and pathway characteristics, the type and frequency of criminal activities are influenced by external forces such as social relations, arrest, and encounters with criminal justice institutions.[12]

Drawing upon insights from social learning theories and neuropsychology, the work of Moffitt and her colleagues represents another developmental criminology perspective.[13] Key to Moffitt's theory is the distinction between "adolescence-limited" and "life-course persistent" offenders. For most, antisocial behavior peaks in adolescence and then diminishes—i.e., the adolescence-limited youth ages out of crime. In contrast, life-course-persistent youth is a relatively small group that engages in antisocial behaviors well into adulthood.

For Moffitt, an etiological theory of adolescence-limited antisocial behavior must account for several empirical regularities: "modal onset in early adolescence, widespread prevalence, lack of continuity, and recovery by young adulthood" (1997a:24). Drawing upon social learning theory, Moffitt maintains that adolescence-limited antisocial behavior is "motivated, mimicked, and reinforced" (ibid.:25). From this view, adolescence-limited delinquents mimic the behavior of life-course-persistent peers. To explain the motivation for such mimicry, Moffitt relies on the notion of maturity:

> If social mimicry is to explain why adolescence-limited delinquents begin
> to mimic the antisocial behavior of their life-course persistent peers, then

logically, delinquency must be a social behavior that allows access to some
desirable resource. I suggest that the resource is mature status, with its con-
sequent power and privilege. (ibid.)

Moffitt elaborates by explaining that modernization has resulted in earlier biological maturity (due to nutrition and health care) and later social
maturity (delaying labor-force participation, sexual activity, etc.). This
means that "contemporary adolescents are thus trapped in a maturity gap,
chronological hostages of a time warp between biological age and social
age" (ibid.:26).

Motivated by a desire to escape this maturity gap, teens begin to notice
the delinquent behavior of peers, particularly life-course-persistent youth,
as a means of asserting adult status. Moffitt explains:
Life-course persistent boys appear relatively free of the apron strings of
their families of origin; they seem to go their own way, making their own
rules. As evidence that they make their own decisions, they take risks and
do dangerous things that parents could not possibly endorse. As evidence
that they have social consequence in the adult world, they have personal
attorneys, social workers, and probation officers; they operate small businesses in the underground economy; they have fathered children. Already
adept at deviance, life-course persistent youths are able to obtain possessions by theft or vice that are otherwise inaccessible to teens who have no
independent incomes (cars, clothes, drugs, entry to "adults only" leisure
settings). Life-course boys are more sexually experienced and have
already initiated relations with the opposite sex. . . . Rumored or real, the
life-course persistents' success in the sexual arena may be a powerful
inducement to other adolescents to mimic their behavioral style. (ibid.:27)

The antisocial precocity or pseudomaturity of life-course-persistent
youths serves as a means to desirable social assets and is therefore mimicked. Moffitt thus sees adolescence-limited delinquency as a "reasonable
adaptation to untoward contextual circumstances" (ibid.:32).

Yet, Moffitt acknowledges that even though almost all adolescents commit some illegal acts, a small minority seems to abstain from criminal acts
altogether and some commit less delinquency than others. She suggests
that this might be so because some might not experience a "maturity gap"
due to late puberty or early initiation into adult roles. Moffitt also claims
that "others may be excluded from *opportunities* for mimicking life-course
persistent delinquent models" (ibid.:33, emphasis added). In terms of
desistence, Moffitt claims that adolescence-limited youth are more capable
of responding to shifting reinforcement contingencies. For healthy youths,
behaviors that are unrewarded or that have relatively high commitment
costs will eventually be extinguished. Additionally, adolescence-limited
youths are able to take advantage of prosocial turning points. Moffitt

points out that "the antisocial behavior of many delinquent teens has been found to decline after they leave high school, join the army, marry a prosocial spouse, move away from the old neighborhood, or get a full-time job" (1997a:36). Moffitt also maintains that desistence is also effected by the "differential accumulation of the consequences of crime":

> Although the forces of cumulative continuity build up less momentum over the course of their relatively short crime careers, many adolescence-limited youths will fall prey to many of the same snares that maintain continuity among life-course persistent persons. Those whose teen forays into delinquency inadvertently attracted damaging consequences may have more difficulty desisting. A drug habit, an incarceration, interrupted education, or a teen pregnancy are snares that require extra effort and time from which to escape. (ibid.:37)

From Moffitt's view, the temporary and situational deviance that characterizes most offenders can be explained via social learning theory.

In contrast to her etiology of adolescence-limited delinquency, Moffitt's explanation of life-course-persistent antisocial behavior draws upon insights from neuropsychology. According to Moffitt, neuropsychology refers to:

> the extent to which anatomical structures and physiological processes within the nervous system engender differences between children in activity level, emotional reactivity, or self-regulation (temperament), speech, motor coordination, or impulse control (behavioral development), and attention, language, learning, memory, or reasoning (cognitive abilities). Toddlers with subtle neuropsychological deficits may be clumsy and awkward, overactive, inattentive, irritable, impulsive, hard to keep on schedule, delayed in reaching developmental milestones, poor at verbal comprehension, deficient at expressing themselves, or slow at learning new things. (ibid.:18)

For Moffitt and her colleagues, neuropsychological deficits are key for distinguishing between those who have temporary and situational antisocial tendencies and those who have stable and persistent antisocial behavior.

Life-course-persistent antisocial behavior, according to Moffitt, begins with "social interactions between problem children and problem parents" (ibid.). Children with neuropsychological deficits are not proportionately distributed across the population. Rather, children with neuropsychological deficits are more likely to have parents who also suffer from neuropsychological deficits. This means that children with neuropsychological deficits are often in environments that are characterized by poor parenting practices, familial disadvantages (e.g., limited material resources, little social capital), and deviant parents. Often, children with neuropsychological deficits are born into environments that will exacerbate rather than relieve problem behavior. Moffitt (ibid.:19) and her colleagues have provided evidence that children who ultimately become "persistently antisocial" suffer from neuropsychological deficits.

According to her view, Moffitt maintains that the children with neuropsychological deficits persist in antisocial behavior for three primary reasons. First, continuity, in part, stems from the fact that the same traits that produced childhood problems (e.g., low impulse control, irritability, low cognitive ability) are carried through into adulthood and produce more problems. Second, life-course-persistent youth "miss out on opportunities to acquire and practice prosocial alternatives at each stage of development" (ibid.:22). That is, irritable and aggressive children are often rejected by parents, other adults, and peers, thereby limiting opportunities to associate with prosocial individuals. Further, as adolescents and adults who have learned to anticipate rejection, these individuals withdraw or act hostilely, again limiting opportunities to interact with prosocial individuals. Third, the consequences of antisocial behavior can virtually lock an individual into a deviant lifestyle. For instance, incarceration, teenaged parenthood, and drug or alcohol addiction could eliminate opportunities to pursue prosocial lifestyles (e.g., good-paying, legitimate employment). Moffitt (1997b) has speculated that these consequences of neuropsychological deficits may vary across environmental contexts such as neighborhoods.

Another developmental approach is advanced by Weis, Catalano, Hawkins, and their colleagues.[14] Integrating social control, learning, and structural theories they offer a "social development model." Similar to our perspective, the social development model argues that environmental-level factors have an impact upon the development of individual antisocial behavior. For example, in communities that are socially disorganized, social control is less effective in averting antisocial behaviors. From this view, the risk for antisocial behavior is controlled by the formation of and reinforcement from prosocial bonds with conforming individuals as well as conventional institutions and beliefs. Adding to Hirschi's (1969) control theory, the social development model asserts that the formation of and reinforcement from antisocial bonds exacerbates the risk for antisocial behavior. From this view, key to determining the trajectories of antisocial behavior is individual perceptions of *opportunities* associated with prosocial and deviant activities, which are shaped rather predictably within particular environmental contexts.

Similar to the social development model is Elliot's "integrated theory," which advances a developmental perspective that weaves together strain, social learning, and control theories of delinquency.[15] From this view, adolescents who live in socially disorganized communities and who receive inadequate conventional socialization are more likely to experience strain, which then weakens bonds with conventional others, activities, institutions, and beliefs. Perceived strain combined with weakened social bonds compels adolescents to reject conforming values and to identify and develop deviant peer associations. Delinquent peers provide models and reinforcements for antisocial behavior. Delinquent associations increase an adolescent's risk for engaging in antisocial behavior.

Yet another developmental perspective is Farrington, Blumstein, and Cohen's delinquent development and criminal career theory.[16] This important and prolific line of inquiry is primarily grounded in the impressive Cambridge Study of Delinquent Development, which is a longitudinal study that has followed the criminal careers of 411 London boys born in 1953. The criminal career approach identifies three distinct groups: "innocents," who have no record of offending, "desisters," who have low recidivism risk, and "persisters," who have high recidivism risk.

Farrington and his colleagues have identified several factors that are manifest by age ten and that predict chronic offending, specifically early conviction (ten to thirteen years of age), low family income, troublesomeness as estimated by teachers, educational attainment at age ten, psychomotor clumsiness, low nonverbal IQ, and the presence of a convicted sibling. Motivated by desires for material goods, sensation seeking, and social status, those with crimogenic tendencies tend to lack opportunities to meet these wants legitimately, and therefore commit criminal acts to satisfy their desires. Further, criminal acts tend to be general rather than specialized. That is, the typical offender commits a variety of criminal acts. For most, the frequency of offending peaks around seventeen to eighteen years of age and decreases in the twenties. The likelihood of committing an offense in a particular situation depends upon the calculation of perceived costs and benefits of that offense vis-à-vis legitimate alternatives. Those who are impulsive are more likely to offend because they are likely to consider only proximal benefits rather than distal consequences. Chronic offenders tend to have disruptive family and work lives, thereby reproducing the kind of deprived and disorderly contexts that they experienced as children for their own children. Over the life-course, the factors that promote or inhibit offending change. Also, there are life events that promote the desistence from offending for some who have engaged in antisocial behavior.

Building on the symbolic interactionist tradition in sociology, several scholars have posited a developmental perspective that revolves around differential association, deviant values, bonding factors, and identity formation. For instance, Thornberry and his colleagues have advanced an interactional theory that contends offending during adolescence results from weakened attachment to parents, commitment to educational attainment, and belief in conventional values, which can be consequences of social disorganization and other structural variables.[17] Borrowing from social learning and differential association theory, Thornberry and his associates maintain that the onset of antisocial behavior occurs in an environment where deviant beliefs, values, and practices can be learned and reinforced by delinquent peers. A central idea to Thornberry's interactional theory is that causal influences are reciprocal. That is, weakened bonds (i.e., attachment to parents, commitment to educational attainment, and belief in conventional values) compel adolescents to develop delinquent associations and engage in deviant behaviors; subsequently, adolescents' delinquent associations and deviant behaviors promote weakened bonds. This dynamic feedback loop underlies the persistence of chronic criminal careers. Thornberry's perspective is age-graded. Thornberry (1987:863) maintains that during early adolescence family attachment is the most important factor associated with delinquency; the "world of friends, school, and youth culture" becomes more important by midadolescence; and during adulthood, offending is determined by individuals' locations in conventional society as well as the development and attachment to families of their own.

A related line of inquiry in symbolic interactionism places greater emphasis on the self and identity formation. For instance, Matsueda, Heimer, and their colleagues have advanced a developmental theory of offending that revolves around self conceptions, role identities, role transitions, and role commitments.[18] According to Bartusch and Matsueda:

> From an interactionist perspective, the important mechanism by which interactants influence each other is role-taking, which consists of projecting oneself into the role of others, and appraising from their standpoint the situation, oneself in the situation, and possible lines of action. The self that emerges through this role-taking process consists of an individual's perception of how others view him or her, and should be somewhat stable across similar situations. . . . The content of the self—that is, the kind of object formed from the standpoint of generalized others—is critical in determining the direction that social control takes. For example, youths who see themselves as bad kids, deviants, or rule violators may be more likely to engage in delinquency than those who see themselves as conformers. Moreover, this self should be rooted in reference groups through a process of informal labeling or social identification. The self, then, is linked to social structure through the organization of reference groups and lines of communication.[19] (1996:147–48)

Symbolic interaction theory thus links the self-concept, meaning, identities, roles, and subcultures.[20]

Matsueda and Heimer specify how an "individual's biographical history—including self-concept, identities, role expectations, and meanings of social locations—"is limited by his or her specific life-course roles, transitions, and trajectories" (1997:175). Matsueda and Heimer explicate how symbolic interactionist role theory can account for the emergence, persistence, and desistence of antisocial behavior in three distinct developmental stages: early childhood identity formation, student and peer roles in adolescence, and family and work roles in adulthood.

Yet another key developmental criminology perspective is Sampson and Laub's age-graded theory.[21] The jumping-off point for Sampson and Laub's age-graded theory can be found in the pioneering longitudinal studies conducted by Glueck and Glueck in the 1930s.[22] The Gluecks identified individual (e.g., biological traits, intelligence, temperament) and social (e.g., parental disciplinary practices, emotional ties, family structure, social economic status) correlates of the onset and persistence of antisocial behavior. Even though their methodology and their integration of biological, psychological, and social factors were path-breaking, their work was dismissed and ignored for over thirty years.[23] Sampson and Laub "rediscovered" the Gluecks' work, bringing it to the attention of criminology scholars and reanalyzing their data in light of contemporary debates and issues.[24]

The key concept for Sampson and Laub's age-graded theory is "turning points." Agreeing with the Gluecks and a host of other developmental perspectives, Sampson and Laub claim that the onset of antisocial behavior is rooted in early childhood socialization at home and school as well as deviant peer associations. They explain discontinuity in deviant behavior by changes in the salience of social bonds within conventional institutions of informal social control, including family (i.e. marriage), the workplace, and the military.[25] Though evidence of change, or "turning points," in the crime associated with any one individual is apparent, it is also well established that previous experiences with delinquency and crime are strong predictors of current experiences with these outcomes. The criminological literature is clear about the fact that childhood delinquency is often a precursor to adult deviance.[26] Sampson and Laub integrate this empirical regularity with the concept of "social capital." Social capital is accrued by successful engagement in conventional institutions and behaviors, and it insulates individuals from deviant activities. By the same token, individuals who engage in antisocial behaviors, particularly those who encounter the justice system (e.g., in terms of arrest and incarceration), undermine their ability to garner social capital, and thereby impede their ability to turn away from offending. The inability to accumulate social capital helps to explain persistent criminal careers.

A DYNAMIC, MULTILEVEL CRIMINAL OPPORTUNITY THEORY

The perspective offered here situates the theory provided thus far within a life-course perspective. Beyond developmental criminology, the socio-logical life-course literature more broadly has traditionally emphasized the role of social structure in influencing stability or change in life path-ways. Social structural mechanisms including rules governing role sequencing, age-grading, and differential allocation of resources shape life trajectories due to their interplay with the aging process of cohorts.[27] In examining life-course transitions and trajectories, issues of continuity, development, and change are key. The plasticity of individuals is empha-sized. Transitions such as school or neighborhood changes, marriage, par-enthood, and participation in the workforce can impose new order and redirect life pathways.[28] This perspective is based upon the assumption that humans are inherently capable of changing as a response to new con-texts,[29] and thus events occurring across life transitions can be viewed as "loosely coupled."[30] Discontinuity from crime across life stages would be an example of loose coupling.

However, close coupling of events is also possible from a life-course per-spective since, despite the possibility for change, there is also a tendency for interdependence to exist between earlier and later life events. For example, as noted earlier, the timing and sequencing of marriage, childbearing, edu-cation, and work can affect subsequent opportunity structures.[31] Similarly, behavior and personality patterns in childhood (e.g., temper and conduct problems) can influence experiences and behaviors through the transition to adolescence, adulthood, and beyond.[32] Selection or transition effects can occur, and due to earlier life statuses, certain doors may be closed in adult life. In this way, similarity or continuity in experiences and action can char-acterize multiple stages of any one life-course. Continuity in offending from adolescence to adulthood would exemplify this close coupling. So, continuity and change can occur when examining experiences and action over time. Neither option is "a given," and empirical examination of tra-jectories is thus an axiom guiding the life-course perspective. Throughout the past decade, there has been a call within the sociological life-course lit-erature for a consideration of both individual-level and environmental-level factors simultaneously in accounting for life-course continuity versus change. Elder (1992), for instance, calls for a bridging of the gap between micro- and macroexplanations regarding life patterns. Featherman and Lerner (1985:659) propose a "developmental contextualism" emphasizing a "person-population" process in accounting for individual development. In extending our theory to incorporate time, the theory becomes one of developmental or dynamic contextualism regarding continuity versus change in crime.

The dynamic contextual model we offer in this chapter is an integration of the ideas regarding time and crime from the three divergent camps in criminology (static, dynamic, and static-dynamic) as well as integration of ideas from the sociological life-course literature emphasizing dynamic contextualism. We clearly adapt the longitudinal or life-course perspective supported by the work of Blumstein, Farrington, Land, Moffitt, Nagin, Sampson, Laub, and others, though much of this work has emphasized individual-level models of change. We believe that individual trajectories should be studied since we operate from the assumption that both continuity and change in experiences and action can occur. Though we assume that offender motivation remains constant in any one individual as well as across individuals, there may still be variation in experiences and action regarding crime since motivated offender exposure, target suitability, and guardianship can change over time. In short, we think that criminal opportunity—the cause of criminal acts and reactions to crime—can be characterized by stability or change when examined longitudinally. As such, criminal acts can be characterized by stability or change.

In focusing on the importance of criminal opportunity, our perspective also draws upon Gottfredson and Hirschi's general theory of crime. While Gottfredson and Hirschi reject the value of longitudinal examinations of crime due to the invariance of "propensity," they also clearly state that it is propensity, *in combination with criminal opportunity*, that impacts crime. As such, they imply that criminal acts may vary over time *as opportunity varies*. In fact, we find this implication of their theory to be incongruent with their strong stance against longitudinal analysis of crime. If opportunity is a crucial ingredient in crime—and we propose that it is *the* critical ingredient—then a dynamic perspective seems very valuable. Further, we propose that opportunity offered at both individual and environmental levels can vary over time, thus suggesting adoption of a dynamic contextualism as advocated by prominent life-course sociologists such as Elder, Featherman, and Lerner. Our suggestion that individual and contextual opportunity are dynamic as opposed to static is illustrated by considering several very simplistic scenarios. These scenarios depict the role of dynamic contextualism in the close versus loose coupling of criminal behavior over time.

In one scenario, imagine a juvenile delinquent (crime at time 1) faced with "ecological constancy," so to speak, in that her or his environmental conditions, especially those contributing to the structuring of criminal opportunity (e.g., population density, urbanness, weak social ties), remain fairly constant through the transition from adolescence to adulthood. Life-course theory predicts that positions and statuses aid in organizing and constraining future positions and their accompanying amount of opportunities.[33] Thus, status as a juvenile delinquent is likely to condition any

adult status; delinquency is unlikely to "open any doors" for this hypothetical individual. So, ambient criminal opportunity structure—"high" or
"strong" to begin with—remains relatively stable for the individual in this
scenario, and the status as "juvenile delinquent" at time 1 might further
limit noncriminal opportunity. This individual's likelihood of experiencing crime at time 2 (e.g., in adulthood) would be rather high. "Life-course
persistence" might characterize this person's offending trajectory, though
we would not link this condition to neuropsychological deficits as would
Moffitt, who made this term so popular. Rather, stability regarding ambient opportunity is key from our theoretical standpoint.

Imagine another scenario in which a juvenile is, again, in a context providing ample criminal opportunity during adolescence. Within this environment, the juvenile is engaging in criminal behavior (crime at time 1).
Disinterested in school and seeing few prospects for jobs, this individual
joins the military, secures steady employment after her/his service, and
resides in a "stable" neighborhood—one with less ambient criminal
opportunity than the neighborhood in which she or he was raised. In this
scenario, individual and ambient criminal opportunity appears reduced.
Based upon this reduction, we predict that this individual's likelihood of
experiencing crime in adulthood (time 2) would be reduced in comparison
to her or his experiences in adolescence. Experiences with criminal acts in
such a trajectory would be "loosely coupled." This offender would more
likely fall into the "adolescent limited" category of offenders.

Of course, the above scenarios are purely hypothetical, and clearly end-
less scenarios could be constructed with variable temporal and spatial
dimensions. For instance, the time period and context under consideration
might be different from the above scenario in which we consider the rather
prolonged individual transition from adolescence to adulthood within the
context of neighborhood. To provide another example, consider the more
truncated transition from middle to high school, experienced by most
individuals over the course of a two- to four-year period during adolescence. Figures 7.1 and 7.2 help depict such a transition hypothetically.

In Figure 7.1, a hypothetical marijuana use trajectory is shown for two
students, both of whom, after the eighth grade, make the transition from
Middle School 1 to High School 1. For ease of interpretation, let us assume
that these two students are also from the same neighborhood. While the
overall level of marijuana use is quite discrepant across these two students,
with Student 1's frequency of use being much higher than that of Student
2, the general shape of the trajectories is similar. Both students experience
elevation in marijuana use frequency as they proceed through middle
school, while their use levels decline upon transition into high school.

In Figure 7.2, the marijuana use of two students is again considered
hypothetically. The two students considered here also attend Middle
School 1 through the eighth grade. But, beginning in ninth grade, these

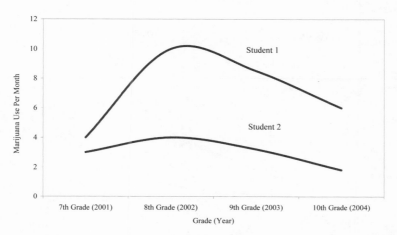

Figure 7.1. Hypothetical delinquency growth trajectories for students embedded within Middle school 1 and High School 1.

two students attend High School 2 as opposed to High School 1. Both use trajectories slowly increase throughout middle school, then increase rather dramatically as the school context changes to that of High School 2. Comparison of Figures 7.1 and 7.2 suggests that something about the High School 2 context enhances marijuana use (in comparison to Middle School 1) whereas something about the High School 1 context diminishes marijuana use (in comparison to Middle School 1). We suggest that changing ambient opportunity (or dynamic contextualism) can possibly account for the increases in use both students experience. In short, ambient opportunity regarding marijuana use can vary; it might be high in High School 2, low in High School 1, and moderate in Middle School 1.

Since contexts were similar for the two hypothetical students in each figure, we might attribute differences in levels of use to differences in individual-level opportunity. The widening gap between Student 1's and Student 2's trajectories, particularly evident in Figure 7.2, further suggests that their individual-level opportunity might be differentially varying ("dynamic individualism," of sorts). So, thinking of other hypothetical scenarios, individual- and ambient-level opportunity might both be time-varying, or individual-level opportunity might be time-varying while ambient-level opportunity is not time-varying, or, finally, ambient opportunity might be time-varying while individual-level opportunity is not time-varying. Any of these possible scenarios, however, is going to affect

A Dynamic Perspective

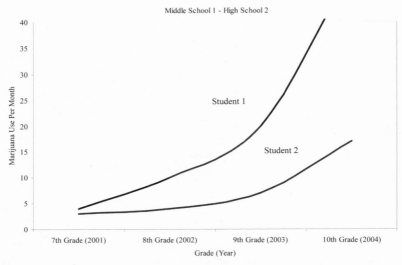

Figure 7.2. Hypothetical delinquency growth trajectories for students embedded within Middle school 1 and High School 2.

the overall mean experience with criminal acts as well as the change/ growth in these experiences over time. Figure 7.3 more comprehensively models the possibilities that exist in a dynamic, multilevel criminal opportunity theory.

Figure 7.3 posits a multilevel growth model of criminal acts and/or reactions to crime in which repeated measures of acts/reactions and opportunity are embedded within individuals who are, in turn, embedded within environmental contexts (schools or neighborhoods, for instance). Arrow 1 in Figure 7.3 suggests that there is within-person historical variation in experiences with criminal acts and reactions to crime. These experiences are viewed as partially a function of time. Because of all of the various ways that time can be operationalized, it is impossible to put forth one proposition that succinctly describes the time-crime (or time-reactions) relationships. If time is operationalized in terms of years, then arrow 1 suggests that there is an age-crime curve, an age-perceived risk curve, an age-fear curve, and an age-constrained behavior curve. The propositions put forth for this operationalization (e.g., propositions regarding the shape or form of the curves) would be very different than if time were operationlized as daily increments within a one-year span of an adolescent's life-course. The propositions regarding the shape of such curves are as limitless as are the operationalizations of "time." Therefore, we simply provide the axiom, to

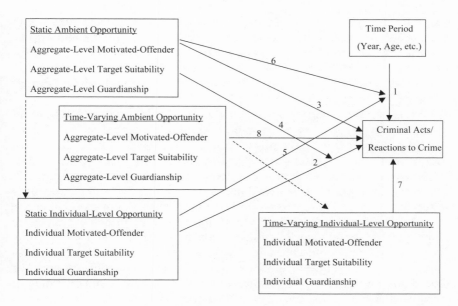

Figure 7.3.   Conceptual multilevel, dynamic model of criminal opportunity.

correspond with arrow 1, that historical fluctuations in crime and reactions to crime are present.

We presume, however, that experiences with criminal acts and/or reactions to crime are not only a function of time but also a function of individual-level and ambient opportunity. These effects are represented by arrows 2 and 3 in Figure 7.3. Arrows 2 and 3 in Figure 7.3 refer to the effects of "static" individual and ambient indicators of criminal opportunity on criminal acts and reactions to crime. These effects have been discussed in previous chapters (e.g., Propositions 4.1 through 4.15 and Propositions 6.1 through 6.6). An important point to stress is that these effects address *cross-individual differences*; *within-individual cross-time differences* are not being considered with these particular effects. So, for instance, arrow 2 in Figure 7.3 represents the effects of individual- or object-level motivated offender exposure on criminal acts or reactions to crime. These are cross-individual "static effects" of covariates (a cross-sectional assumption); they imply that exposure varies across individuals or objects and this variation affects the respective probabilities that these different individuals or object experience crime or reactions to crime.

Further, as discussed in Chapters 5 and 6, individual and ambient opportunity can interact in affecting crime and reactions to crime. These potential micro-macro moderating effects are represented by arrow 4 in Figure 7.3. Arrow 4 represents the conditioning effects of ambient opportunity indicators on the relationships between individual-level opportunity indicators and criminal acts and/or reactions to crime. These effects have been addressed explicitly in Propositions 5.1 through 5.9 and Propositions 6.7 through 6.15.

While previous chapters have already discussed the effect of individual and ambient opportunity on cross-individual level of criminal acts and/or reactions to crime, we have not yet allowed for the possibility that these opportunity factors affect change or growth in criminal acts and/or reactions to crime. These effects are represented by arrows 5 and 6 in Figure 7.3. As shown in Figure 7.3, arrows 5 and 6 point to arrow 1—they affect the effect of time on crime (representing the growth parameter). In other words, opportunity (both individual and ambient) interacts with time (time period, age, etc.) in affecting criminal acts and/or reactions to crime. While we recognize that these interactions probably exist, it is difficult to offer precise theoretical propositions for these interaction effects since we could not offer a precise proposition regarding the time-crime relationship (or growth). Given that the posited time-crime relationship is so variable, depending upon operationalization of time (see above discussion), we can offer no real concrete propositions regarding the effects of opportunity on this time-crime relationship. However, for purposes of discussing how this interaction *might* work according to our theory, we offer several scenarios. Consider first how individual and environment differences might affect within-individual historical change (or growth) in criminal acts and reactions to crime, *assuming a tendency for crime to decline with time (negative growth)*. Such a growth curve might emerge among individuals in a sample studied annually throughout the transition from adolescence to adulthood (e.g., a ten-year study spanning ages fifteen through twenty-five). Given this hypothetical negative time-crime relationship, we might observe that, all else equal, individual- or object-level motivated offender exposure exacerbates this negative relationship. The decline in crime would be more discernible as cross-individual static exposure (exposure at $t = 0$) increased. At the highest levels of baseline exposure, where risk is greatest (see Chapter 4), the potential for decline in criminal acts is also greatest. At low levels of exposure (at $t = 0$), criminal opportunity is low (holding all else constant), and thus experience with criminal acts should be low initially, with declines thereafter seemingly minimal. Now, assume for the purposes of another example that the time-crime relationship is positive. This might appear in a sample of middle-school students, with repeated measures available from years eleven through thirteen, for instance. Given this hypothetical time-crime relationship, we might observe that individual- or object-level motivated offender exposure tempers this positive growth. The increase in crime would be less discernible as static exposure (exposure at $t = 0$) increased. At the highest levels of baseline exposure, where risk is greatest (see Chapter 4), the potential for increase is less.

The effects of opportunity on either levels of crime/reactions to crime or growth in crime/reactions to crime considered up to this point have been static effects. But, just as crime and criminal reactions might change over time, so might the covariates of crime and reactions to crime. More specifically, arrows 7 and 8 represent the effects of *within-person* variation in levels of individual-level opportunity indicators and environmental-level opportunity indicators on criminal acts and reactions to crime. We assume that within-individual or within-object motivated offender exposure is positively related to criminal acts, risk perception, fear of crime, and constrained behavior. We also assume that within-individual or within-object target suitability is positively related to criminal acts, risk perception, fear of crime, and constrained behavior. And, we finally assume that within-individual or within-object guardianship is negatively related to criminal acts, risk perception, fear of crime, and constrained behavior. It should be clear that these assumptions appear very similar to the theoretical propositions offered in Chapter 4 regarding the main effects of individual and ambient opportunity. Again, however, previous chapters were considering cross-sectional, between-individual differences. They did not consider longitudinal differences in repeated measures within individuals. Yet, it is this intraindividual change in levels of opportunity and levels of crime/reactions that is being considered by arrows 7 and 8 in Figure 7.3. Notice that, theoretically, we offer no reason to suspect that individual-level or ambient opportunity act differently in explaining within-individual change as opposed to between-individual cross-sectional differences. However, the distinction of these respective effects, in a modeling sense, is an important one.

Finally, the introduction of time into the multilevel model allows for the consideration of possible mediating effects. Ambient opportunity may influence individual-level opportunity, which can, in turn, affect criminal acts and/or reactions to criminal acts. Such potential mediation is represented by Figure 7.3's dashed arrows. Additional mediation *not* depicted in Figure 7.3, but very plausible nonetheless, includes the interdependence among several of the outcome variables. As discussed in Chapter 6, criminal acts might affect subsequent risk, fear, or constrained behavior. Likewise, risk probably mediates the effects of opportunity and crime on fear. So, some of the outcome variables may be "more endogenous" than others; some may be involved in reciprocal relationships or feedback loops not depicted. For simplification purposes, we focus instead on the role of time and time-varying covariates in the conceptual model already presented in the previous chapters. We focus here on the possible mediating and moderating processes among exogenous parts of the model rather than the endogenous parts of the model (though we recognize that the latter probably exist).

THEORETICAL IMPLICATIONS

So, what are the overall implications of adding a temporal element to a multicontextual criminal opportunity theory? The theory and the modeling thereof allow for crime and criminal reactions to vary over time—to have a "growth curve," so to speak. It recognizes that opportunity, predicting crime, may not only be individual-level or environmental-level in terms of spatial context, but it also may be static or time-varying at either level in terms of temporal context. Having mapped these possibilities out in a conceptual model that builds upon the model started in earlier chapters, we conclude with a more general theoretical discussion of the implications for criminal acts given spatially *and* temporally situated criminal opportunity.

First, the notion of temporally situated criminal opportunity affecting criminal acts suggests that there is, indeed, a time dependence to criminal acts. We recognize the possibility for both individual trajectories as well as general, aggregate age-crime curves. Let us consider how criminal opportunity theory can account for the aggregate age-crime curve (e.g., peak in midadolescence with sharp decline thereafter). Why and how do opportunities change from childhood to adolescence to young adulthood and then to mature adulthood? We suggest that exposure to motivated offenders, target suitability, and especially capable guardianship are age-graded. For instance, there is a decrease in capable guardianship as children move through adolescence, distancing themselves from parents, teachers, etc. These social ties are not automatically replaced but are replaced when an individual chooses to pursue a life transition, such as marriage, military involvement, or employment. Further, the notion of spatially situated criminal opportunity suggests that these choices regarding individual-level social ties are conditioned by environmental context. Ambient opportunity clearly plays a role. One may choose to be employed, yet high unemployment in the community prevents such a thing, thus contributing to overall criminal opportunity.

Given an overall aggregate age-crime curve, our approach recognizes that individual-level trajectories will be variable, with some desisting from crime while others persist. How does the notion of temporally and spatially situated criminal opportunity account for these differences in individual trajectories? Our answer is that those who persist have failed to make a transition—either at the individual level or the environmental level —to a context of diminished opportunity. Thinking about the hypothetical life-course scenarios presented earlier, one individual escapes a crime-ridden neighborhood by joining the military (a transition in terms of higher guardianship), the other's opportunity contexts remain static. A middle-school students who uses drugs may make the transition into a college-preparatory high school with strong parental involvement while another drug-using middle-school student makes the transition into a high school with a drug culture among students and an alienated faculty. Some might ask why some individuals fail to make the transition into low-opportunity contexts. If our job is to explain criminal acts (which it has been, as stated, from the outset) then we have accomplished our task with the answer centered on differences in opportunity (particularly guardianship). If our task were to explain differences in life transitions, then we would need, perhaps, to look at issues of self-control, neuropsychological deficits, etc. However, the relationship between these antecedent conditions and opportunity contexts would require a different book—one that tries to explain criminal opportunity, not criminal acts.

Even though we have not set out to explain criminal opportunity per se, we do not mean to suggest that criminal opportunity is a purely exogenous factor in the explanation of criminal acts. In elaborating this point, it would be useful to provide a synopsis of our theoretical perspective, giving special attention to Cook's (1986) idea of feedback loops in conjunction with the temporal dimensions we have discussed.

As we have stated, at any moment in time, an ambient criminal opportunity context can be characterized in terms of aggregated supplies of motivated offenders, suitable targets, and capable guardians. The particular manner in which these three macrovariables converge produces environmental-level criminal opportunity that influences the likelihood of criminal acts occurring in that bounded locale in ways that we have specified. At any moment in time in such a bounded locale there are individuals who are engaged in routine activities and who can be characterized in terms of motivated offender exposure, target suitability, and capable guardianship. The ways in which these three microvariables converge produce individual-level criminal opportunity contexts that influence the probability of individuals experiencing criminal acts, which we have also detailed. Numerous interactions between ambient conditions and individual factors affect the chances of individuals experiencing criminal acts in a bounded locale. We have also delineated how environmental-level opportunity, individual-level opportunity, and cross-level interactions affect reactions to crime (i.e., cognitive risk perception, fear of crime, and precautionary measures).

Our discussion of temporal dimensions of multilevel contexts and criminal acts has suggested that criminal opportunity is constantly shifting, it is in a state of ever-becoming. But how? Why? Some reasons are completely beyond our focus on criminal opportunities and acts (e.g., birth rates could eventually influence the supply of motivated offenders, real wages could have an impact upon suitable targets, or technological changes in surveillance could influence guardianship). Other changes, however, are produced by the feedback loops associated with criminal opportunities and acts. For instance, imagine a neighborhood context that is characterized by a relatively high rate of crime, which produces cognitive and emotionally based fear among many of its residents and which then leads them to take protective measures (e.g., invest in home alarms, limit their public exposure). Such a collection of reactions to crime can literally change the unfolding ecological context. In this case, perhaps, these reactions lead to greater ecological and individual guardianship which diminishes criminal opportunities and thereby reduces criminal acts. Or perhaps the increased fear of crime leads to a flight of residents, thereby causing informal social controls in the community to deteriorate, which then produces an increase in criminal opportunities and subsequently, acts. Given the time-varying nature of the covariates and feedback loops, our theory would greatly benefit from empirical applications that pay specific attention to the issues of temporality that we have discussed.

NOTES

1. For example, see Adams (1997), Blumstein, Farrington, and Moitra (1985), Blumstein, Cohen, and Farrington (1988a, 1988b), Blumstein, Cohen, Roth, and Visher (1986), Caspi (1993), Caspi and Moffitt (1995), Catalano, Kosterman, Hawkins, Newcomb, and Abbott (1996), Cerkovich and Giordano (2001), Cline (1980), Conger and Simons (1997), D'Unger, Land, McCall, and Nagin (1998), Elliot (1994), Farrington (1979, 1986a, 1986b, 1988a, 1988b, 1989a, 1989b, 1991, 1992, 1993, 1995), Farrington and Hawkins (1991), Farrington and Loeber (1990), Farrington, Loeber, Elliot, Hawkins, Kandel, Klein, Rowe, and Tremblay (1990), Farrington and West (1981), Hagan (1997), Horney, Osgood, and Marshall (1995), Kagan (1980), Land (1992), Land and Nagin (1996), Laub, Nagin, and Sampson (1998), Laub and Sampson (1993, 1995, 2001), Lauritsen (1998), LeBlanc (1997), Loeber (1982, 1990), Loeber and Hay (1997), Loeber and LeBlanc (1990, 1998), Loeber and Stouthammer-Loeber (1998), Loeber, Stouthammer-Loeber, Van Kammen, and Farrington (1991), Loeber et al. (1993), Lynam (1996), Matsueda and Heimer (1997), McCord (1979, 1991, 1995), Moffitt (1990, 1993, 1997a, 1997b), Moffitt, Caspi, Dickson, Silva, and Stanton (1996), Nagin and Farrington (1992a, 1992b), Nagin and Land (1993), Nagin and Paternoster (1991), Nagin and Tremblay (1999), Nielson (1999), Paternoster and Brame (1997), Paternoster, Dean, Piquero, Mazerolle, and Brame (1997), Patterson, DeBaryshe, and Ramsey (1989), Piquero, Blumstein, Brame, Haapanen, Mulvey, and Nagin (2001), Piquero, Brame, Mazerolle, and Haapanen (2002), Piquero and Mazerolle (2001), Rand (1987), Sampson and Laub

(1990, 1993, 1995, 1997), Shover and Thompson (1992), Simons, Johnson, Conger, and Elder (1998), Simons, Wu, Conger, and Lorenz (1994), Smith and Brame (1994), Smith and Paternoster (1990), Thornberry (1997), Uggen (2000), Warr (1998), Weis and Hawkins (1981), West and Farrington (1973), and Wright, Caspi, Moffitt, and Silva (1999, 2001).

2. See Gottfredson and Hirschi (1986, 1987, 1988, 1990) and Hirschi and Gottfredson (1983, 1995).

3. For example, see Blumstein et al. (1986, 1988a, 1988b), Farrington (1986a, 1986b, 1988a, 1988b, 1989a, 1989b, 1995), Land (1992), Laub and Sampson (1993), and Petersilia (1980). Compare these with Hagan and Palloni (1988) and Tittle (1988).

4. See Farrington (1986a), Greenberg (1985), Steffensmeier, Allan, Harer, and Streifel (1989), Steffensmeier, Allan, and Streifel (1989), and Steffensmeier and Streifel (1991).

5. For example, see Laub, Nagin, and Sampson (1998), Laub and Sampson (1993), and Sampson and Laub (1990, 1993, 1996, 1997).

6. For example, see Blumstein et al. (1985, 1986, 1988a, 1988b), Farrington (1979, 1986a, 1986b, 1988a, 1988b, 1989a, 1989b, 1991, 1992, 1993, 1995), Farrington and Hawkins (1991), Farrington and Loeber (1990), Farrington et al. (1990a, 1990b), Farrington and West (1981), Loeber et al. (1991), Nagin and Farrington (1992a, 1992b), and West and Farrington (1973).

7. For example, see Moffitt (1990, 1993, 1997a, 1997b), Moffitt et al. (1996), and Wright et al. (1999).

8. For example, see D'Unger et al. (1998), Fergusson, Harwood, and Nagin (2000), Land (1992), Land and Nagin (1996), Nagin, Farrington, and Moffitt (1995), Nagin and Land (1993), Nagin and Paternoster (1991), Nagin and Tremblay (1999), and Piquero et al. (2001).

9. For a fuller account of the limitations of nondevelopmental theories and the strengths of developmental approaches see Thornberry (1997:1–5).

10. See Loeber and LeBlanc (1990, 1998).

11. See Loeber et al. (1991).

12. See Paternoster et al. (1989, 1995, 1997), Larzelere and Patterson (1990), and Patterson and Dishion (1985).

13. See Caspi and Moffitt (1995), Lynam (1996), Moffitt (1990, 1993, 1997a, 1997b), Moffitt et al. (1996), Nagin et al. (1995), and Wright et al. (1999, 2001).

14. See Catalano et al. (1996), Hawkins et al. (1988, 1991, 1992, 1995), O'Donnell et al. (1995), and Weis and Hawkins (1981).

15. See Elliot (1994) and Elliot et al. (1979, 1985, 1996).

16. See Blumstein et al. (1985, 1988a, 1988b), Farrington (1979, 1986a, 1986b, 1988a, 1988b, 1989a, 1989b, 1991, 1992, 1993, 1995), Farrington and West (1981), Nagin and Farrington (1992a, 1992b), Nagin et al. (1995), Piquero et al. (2001), and West and Farrington (1973).

17. See Jang (1999), Jang and Smith (1997), Thornberry (1987), and Thornberry, Lizotte, Krohn, Farnworth, and Jang (1991, 1994).

18. See Bartusch and Matsueda (1996), Heimer (1995, 1996), Heimer and Matsueda (1994), Jang and Thornberry (1998), Matsueda (1992), and Matsueda and Heimer (1997). Compare with Kaplan (1980) and Kinch (1963).

19. See Blumer (1969), Cooley (1902), Lofland (1969), Mead (1934), and Shibutani (1955).

20. See Stryker (1980).

21. See Laub et al. (1998), Laub and Sampson (1993, 1995, 2001), Sampson (1992, 1997), and Sampson and Laub (1990, 1993, 1995, 1996, 1997).

22. See Glueck and Glueck (1930, 1934, 1950, 1964, 1967, 1968).

23. See Laub and Sampson (1991).

24. See Laub and Sampson (1988).

25. Horney et al. (1995) demonstrate that it may be fruitful to think of "turning points" in smaller time units than what is implied by "marriage" and "enlistment or inscription into the military." To illustrate, during the course of a year an individual may experience attachments to prosocial institutions episodically. That is, an individual may be employed for several weeks, followed by unemployment for several weeks, followed by a period of employment, and so on. Or an individual may be engaged in a committed relationship for several weeks, followed by being unattached for several weeks, followed by a period of relational commitment, and so on. During the times when individuals are disconnected from prosocial institutions, we would expect their offending to increase; similarly, during those times when they are engaged in prosocial institutions, we would expect their offending to decrease. Consequently, questions that ask respondents to report on their attachments and offending during a year might be too grossly measured to reveal the real impacts conventional institutions and turning points have on criminal activity.

26. For example, see Shannon (1988), Tracy, Wolfgang, and Figlio (1990), and Wolfgang, Thornberry, and Figlio (1987).

27. For example, see Elder and O'Rand (1995), O'Rand (1990), and Riley (1987).

28. For example, see Dannefer and Sell (1988), Elder, Gimbel, and Ivie (1991), and Elder and O'Rand (1995).

29. See Alwin (1994).

30. See Elder and O'Rand (1995).

31. For example, see Brooks-Gunn and Furstenberg (1987), Hogan and Astone (1986), and O'Rand (1990).

32. For example, see Caspi, Elder, and Herbener (1990), and Farrington, Loeber, and Van Kammen (1990).

33. For example, see Dannefer (1984).

8

Possibilities and Limitations for Empirical Research

Thus far, we have presented a dynamic, multilevel model of criminal acts and reactions to crime. We have specified propositions and general hypotheses, using neighborhoods and schools as examples of environmental contexts that could be researched. In this chapter, we address some methodological issues relevant to our theory. Considering methodological issues is important because assessing the adequacy of a theory depends, in part, upon understanding *both* the possibilities *and* the limitations it presents for empirical investigation. Methodological concerns are particularly germane for our theory because the impetus for advancing a *multilevel* theory of criminal acts has been greatly influenced by relatively recent developments in hierarchical regression modeling procedures. We saw the need to advance a truly multilevel theory because criminology has been in a state where "the methods lie ahead of the theory." That is, researchers were investigating multilevel phenomena with nominal, post hoc, or, at best, incomplete theoretical justifications for such explorations. We believe that our multiple-level, dynamic criminal opportunity theory provides a sound theoretical foundation for empirical investigation.

To further this claim, we present how our theory could be tested via a variety of methods. First, we consider hierarchical regression modeling procedures, which are the most compatible with our perspective. In this discussion we explain the details of a simple, cross-sectional, multilevel analysis. From there we consider more intricate, longitudinal designs. It should be noted that multilevel, longitudinal designs represent the gold standard of methods. That is, such designs would provide the most thorough and suitable tests of our theory. However, the utility of our theory is not limited to only those empirical investigations that use multilevel, longitudinal designs. As suggested earlier, we consider how multilevel, cross-sectional designs could be used to empirically examine our theory. In fact, we argue that case study designs (both quantitative and qualitative in nature) could be useful in exploring our concepts and propositions. We detail several qualitative approaches (i.e., ethnography, qualitative individual interviews, focus or peer group interviews, and strategies using multiple qualitative methods) that could be useful in testing and building our theory. For each methodological approach we consider its relative strengths and weaknesses. It is our desire and belief that our multilevel criminal opportunity theory is not only logically sound but will also stimulate ample research that uses a wide variety of the methodological tools found in the social sciences.

TESTING A DYNAMIC, MULTICONTEXTUAL CRIMINAL OPPORTUNITY THEORY: MULTILEVEL MODELING

In previous chapters we have presented various aspects of a multilevel model of criminal acts and reactions to crime. This process culminated in the dynamic, multicontextual model of criminal opportunity presented in Chapter 7 (see Figure 7.3). Again, the paths in this model suggest that interindividual differences are a function of both individual and ambient characteristics. Furthermore, this model suggests that the effects of individual-level characteristics are not constant across different environmental settings. Instead, these effects vary according to the characteristics of the social settings in which such individual differences are nested. To complicate matters further, these individual- and ambient-level main and moderating effects are embedded in time. As such, the interindividual characteristics, environmental characteristics, and the interplay between the two are dynamic and can change as individuals progress through the life course. The results of this dynamic contextualism are, of course, individual "trajectories" regarding crime, victimization, risk perception, fear of crime, or other such outcomes discussed herein.

While conceptually complex, statistical procedures are available for integrating and modeling such multilevel effects when examining these outcomes and/or their corresponding individual trajectories. Hierarchical regression modeling procedures provide a statistically sound way of integrating micro- and macrolevel variables by incorporating submodels for each level involved in the structure of data.[1] As such, they provide an ideal option for the estimation of the multilevel model proposed here. Error structures in conventional regression analyses of crime are modeled such that the estimations of outcomes for individuals within the same social groups are assumed to be unrelated. Yet, it is simply unrealistic to ignore group membership and neglect the dependent error structure. In fact, doing so (i.e., using single-level regression models) is posited to cause inefficient estimates and actual Type I error rates that greatly exceed the nominal rate.[2] Given the implicit nested structure involved in much crime and/or criminal reactions data—with individuals grouped within schools and/or neighborhoods, and schools and neighborhoods clustered within districts, counties, or other social units—a hierarchical analytic approach is useful. This approach has, in fact, been employed in a series of previous studies on victimization and fear of crime conducted by the authors of this book. Here, we review some of the methodological and statistical procedures used in these previous studies. More specifically, we illustrate use of hierarchical models employing criminal victimization (e.g., number of victimizations) as the specific crime-related outcome of interest. We start by presenting examples using cross-sectional data (without repeated measures), and then discuss how longitudinal data can be utilized within these same types of models.

Two-Level Hierarchical Regression Models

Ignoring repeated measures for now, the general form for a level-one or individual-level component of a two-level hierarchical, cross-sectional regression model predicting victimization (Y) for individual i in neighborhood j, for instance could be written as follows:

$$Y_{ij} = \beta_{0j} + \beta_{1j}X_{1ij} + \beta_{2j}X_{2ij} + \cdots + \beta_{kj}X_{kij} + e_{ij} \tag{1}$$

where β_{0j} is the intercept and represents the mean level of victimization for neighborhood j, β_{kj} ($n = 1, \ldots, k$) represent regression coefficients for the effects of X_{kij} on Y_{ij}, X_{kij} represent individual-level predictors of victimization, and e_{ij} represents the individual-level error term. Given the opportunity theory discussed throughout this book, an example of a *level-one model of victimization* would be:

Level-One (Within-Neighborhood, Between-Individual) Model:

Frequency of Victimization$_{ij}$ = β_{0j} + β_{1j}Age$_{1ij}$ + β_{2j}Gender$_{2ij}$ + β_{3j}Race$_{3ij}$ + β_{4j}SES$_{4ij}$ + β_{5j}Nighttime Activities$_{5ij}$ + β_{6j}Carried Valuables$_{6ij}$ + β_{7j}Household Goods$_{7ij}$ + β_{8j}Safety Precautions$_{8ij}$ + β_{9j}Ties to Neighbors$_{9ij}$ + e_{ij} \hfill (2)

Thus, within-neighborhood, individual-level frequency of victimization is specified as a function of age, gender, race, SES, nighttime activities, carried valuables, household goods, safety precautions, and ties to neighbors. These individual-level effects and errors could be modeled for any number of neighborhoods. With these models and iterative generalized least squares methods, we can estimate the variability in intercepts and slopes across neighborhoods employing random-coefficient regression techniques. Neighborhoods may differ with respect to mean victimization, and neighborhoods may vary in the exhibited relationships between individual-level predictors and victimization. Further, such variability across neighborhoods may be "systematic" in that it is nonrandom, dependent upon neighborhood-level characteristics. If the intercept and the slopes are variable across neighborhoods and part of the variation is predicted by a certain neighborhood-level characteristic N, then these slopes and intercepts are *nonrandomly varying* and are modeled as follows:[3]

Level-Two (Between-Neighborhood) Model:

$$\beta_{kj} = \Theta_{k0} + \Theta_{k1}N_j + u_{kj} \tag{3}$$

In such cases of nonrandom or systematic variability, once N is controlled in the level-two model, much of the residual variance of β_{kj} approaches zero.[4] So, for example, it may be that individual victimization varies significantly across neighborhoods. Further, it may be that the "carried valuables" measure from the individual-level model (represented by β_{6j}) relates to victimization differently according to neighborhood-level variables. If these hypothetical scenarios of nonrandom variation were apparent, we would want to understand this variability as a function of neighborhood-level characteristics. Using only a few measures from concepts outlined in the conceptualization and operationalization of a multi-contextual criminal opportunity theory (see Chapter 4), we could hypothetically estimate this variation as follows:

Level-Two (Between-Neighborhood) Model:

$\beta_{0j} = \Theta_{00} + \Theta_{01}$Neighborhood Mobility$_j$ + Θ_{02}Neighborhood Racial Composition$_j$ + Θ_{03}Neighborhood SES$_j$ + Θ_{04}Neighborhood Organizational Participation$_j$ + u_{0j}

$\beta_{6j} = \Theta_{60} + \Theta_{61}$Neighborhood Mobility$_j$ + Θ_{62}Neighborhood Racial Composition$_j$ + Θ_{63}Neighborhood SES$_j$ + Θ_{64}Neighborhood Organizational Participation$_j$ + u_{6j} $\tag{4}$

There can be any number of individual-level characteristics in the within-neighborhood model, and any number of individual-level characteristics (including the intercept) may vary across level-two units. Likewise, multiple neighborhood-level variables may impact the variability in intercepts and slopes, and these neighborhood-level predictors may impact this variability differentially, depending on the β_{kj}. Thus, the between-neighborhood models may not be the same for all β_{kj}. Finally, the neighborhood is only one of several possible level-two units in this cross-sectional example. As indicated within this book, other environmental contexts could also be treated as level-two units in a cross-sectional, two-level hierarchical analysis of individual victimization.

Three-Level Hierarchical Regression Models

Cross-sectional, hierarchical data may involve more than two nested levels. For instance, individuals are not only nested within neighborhoods, but such neighborhoods are grouped, in turn, within larger communities, which can exert contextual effects as well. If we are interested in how victimization varies across neighborhoods and cities, for instance, the data structure demands a three-level model. The three-level design is similar to the previously outlined two-level model. A general level-one model estimates individual victimization for individual i in neighborhood j and city k as a function of individual-level variables. As in the two-level model, the intercepts and slopes of the individual-level model may be nonrandomly varying. In cases in which the coefficients are nonrandomly varying, again, the variability may be explained with neighborhood-level (level-two) models [e.g., see model (4)]. However, nonrandomly varying slopes and intercepts can also be explained by city-level properties, thus necessitating a level-three model. In such instances, the variability in the coefficients could be determined by an intercept (a mean risk) plus city-level characteristics. A generic level-three model depicting this is as follows:

Level-3 (Between-City) Model:

$$\Theta_{pqk} = \pi_{pq0} + \pi_{pq1}C_{1k} + \pi_{pq2}C_{2k} + \cdots + r_{pqk} \tag{5}$$

where C, in the specific case of this study, might be city-level population density or city-level police expenditures. The level-three model indicates that within-neighborhood means or slopes vary randomly according to an overall city mean and various city-level characteristics. So, taking the level-one, level-two, and level-three models together, the total variability in the outcome, Y_{ijk} (victimization, in this case), is partitioned into three components. Victimization can vary among individuals within neighborhoods, it can vary among neighborhoods within cities, and it can potentially vary among cities. Further, individual-level predictors of victimization may have effects which vary according to conditions characterizing level-two and level-three units.

Variation on Basic Two- and Three-Level Hierarchical Models: Cross-Classified Models

Some environmental contexts are perfectly nested within other environmental contexts, as in the above three-level hierarchical example, with individuals nested within neighborhoods nested within cities. However, there are other instances in which individuals are nested within multiple environments that are, in turn, not perfectly nested within one another. Individuals grouped within schools and neighborhoods provide a good example of this imperfect nesting. There are often instances in which not all students in a school live in the same neighborhood, and, conversely, not all students in the same neighborhood attend one school. The contextual units of interest in such cases are not perfectly nested in structure, but are cross-classified instead. Therefore, cross-classified models are most appropriate when multiple types of contexts—but imperfectly nested contexts—are being considered simultaneously.[5] The individual-level component of a general cross-classified model of victimization (Y) for individual (i) in (jk) school/neighborhood combination can be written as follows:

$$Y_{i(jk)} = \text{\ss}_{0(jk)} + \text{\ss}_{1(jk)}X_{1i(jk)} + \text{\ss}_{2(jk)}X_{2i(jk)} + \cdots + u_j + u_k + e_{i(jk)} \tag{6}$$

where $\text{\ss}_{0(jk)}$ is the overall mean level of victimization, $\text{\ss}_{1(jk)}$, $\text{\ss}_{2(jk)}$, ... represent individual-level effect coefficients, u_j represents random error due to school j, u_k represents random error due to neighborhood k, and $e_{i(jk)}$ is the individual-level error term.[6] As illustrated in the two- and three-level hierarchical models described above, any of the β can vary across neighborhood/schools, with characteristics of these units potentially accounting for such variation.

Variation on Basic Two- and Three-Level Hierarchical Models: Growth-Curve Models

Finally, a very important variation on the traditional two- and three-level hierarchical linear models is the growth curve model. As discussed in Chapter 7, our theory ultimately suggests that it is important that we study crime from a developmental or life-course perspective and discern intra- and interindividual heterogeneity in trajectories regarding crime-related outcomes. However, in examining such trajectories, we do not want to abandon the notion that such individual trajectories are embedded in various ecological contexts. Such contexts, along with individual-level characteristics, may be of great importance in understanding pathways and turning points or transitions in any "career." Thus, it is often helpful to employ two-, three-, and four-level growth curve models. Such models are structured similarly to n-level hierarchical models, except that the level-one model represents the individuals' developmental trajectories (or intraindividual growth), the level-two model represents the individual-level characteristics that may affect growth trajectories, and level-three, level-four, . . . , level-n models represent variation in growth parameters across the various (n) ecological contexts in which the individuals are nested.[7] As an example, suppose we are interested in the individual growth model of victimization for individual i in neighborhood j at time t. A level-one model, capturing the change over time in individual victimization, could be expressed as:

Level-1 (Within-Individual) Model:

$$Y_{tij} = \pi_{0ij} + \pi_{1ij}\text{age (or time period)}_{tij} + e_{ti} \tag{7}$$

where Y_{tij} represents the victimization status (e.g., frequency, amount) of individual i in neighborhood j at time t; π_{1ij} represents the growth rate for person i over the longitudinal study period and the intercept π_{0ij} is the victimization status of individual i at age(or time period)$_{tij} = 0$. It should be noted that, given a lengthy time series, the effect of age or time period will probably not be first-order in nature. In other words, the growth will probably not be linear. However, without empirical investigation, it is impossible to specify precisely the most appropriate order.

A level-two model is then specified in order to address the fact that both the intercept and the growth-rate parameter can vary depending upon individual-level characteristics. Using individual-level constructs from the theory presented here, a level-two model for this growth curve example could be written as follows:

Level-Two (Between-Individual) Model:

$$\pi_{0ij} = \beta_{00j} + \beta_{01j}\text{Gender}_{ij} + \beta_{02j}\text{Race}_{ij} + \beta_{03j}\text{SES}_{ij} + \beta_{04j}\text{Nighttime Activities}_{ij} + \beta_{05j}\text{Carried Valuables}_{ij} + \beta_{06j}\text{Household Goods}_{ij} + \beta_{07j}\text{Safety Precautions} + \beta_{08j}\text{Ties to Neighbors}_{ij} + r_{0ij}$$

$$\pi_{1ij} = \beta_{10j} + \beta_{11j}\text{Gender}_{ij} + \beta_{12j}\text{Race}_{ij} + \beta_{13j}\text{SES}_{ij} + \beta_{14j}\text{Nighttime Activities}_{ij} + \beta_{15j}\text{Carried Valuables}_{ij} + \beta_{16j}\text{Household Goods}_{ij} + \beta_{17j}\text{Safety Precautions}_{ij} + \beta_{18j}\text{Ties to Neighbors}_{ij} + r_{1ij} \tag{8}$$

where β_{00j} represents the mean initial victimization status in neighborhood j, β_{10j} represents the mean growth rate in victimization in neighborhood j, $\beta_{01j}, \ldots, \beta_{08j}$ represent the effects of sex, race, etc. on the initial victimization status in neighborhood j, and $\beta_{11j}, \ldots, \beta_{18j}$ represent the effects of sex, race, etc. on the growth rate for victimization in neighborhood j. Now, suppose that mean initial victimization status, mean growth rate, and the effect of carried valuables on the growth rate vary significantly across neighborhoods and that a neighborhood characteristic such as neighborhood SES can account for this variation. Using this scenario, we could write a level-three model as follows:

Level-three (Between-Neighborhood) Model:

$$\beta_{00j} = \gamma_{000} + \gamma_{001}(\text{Neighborhood SES})_j + u_{00j}$$
$$\beta_{10j} = \gamma_{100} + \gamma_{101}(\text{Neighborhood SES})_j + u_{10j} \qquad (9)$$
$$\beta_{15j} = \gamma_{150} + \gamma_{151}(\text{Neighborhood SES})_j + u_{15j}$$

with all other β_{qkj} being specified as fixed (across level-three units). City-level characteristics could also be incorporated into a similar level-four model. In essence, these growth curve models employing hierarchical regression techniques represent an integration of the best features of a straightforward two- or three-level contextual model with repeated-observations models. In short, change can be detected, but most importantly, it can be understood within appropriate individual and environmental contexts. Such a growth curve approach in which we can not only estimate the change but also individual- and contextual-level influences on variation in such change across schools, communities and other environmental contexts epitomizes "dynamic contextualism" and, if employed in conjunction with a dynamic, multicontextual opportunity perspective, can help chart a new frontier for understanding trajectories of crime, victimization, risk perception, fear of crime, and crime-avoidance behavior.

Research Design Issues

While the above discussion on hierarchical regression modeling (including growth curve modeling) illustrates an appropriate quantitative analytic technique for estimating the theoretical model proposed in this book, there are obviously multiple methodological concerns that must be addressed prior to quantitative data analysis—issues that must be considered if one is to even get to the stage of such model estimation. After all, one must have appropriate data in order to analyze it using hierarchical regression techniques. The obtaining of such appropriate data entails careful thought regarding research design issues such as sampling, measurement, and data collection procedures.

Sampling. Regarding sampling, the dynamic multicontextual criminal opportunity theory and the hierarchical regression analytic technique for estimating such a theory are both premised on the notion of multiple units of analysis. Not only are individual units important, but so are contextual units. The whole notion of multiple units of analysis implies multistage sampling. Sampling for research purposes must involve both the sampling of contextual units and the sampling of individuals within those contextual units. This obviously makes sampling a more complex endeavor, particularly if quantitative analysis of data from such sampling is the ultimate goal. In order to conduct adequate tests of the theory using analytic techniques such as hierarchical regression modeling, a sufficiently large number of contexts need to be sampled, with a sufficiently large number of individuals within contexts sampled in turn. As such, sampling for multilevel research designs has the potential to be both expensive and expansive. Sampling for such projects may be more expensive than, say, a typical single-level research design involving individuals, since a larger total number of individuals is typically required for multilevel projects. Because the contexts in which individuals are embedded are also important in multilevel designs and must therefore also be sampled, with enough individuals within each context for model estimation purposes, the number of total individuals sampled can become large rather quickly.

An example of this phenomenon is perhaps in order. Consider, first, a single-level design in which a researcher randomly samples individuals. A sample of one thousand would clearly seem adequate given probability selection techniques, an acceptable and nonbiased response rate, and the like. But, suppose the researcher was also interested in the neighborhood contexts in which these individuals were embedded. If the one thousand sampled individuals were nested within one thousand unique neighborhood contexts, the researcher could not adequately partition between-individual and between-neighborhood effects. The researcher would need more individuals within each context in order to do so. If the researcher obtained, on average, twenty respondents from each neighborhood context for such purposes, the sample size is suddenly increased to twenty thousand. The number of contexts examined could be and probably would be decreased given the improbability of being able to really handle (expensewise) a sample size of twenty thousand individuals, but decreasing the number of neighborhoods comes with costs in terms of being able to discern cross-neighborhood variation within statistical models.

The placement of the sampled neighborhood contextual units in space is also a consideration with potentially far-reaching implications. As a

solution to the inability to realistically sample twenty thousand individuals nested within one thousand neighborhoods, a researcher might settle
on sampling about twenty to thirty individuals from one hundred to three
hundred neighborhoods, for a total individual-level sample size in the
two-thousand to nine-thousand range. Sampling designs of similar scope
and magnitude have been employed in benchmark criminological studies,
including the Seattle study of criminality and victimization, the project on
Human Development in Chicago Neighborhoods, the Rochester Youth
Developmental Study, the Denver Youth Survey, the Pittsburgh Youth
Study, the Cambridge study, and the 1972–1973 Dunedin Health and
Development Cohort Study in New Zealand.[8] As can be seen from the
titles of these data collection efforts, the neighborhoods sampled all come
from one city. For data collection ease, nested designs are often done in
such a fashion. It is not easy for researchers to travel to multiple locations
for data collection purposes, and such an endeavor would also greatly
increase costs. However, restricting sampled neighborhoods to one city
probably restricts neighborhood-level variation. While there may be
tremendous variation across neighborhoods within Seattle, Chicago, or
Rochester (for example), there is undoubtedly more cross-neighborhood
variation introduced when neighborhoods from Seattle, Chicago, and
Rochester are considered simultaneously in one research design. We
restrict our ability to discern neighborhood-level variation and neighborhood-level contextual effects when we restrict the heterogeneity of the
neighborhood-level sampling frame.

Of course, widening the sampling frame to include neighborhoods in
multiple cities opens up additional issues beyond the "expense and
expanse" of the sample. Such a strategy adds a third unit of analysis. The
individuals sampled would be nested nonrandomly within neighborhoods, within cities. Ignoring the nonrandom clustering within cities
when conducting quantitative analysis of such data may lead to inefficient
estimates of individual or neighborhood effects. As such, the third unit of
analysis should be explicitly incorporated into statistical modeling of such
data. Doing this, of course, necessitates a sufficient number of level-three
(city-level, following this example) units. Estimating three-level hierarchical regressions models using data on individuals sampled from neighborhoods within the cities of Seattle, Chicago, and Rochester would not be
possible given the small number of level-three units. Yet, ignoring the city
level when modeling the nested nature of the data is problematic as well.
So, sampling individuals within neighborhoods across a sufficient number
of cities would be the best approach in accurately discerning cross-context
variation. The expensiveness and expansiveness of such a sample is easy
to imagine; these factors are undoubtedly integral in determining the
absence of such datasets in the criminological field. In order to cut costs

and ease the logistics involved in collecting data, we often "settle" for data from multiple neighborhoods within one city. While this strategy allows us to at least begin to disentangle individual from contextual effects, we should also be aware that the unearthing of contextual effects, in particular, is hindered by such sampling strategies, and therefore employ caution when reporting results from studies using these sorts of samples. In short, comprehensive tests of multilevel effects that are based on samples that optimize the likelihood of discerning cross-environment heterogeneity are indeed rare if not altogether absent from the extant literature.

Data Collection and Measurement. Sampling is not the only aspect of research design that is necessarily complex in testing the dynamic multicontextual criminal opportunity theory proposed here. The "dynamic" component of the theory suggests that observations and measures should be gathered at multiple time points. Longitudinal data collection is another expensive venture—expensive in terms of both money and time. Additional methodological concerns also present themselves when a time series of data is being collected. For instance, attrition of sampled individuals is likely as the period of the study extends beyond one time point. Participants are likely to drop out of the sample for a variety of reasons, including mobility (moving to another location), disinterest, and death, to name but a few examples. If individuals drop out in some sort of systematic fashion, then the representativeness of the sample is likely to diminish as the study progresses over time. Complicating the problem of attrition is the fact that multiple sampling units are involved in a test of this theory. So, attrition can occur at multiple levels. Not only may sampled individuals drop out over time, but so may environmental contexts. While it is difficult to conceive of a geographic unit like a neighborhood "disappearing," processes of construction, gentrification, etc., could, in fact, lead to such a possibility. Other possible contextual units also illustrate this issue. If schools, for instance, were a contextual unit, it would be necessary to get the cooperation of school administrators for sampling within such schools (such context-level "permission" does not really exist in most studies using neighborhoods). Over time, schools may simply refuse to participate, and if cooperation of the school is necessary in order to collect data on sampled students therein, then data on possibly large numbers of individuals would be systematically missing from portions of the time series.

The problem of attrition is perhaps most felt when a research design entails observations and measurements being gathered primarily and directly from individuals, through survey administration, for instance. In such cases, without the presence and participation of the individual, data would not exist. Use of secondary or archival data, on the other hand, is not as susceptible to problems of attrition. However, the best measures of individual-level exposure, target suitability, and guardianship are likely to be obtained through primary data collection rather than use of existing data (e.g., data from school records). We know of no sources of existing data available for all individuals that directly measure target suitability, guardianship, accessibility, etc. Individual-level data that might be available to researchers without primary data collection would likely be proxy measures, including sociodemographic information, information on school performance (e.g., GPA or standardized test scores). As discussed in earlier chapters, these proxy measures are often limited since they can seemingly represent multiple concepts within the theory. A test of the theory that relied solely upon such measures would probably yield unconvincing and uninformative results. Primary data collection at the individual level therefore seems essential to comprehensive tests of a dynamic, multicontextual criminal opportunity theory.

Comprehensive measurement of ambient opportunity will also probably entail primary data collection. Proxy measures of ambient opportunity may be available using existing data sources, depending upon the environmental unit of interest. For instance, there is a long history in the social disorganization theoretical tradition of measuring "neighborhood disorganization" (a facet of ambient opportunity, in our view, as discussed in Chapter 4) with census-based indicators, including community poverty rates, population racial heterogeneity, and population stability/mobility. However, similar to the situation involving individual-level sociodemographic characteristics, these aggregate-level sociodemographic characteristics are often ambiguous operationalizations of opportunity concepts. As discussed in previous chapters, aggregate-level poverty (or SES) or racial composition could seemingly represent aggregate-level exposure, aggregate-level target attractiveness, and aggregate-level guardianship. Interpreting results within the conceptual framework is therefore difficult when such proxy measures are used. More direct measures, with less conceptual overlap, are preferred in rigorous tests. Obtaining such measures will probably entail some sort of primary data collection. For instance, measures of routine activities, household goods, safety precautions, and social ties can be asked in individual-level surveys, with individual responses then aggregated within the environmental unit of interest in order to create alternative measures of context. This alternative measurement strategy has the added benefit of being more flexible in terms of aggregate unit of analysis. Just about any contextual unit is susceptible to such aggregated measures, assuming enough individuals within contextual units have been sampled. Existing data, on the other hand, is often only available at units of analysis recognized by official collection agencies, including units such as census blocks, census tracts, counties, or states. Regarding multilevel studies of students within classrooms, "official data" are often only available at the school or school district level. So, a researcher interested in classroom-level contextual measures might be forced to rely upon primary data collection strategies.

One of the more innovative data collection strategies has been the use of systematic social observation in the Human Development in Chicago Neighborhoods study.[9] In this study, a multilevel survey design (similar to the ones suggested above) was used in conjunction with systematic, qualitative direct observations, which were then quantified. The qualitative component consisted of observers driving "a sport utility vehicle at a rate of five miles per hour down every street" within a sample of neighborhood clusters, videotaping as well as logging their observations of the social activities and physical environments (Raudenbush and Sampson 1999:13). Eventually, over one hundred quantitative variables were constructed from the coding of these observations, providing data on "physical conditions, housing characteristics, business, and social interactions" (ibid.:14). Similar efforts at systematic direct observation have been made by Taylor and his colleagues, particularly in the Baltimore neighborhood studies. Essentially, they too walked the streets of neighborhoods, coding, for instance, land use within the area (e.g., number and type of businesses, number of schools, churches) and signs of social and physical disorder.[10]

DYNAMIC, MULTICONTEXTUAL CRIMINAL OPPORTUNITY THEORY: OTHER METHODS

Without a doubt, the most appropriate way to test our dynamic, multicontextual, criminal opportunity theory is to use hierarchical regression modeling techniques on data derived from longitudinal research designs that frequently gather information on a sufficient number of individuals embedded in an ample number of well-defined spatial environments. The more frequently data are collected the better, all else being equal. Undoubtedly, this is the research design gold standard for testing our theory. Even though a multilevel, longitudinal design presents some serious challenges in terms of sampling, data collection, and resource costs, it truly could provide the fairest and most comprehensive test of our theory. However, the utility of our perspective would be extremely limited if this were the *only* way our theory could be empirically investigated.

Fortunately, we believe that other research designs could be used to test and explore crucial aspects of our theory. For instance, in our discussion of multilevel designs above, we began with a cross-sectional design. We did this primarily to illustrate the fundamentals of multilevel analysis before discussing the details of more complex longitudinal, multilevel designs. Here we would like to make explicit what our earlier discussion implied:

a simple (i.e., one-time), multilevel, cross-sectional design could provide data to test key elements of our theory. Granted, a weakness of cross-sectional designs is that they typically do not incorporate temporal dimensions into their analysis. Therefore, cross-sectional designs would not be able to investigate completely those elements of our theory that deal with criminal opportunity contexts across time. However, it is possible to incorporate some temporal components into cross-sectional analyses. For instance, cross-sectional designs can approximate longitudinal designs if they are repeated (e.g., a repeated cross-sectional design) with different samples at each time point. Even simple, one-time cross-sectional designs could illuminate important temporal dimensions of our theory by asking either time-sensitive questions (e.g., Do you walk in your neighborhood at night?) or retrospective questions (e.g., When your house was burglarized did you have a home alarm system?). While these cross-sectional approaches are not as desirable as longitudinal data that could provide a more precise picture of the temporal dimensions of criminal opportunity, they represent reasonable and cost-effective alternatives.

Additionally, cross-sectional designs could be single-level and still explore crucial components our theory. Our theory offers not only multilevel propositions and hypotheses, but we have also specified purely individual-level and purely aggregate-level propositions and hypotheses. Admittedly, a *single-level* exploration of a theory purported to be *multilevel* seems conspicuously inadequate. Yet, single-level designs could explore some of the concepts and propositions that we have advanced. Such efforts would not offer definitive tests of our perspective. Nonetheless, data derived from cross-sectional designs solely focusing on the individual or environment level could provide evidence that could support or fail to support our perspective.

Thus far, we have discussed quantitative approaches to examining our multilevel theory of crime. We also believe that qualitative studies could be informed by our theory. The Chicago and Baltimore studies both suggest how qualitative and quantitative data can be integrated into an analysis.[11] Both of these studies use qualitative data collection techniques (i.e., direct observations) to construct quantitative measures. We contend that analysis of qualitative data as such (i.e., without quantifying them) could be useful in exploring the adequacy and utility of our theory. These efforts alone would not provide definitive tests of our perspective. Regardless, data derived from qualitative studies could also provide evidence that could support or fail to support our perspective. To illustrate some of the possibilities these studies hold for investigation of our theory we consider ethnography and qualitative interviews.

Actually, ethnography uses a variety of qualitative data collection techniques, and is therefore not easily defined. Ethnography can trace its origins to the emergence and development of the discipline of anthropology as well as the era of exploration and colonization. To study a "tribal" or so-called "primitive" society, cultural anthropologists felt it was necessary to immerse themselves in the social and natural environments of "a peo-ple"—*ethnos* refers to "a nation" or "a people." This underlying orienta-tion is compatible with our theoretical framework in that it emphases the importance of ecological context. The study of "a people" is more than just an examination of a collection of individuals. Rather, "a people" shares a culture and exists in more-or-less relatively well-defined temporal and spatial contexts. The general underlying orientation to ethnography is that to understand "a people," researchers must examine their words and deeds in situ, that is, in their social and natural environments. Originally, it was considered necessary to conduct an ethnographic study for at least a year. This was so because it was believed that a year would give researchers a chance to observe the entire spectrum of seasonal rhythms and rituals of "a people," a particularly germane issue given that anthro-pologists at the time focused on nonmodern, agrarian societies. Contem-porary ethnographers have not emphasized the need to immerse themselves completely in a context and observe for at least a year—a response to a publish-or-perish reality. Regardless, ethnography, at its core, requires systematic, in-depth observation of "a people" in its spatial and temporal contexts.

The comparative advantage of ethnography as a research method is that it allows for a relatively "thick description" of a people.[12] Data in ethnographic studies can be and usually are derived from a variety of sources, including the researcher's field notes—which typically consist of observational notes, records of oral communications, and analytical notes—written documents, audiotapes, and videotapes.[13] The fieldwork phase of an ethnography is complete at the point of theoretical and/or empirical saturation—that is, when the researcher is relatively certain that the collection of additional data will not yield additional theoretical insight or empirical clarification.[14] Ethnographies, as well as other quali-tative methods, often suffer from an embarrassment of riches in terms of data.

While ethnographic data lend themselves to "thick description," it is not accurate to characterize ethnography as a method that produces only descriptive analyses. Ethnography can also be used in theory testing and building.[15] While ethnographers should enter the field with an open mind, they are not "mindless empiricists," recording information without any conceptual guidance. Rather, ethnographers use "sensitizing concepts" to guide their data collection and analysis.[16] Precisely because it is not based on a mindless empiricism, ethnographic data can confirm or call into ques-tion theoretical concepts and propositions. They can help to create and modify both concepts and measures. As but one component in a scientific effort, ethnography can serve important functions for theory testing and building.

The theory we have presented provides a set of interrelated concepts and propositions upon which ethnographic studies could be conducted. To illustrate, our multilevel orientation suggests that ethnographers would be sensitized to temporal and spatial aspects of "a people" in a bounded locale.

Being sensitized to examine spatial contexts would entail an examination and description of the physical environment of a bounded locale. Numerous studies compatible with our theory have used ethnographic or direct observational techniques to examine the relationship between physical environment—including land use, street layout, building design, and physical deterioration—and criminal acts. As we noted earlier, physical properties may, along with social characteristics, affect the emergence of strong informal social control.[17] In fact, in his seminal work, Newman states that elements of "defensible space"—consisting of natural surveillance, territoriality, and image/milieu—create "the physical expression of a social fabric that defends itself" (1973:3). Newman adds that "all the different elements which combine to make a defensible space have a common goal—an environment in which latent territoriality and sense of community in the inhabitants can be translated into responsibility for ensuring a safe, productive, and well-maintained living space" (ibid.). Later formulations of these ideas still implicitly rely upon the notion that the physical environment affects crime indirectly by affecting how residents/occupants self-police and prevent crime within the local area,[18] though the name attached to the theory has been varied, including most notably Newman-coined "defensible space" as well as "crime prevention through environmental design" (CPTED). The point to be made here is that our multilevel theory has already benefited and could continue to benefit from ethnographic or direct observations.

Providing data on the physical environments of bounded locales is not the only aspect of our theory that ethnographic investigations could examine. In terms of temporal contexts, ethnographers could observe and record the routine activities of individuals, paying particular attention to rhythm, tempo, and timing. These observations could provide data at both the individual and environmental level of analysis. Researchers could also observe and record the characteristics of the physical environment as well as the presence or absence of motivated offenders, suitable targets, and capable guardians in time and space. In such a design, researchers would need to record the circumstances present when criminal acts are realized and when they are not. When criminal acts occur, ethnography's ability to capture multiple perspectives could allow for examinations of both offending and victimization. In addition, because of its on-the-ground presence, ethnography is particularly well-suited to capture the precise unfolding of the various reactions to crime after a criminal act is discovered by individuals in a bounded locale. While ethnographic efforts could not offer definitive tests of our perspective, they can nevertheless provide evidence that could support or fail to support our perspective.

In addition to ethnographic studies, the testing and building of our theory could be advanced by qualitative interviewing: by asking questions that are relatively open-ended, inviting respondents to elaborate in as much detail as possible. Responses from such questions are subjected to the same sort of coding and content analysis that is used with ethnographic fieldnotes, documents, or other texts.[19] Data derived from qualitative interviews could be used in conjunction with other data sources (both qualitative and quantitative) in either a single-level or multilevel fashion. Alternatively, qualitative interviews could be used alone. Using the concepts of our multilevel opportunity theory of crime, qualitative interviews could explore perceptions of physical environments, routine activities (including examinations of their rhythms, tempos, and timings), exposure and proximity to motivated offenders, suitable targets, and capable guardians, offending, victimization, as well as cognitive, emotional, and behavioral reactions to crime. As with other analyses derived from other types of data collection strategies, qualitative interviews would not provide definitive tests of our theory. However, they too can provide evidence that could support or fail to support our perspective.

A rather effective qualitative interviewing strategy that could prove useful involves focus groups.[20] One use of focus groups is to allow the recording of subjects as they discuss topics or questions presented to them by facilitators. The composition of focus groups can be manipulated to make comparisons between and within groups (e.g., structuring groups by criteria based on age, sex, race, SES, religion, political orientations, and so on). Compared to qualitative interviews conducted with one individual at a time, focus group permit researchers to more efficiently explore topics and questions with a greater number of individuals.

An interesting variant of this basic focus group strategy, and one that has important implications for exploring our theoretical concepts and propositions further, has been developed by Gamson (1992). Gamson specifically uses "peer" groups, consisting of individuals who either know one another or have some connection outside the research setting (e.g., those who work for the same employer, live in the same neighborhood, or attend the same school).

Using peer group interviews, Sasson (1995) explores Bostonians' perceptions of crime as evidenced by their reactions to and discussions about a sample of newspaper commentaries on crime and criminal justice.

Sasson suggests that peer group interviews have two advantages when compared to focus group interviews:

> First, peer group participants typically interact with greater intensity and less reserve than their focus group counterparts. This, in turn, permits the facilitator to minimize his or her involvement in the discussion and results in richer transcripts. Second, because the peer groups have a social existence independent of the sociologist's contrivance, their discourse can be regarded with greater confidence as reflective of the particular subcultures from which they are drawn. (ibid.:20)

Data derived from peer groups (or focus groups more generally) would be coded and subjected to content analysis in order to explore themes and relationships of interest to the researcher.

Similar to individual qualitative interviews, focus or peer group interviews could be informed by our theory, providing the topics and questions for discussion. Peer group interviews would be particularly compatible with our theory in that subjects could be systematically selected from some identified bounded locale (e.g., neighborhoods or schools). Then, concepts from our multilevel opportunity theory of crime could be used to generate discussion about offending, victimization, and reactions to crime as well as the conditions of physical environments, routine activities (including issues relevant to rhythm, tempo, and timing), and exposure to motivated offenders, suitable targets, and capable guardians. Once again it should be noted that even though focus or peer group interviews could not provide absolute tests of our theory, they would yield data that might support or fail to support our perspective.

Finally, an effective strategy to make a study more robust methodologically is to employ multiple methods. The work conducted by researchers at the University of Michigan exemplifies the use of multiple methods.[21] Additionally, although this work is not informed by criminal opportunity theory, it illustrates how qualitative methods could explore criminal acts and reactions to crime in spatial and temporal contexts (in this case, individuals in schools). Drawing upon the CPTED literature and using maps, semistructured interviews, and focus groups, scholars involved in this project have been able to identify structural and cultural reasons why students identify certain school subenvironments or "subcontexts" as particularly dangerous and/or feared. The maps used by Astor and colleagues have revealed that certain "hot spots" in schools—such as hallways, bathrooms, cafeterias, and parking lots—are the sights of more incidents and greater fear among students. Interviews with students and teachers revealed that incidents occurred in these areas when adults were typically not present. The interviews also revealed that these areas tended to be "unowned" by either students or school staff. Further, school organization appeared to affect territorial functioning. Astor, Meyer, and Pitner (2001) found that sixth-graders in middle schools were more likely than sixth graders in elementary schools to perceive particular school subcontexts as risky. This suggests that middle schools may have more undefined areas not only because they are larger, but because teachers in these schools display "isolated" or specific territoriality—a territoriality that does not extend far beyond the boundaries of their specific classroom or subject area. As such, many physical spaces in the school are poorly monitored, unkempt, and potentially dangerous. This research provides some support for our theory and could provide the basis for other explorations (both quantitative and qualitative).

To conclude, qualitative methods could make useful contributions to the testing and building of a multilevel, dynamic criminal opportunity theory. The strengths of qualitative research include the ability to generate "thick descriptions" and provide an on-the-ground perspective of events. However, it must be noted that qualitative research has some key weakness as well. For instance, even though researchers may immerse themselves in a context, their observations might be influenced by the time of day or year. For instance, the physical environment of a school might appear completely orderly if it were observed the first day of a new school year; the same school might appear severely disordered if it were observed on the last day of a school year. Consequently, even though qualitative researchers may immerse themselves in a context, they must be acutely aware that their observations are time sensitive.

Another limitation is that qualitative research is typically resource costly in terms of labor time and money. Simply, the use of qualitative methods usually means data collection takes longer and is limited in the number of individuals and contexts it can study. In addition, qualitative research may involve hours upon hours of direct observations, in-depth interviews, audio tape transcriptions, and audiotape recordings as well as reams of documents. After investing in the collection and recording of all this information, the raw data then must be coded into some form that is amenable to analysis. Of course, all of this adds to resource costs.

Finally, sound qualitative designs are commonly understood to be strong on validity but weak in terms of reliability and generalizability. One reason qualitative methods is thought to be weak in terms of reliability is that such studies are usually "lone ranger" operations—i.e., one person designs the study, collects the data, records the data, codes the data, and performs the analysis. In this process, there is no systematic way to determine if the study's measures are reliable. This problem can be partly addressed by using two or more coders. While this strengthens reliability, it exacerbates the problem of resource costs. Because most qualitative methods do not lend themselves to random sampling procedures, they do not produce results that are generalizable. Even if a study is not generalizable, it can still provide evidence that confirms or challenges a theory, as long as it was conducted in a rigorous and systematic manner. Further, the analysis of findings from a collection of qualitative studies (i.e., meta-analysis) can be another rich source for theoretical confirmations and challenges. Therefore, qualitative studies have the potential to be important sources for theoretical refinement, revision, and testing.

NOTES

1. For a discussion of *linear* hierarchical modeling see Bryk and Raudenbush (1992). For a treatment of *logistic* hierarchical modeling see Wong and Mason (1985).

2. See Hox and Kreft (1994).

3. See Bryk and Raudenbush (1992).

4. See Bryk and Raudenbush (1992).

5. See Rasbash and Woodhouse (1995).

6. See Rasbash and Goldstein (1994).

7. See Bryk and Raudenbush (1992), Goldstein, Healy, and Rasbash (1994), and Laird and Ware (1982).

8. Not all of these studies are suited for both growth curve *and* individuals-in-environments analyses. This is not an exhaustive enumeration of datasets that provide the potential for growth curve and/or individuals-in-environments analyses. These studies are mentioned here merely to provide interested readers with examples of the scope and magnitude of the samples necessary for contextual studies. For a description of the Seattle study of criminality and victimization, see Miethe (1992). For the project on Human Development in Chicago Neighborhoods, see Earls and Visher (1997). For the Rochester Youth Developmental Study, see Browning, Thornberry, and Porter (1999). For the Denver Youth Survey, see Huizinga, Esbensen, and Elliott (1988a, 1988b). For the Pittsburgh Youth Study, see Browning and Loeber (1999). For the Cambridge study, see Farrington and West (1981). For the 1972–1973 Dunedin Health and Development Cohort Study in New Zealand, see Moffitt and Silva (1988).

9. For a discussion of this project, see Raudenbush and Sampson (1999) and Sampson and Raudenbush (1999). For a discussion of systematic social observation, see Reiss (1971).

10. For example, see Taylor (1987, 1988), Taylor and Brower (1985), Taylor and Covington (1988), Taylor et al. (1981, 1984, 1995), and Taylor and Hale (1986).

11. See also Sampson and Laub (1998).

12. See Geertz (1973:3–32).

13. In this discussion we equate ethnography with purely qualitative analysis. This is not entirely accurate. Ethnographic research can and has produced both qualitative and quantitative analyses. Our glossing over of this detail has been done for the sake of presentation clarity.

14. See Corbin and Strauss (1998) and Glaser and Strauss (1967).

15. See Corbin and Strauss (1998) and Glaser and Strauss (1967).

16. See Blumer (1969).

17. For example, see Heinzelmann (1981) and Murray (1995) for reviews of this perspective.

18. For example, see Angel (1968), Appleyard (1981), Baum et al. (1978), Brantingham and Brantingham (1981), Brown and Altman (1981), Cisneros (1995), Clarke (1997), Crowe (2000), Donnelly and Kimble (1997), Duffala (1976), Fowler and Mangione (1986), Fowler, McCalla, and Mangione (1979), Greenberg et al. (1982), Jacobs (1961, 1968), Kurtz, Koons, and Taylor (1998), La Vigne (1997), Ley and Cybriwsky (1974), Mawby (1977), Merry (1981), Newman (1995, 1996), Newman and Franck (1982), Roncek and Faggiani (1985), Roncek and LoBosco (1983), Roncek and Maier (1991), Roncek and Pravatiner (1989), Sherman, Gartin, and Buerger (1989), Skogan (1990), Smith (1996), Speer, Gorman, Labouvie, and Ontkush (1998), Taylor (1987, 1988, 2001), Taylor and Brower (1985), Taylor and Covington (1988), Taylor and Gottfredson (1986), Taylor et al. (1981, 1984, 1995), Taylor and Harrell (1996), Taylor, Shumaker, and Gottfredson (1985), Tucker and Starnes (1993), Westinghouse Electric (1977a, 1977b), White (1990), Wilcox Rountree et al. (2000), Wilson and Kelling (1982), and Wood (1961). For a similar line of research focusing on schools, see Astor and Meyer (1999, 2001), Astor, Meyer, and Behre (1999), Astor, Meyer, and Pitner (2001), Schneider, Marschall, Roch, and Teske (1999), Toby (1994), and Wallis and Ford 1980.

19. For an explication of both coding and content an analysis as it is used in quantitative studies, see Neuendorf (2002).

20. For a treatment of qualitative interviewing using focus groups, see Morgan (1988).

21. For example, see Astor and Meyer (1999, 2001), Astor et al. (1999), and Astor et al. (2001).

9

Implications for Policy and Practice

The previous eight chapters have presented assumptions, propositions, and methods for testing a dynamic multicontextual criminal opportunity theory. In this chapter, we turn to the question of what this theory means for policy and practice. Although there are some fundamental differences in terms of orientations toward theoretical explanation (i.e., crime specific vs. general), our multilevel criminal opportunity theory and "situational crime prevention" are quite similar in regard to policy and practice.[1] Felson and Clarke succinctly summarize this view:

> Situational prevention is a radically different approach to crime control. It is focused on the immediate environments in which crime occurs, rather than upon those committing criminal acts. It seeks to forestall the occurrence of crime, rather than to detect and sanction offenders. It seeks, not to eliminate criminal or delinquent tendencies, but merely to reduce opportunities for crime. Central to this enterprise is not the criminal justice system, but a host of public and private organizations and agencies—schools, hospitals, transport systems, shops and malls, manufacturing businesses, and phone companies, banks and insurance companies, local parks and entertainment facilities, pubs and parking lots—whose services, products, and modes of operation spawn opportunities for a vast range of different crimes. Proceeding from an analysis of the circumstances giving rise to specific kinds of crime, situational prevention introduces discrete managerial and environmental change to make criminal action more difficult and risky, less rewarding and less excusable. (1997:197)

If criminal opportunity—temporally and spatially situated—lies at the heart of criminal acts, what can we do about it? We begin the process of exploring this question by examining the compatibility of various philosophies of crime control.

SOCIAL CONTROL OF CRIME

Traditionally, societywide crime control has been based upon several competing or differing philosophies, including retribution, incapacitation, deterrence, and rehabilitation. While the purpose of this book is not to provide an exhaustive discussion of these philosophies, a brief overview of each is in order.

Retribution is a nonutilitarian philosophy suggesting that the purpose of crime "control" (used loosely to refer to societal responses to crime) is to punish. Crime reduction is not a necessary by-product of the response. Rather, punishment is simply deserved; a "wrong" has been committed. Regardless of whether future crime is prevented because of the response, the response (punishment) is deserved and should happen for that reason alone. The punishment should be proportional to the crime committed, thus representing a sort of "just deserts." Retribution is morally based and thus it is impossible to refute its "effectiveness."

Incapacitation, in contrast, is a utilitarian philosophy of social control. The incapacitation argument suggests that social control should serve to improve society by keeping people who commit criminal acts from continuing to do so. Crime control strategies should therefore not merely punish, but should reduce the likelihood of future criminal acts. This reduction comes about by making it physically impossible for offenders to commit more crime; they are essentially removed from society.

Deterrence is another utilitarian philosophy, aimed at reducing crime in society. Punishment is not done for punishment's sake (as in the case of retribution), but is done for the sake of preventing future crime. Deterrence is based upon a classical or rational choice assumption regarding human nature and human behavior. It is believed that individuals commit criminal acts because of hedonism—the pleasure associated with the acts outweigh the costs associated with the acts. As a result, deterrence advocates an approach to social control whereby the costs associated with crime are perceived as outweighing the benefits. According to the deterrence doctrine, crime would be low in such a society since rational actors would avoid costly consequences—in other words, potential offenders would be deterred. Criminologists focus on three aspects of punishment that serve to make the response adequate in terms of its deterrent value: certainty of punishment, severity of punishment, and celerity, or swiftness, of punishment.[2] It is assumed that certain, severe, and swift punishments will serve to both diminish future crime among those experiencing punishment (specific deterrence) and prevent potential offenders throughout society, who presumably are knowledgeable of the costs of crime, from engaging in criminal acts (general deterrence).

Rehabilitation is yet another utilitarian philosophy in which the objective is to reduce crime. However, this philosophy is based on an assumption of human nature and human behavior that is very different from that of the deterrence doctrine. Rehabilitation theorists suggest that individuals have much less free will than is assumed by deterrence theorists. Human behavior is assumed to be largely predicted (determined) by forces outside individual control, a myriad of factors including chemical imbalances, psychological problems, and peer pressure. The solution in controlling crime, therefore, lies in "fixing" the external factors that are causing the criminal behavior.

Various specific social control mechanisms can be justified by one or more of these underlying philosophies. For instance, the response of imprisonment within the criminal justice system can be supported with retributive, incapacitative, deterrent, and rehabilitative arguments. From a retribution standpoint, incarceration could be viewed as deserved punishment. Locking up offenders for long sentences can also be seen as an example of an incapacitative strategy in that it should reduce crime since offenders will be removed from society, thus disabling them from committing more crime. Of course, for incapacitation to work in this way, various assumptions must hold. For instance, locking up offenders only reduces crime to the extent that there is no replacement on the outside. To the extent that other individuals step into the "criminal roles" occupied by those incarcerated, then imprisonment will fail as an incapacitation tool. Incarceration can also be justified on the grounds that it is a potential deterrent. Many policymakers believe that harsh sentencing guidelines will prevent rational actors from risking such costs. Finally, incarceration could be supported on the grounds of rehabilitation *if* prison programming aimed at fixing the offender (e.g., education programs, job-skills training, drug treatment programs) is presumed to be a component of the imprisonment experience.

Other specific social-control practices can be justified using some of these philosophies, but not others. Capital punishment, for instance, can be argued, in theory, to be a tool of retribution, incapacitation, and deterrence, but it is clearly not viewed as a means of rehabilitation.[3] Policing, while helpful in eventually bringing about retribution and incapacitation, is most easily linked to deterrence. Effective police patrol and investigation is presumed to enhance the certainty and celerity of punishment, and is thus vital in ensuring that crime can be deterred.

SOCIAL CONTROL AND CRIMINAL OPPORTUNITY

So, how do these various philosophies and some of the specific practices they support relate to the dynamic criminal opportunity theory offered here? Being based upon classical, rational choice assumptions, criminal opportunity theory is perhaps most compatible with classically based deterrent strategies of social control. Incapacitation makes no assumption about the origin of criminal acts, but simply presumes that the number of criminal acts in society will decline if offenders are "disabled." Rehabilitation, on the other hand, is based upon assumptions that presume determinism rather than free will on the part of individuals. As such, rehabilitation strategies are not aimed at altering choice.

Both deterrence and criminal opportunity theories assume that crime will occur if the benefits outweigh the costs, and as such, they are clearly "relatives." Yet, there are some very important differences between the practices consistent with the deterrence doctrine and the practices consistent with the tenets of a dynamic, multicontextual criminal opportunity theory. The idea of deterrence suggests that certain, severe, and swift punishments are key in the cost-benefit calculation that is behind criminal acts. Criminal opportunity theory, on the other hand, suggests that exposure to motivated offenders, suitable targets, and capable guardians are the key factors involved in the calculation. Several of these key factors intersect with the key factors outlined by the deterrence doctrine. For instance, "certain and swift punishment" usually happens through formal "guardianship." As such, some "deterrent strategies" are compatible with criminal opportunity theory. More specifically, deterrent strategies that are aimed at enhancing the certainty and celerity of punishment (e.g., policing) are consistent with criminal opportunity theory, since they address its guardianship component. In contrast, the "severity of punishment" component of deterrence does not intersect with any of the components of criminal opportunity, and thus strategies aimed at enhancing punishment severity specifically are much less compatible with criminal opportunity theory. As an example of such a difference, the policy of extending the death penalty to violent juvenile offenders follows, at least in part, the idea of deterrence. The severity of the punishment (especially in contrast to lenient juvenile sentences) is presumed to make kids think before committing violence. We have all heard many a politician say something to the effect of "We need to send a message to kids that they cannot get away with murder." Such a policy, however, should have no real effect on crime according to the criminal opportunity theory. It does not influence exposure, target suitability, or guardianship.

So, while there is some compatibility between criminal justice policies based upon deterrence and criminal opportunity theory, there are also important differences. The differences between deterrence and criminal-opportunity-related policy are also evident when we examine extralegal forms of social control. Deterrent strategies are largely based within the criminal justice system, since punishment is actually sanctioned by this official agency. However, affecting exposure, target suitability, and guardianship can clearly take place outside the criminal justice system. The community, for instance, can be a very important source of crime-reduction practices according to criminal opportunity theory.

Community-Based Control

Given that community-level informal social control practices were an important part of the operationalization of our dynamic multicontextual criminal opportunity theory,[4] it is no surprise that we advocate such practices as compatible with the tenets of the theory. Recall that community-based control intersects with the aggregate-level guardianship aspect of criminal opportunity most specifically. If communities exhibit cohesiveness and collective efficacy (thought to be related to structural factors such as low poverty and low mobility), then supervision and intervention regarding criminal acts are likely, and criminal opportunity—at least at the community context level—will be slight.[5] As such, programs aimed at building or strengthening communities are in line with our theory.

While community-level collective efficacy is clearly extralegal in the sense that it involves informal rather than formal control, efforts at building such community efficacy can take place in conjunction with policies inside the bounds of the criminal justice system. Community policing and community corrections represent two such examples of criminal justice policy that have repercussions for informal community control.

Community Policing.   Community policing is often viewed as founded upon the notion that community members rather than the police represent the first line of defense against crime. Advocates of community policing initiatives thus see community building as an integral part of policing. Many community policing activities are thus aimed at helping communities help themselves. An activity such as educating communities about the fundamentals of "neighborhood watch" helps to strengthen aggregate-level informal guardianship. An activity such as foot patrol can have multiple benefits compatible with a dynamic multicontextual criminal opportunity theory. First, since foot patrol is presumed to be a more "visible" form of police patrol than is traditional beat patrol from the police cruiser, then formal guardianship in the community should be enhanced through this practice. Second, since foot patrol can have the advantage of allowing and even encouraging conversation between police and neighborhood residents and among neighborhood residents themselves, then foot patrol can indirectly enhance informal social control through a strengthening of the social fabric necessary (e.g., social ties) for such community-based guardianship. A community policing activity as "neighborhood clean-up" focuses on the maintenance of order and "civility" and is compatible with a multicontextual criminal opportunity theory to the extent that order does suggest and promote strong informal social control. This idea is, of course, premised on the notion of Wilson and Kelling's (1982) "broken windows thesis"—that disorder and disrepair signal to potential offenders the vulnerability of an area. If, on the other hand, order is present, the perception of offenders is that community members are watching and participating in community wellness. The perception of would-be offenders in such instances is that aggregate-level criminal opportunity is lacking.[6]

Community Corrections. Community corrections was not necessarily premised on the notion of community-building. Rather, it is largely viewed as a relatively inexpensive way to incapacitate, deter, or rehabilitate offenders while relieving some of the burden of our overcrowded prison system. Community corrections takes on a variety of forms, including home incarceration, community service programs, and community-based drug treatment. The logic is simple: save dollars and prison bed space by keeping less serious offenders in the community for their sentences. But, the logic of community corrections can also be extended to incorporate ideas compatible with aggregate-level criminal opportunity. In short, keeping people in the community can be beneficial to the maintenance of strong informal social control. Rose and Clear (1998) have discussed the merits of keeping men, in particular (they are, after all, the bulk of those incarcerated), in their communities by showing the detrimental effect of incarceration rates on area crime. From their vantage point, incarcerating people in the prison system takes them out of the community and thus disrupts the social fabric of the community necessary for effective informal community-based guardianship.

Crime Prevention Through Environmental Design (CPTED). While community policing and community corrections programs are formal practices of the criminal justice system that have important implications for informal community-level guardianship, other community-level initiatives compatible with criminal opportunity theory are more fully outside the purview of the legal system. Crime Prevention Through Environmental Design (CPTED) is one such initiative.[7] The CPTED approach attempts to alter the community crime rate by altering the physical or built environment. We suggest that this approach is very compatible with a multicontextual criminal opportunity theory. Further, given its relative lack of ties to the criminal justice system, we see this as a more readily implemented practice. Implementing CPTED typically requires no legislative approval, no official sanctioning, and no system- or societywide adherence. Because of this greater practicality, we devote a bit more space to the discussion of this policy.

According to the tenets of CPTED, the physical environment—including land use, street layout, building design, and physical deterioration—can affect crime through influences on natural surveillance, territoriality, and image/milieu.[8] In short, physical environment affects crime indirectly by affecting how residents self-police and prevent crime within the community.

Jane Jacobs (1961, 1968) originally posited the idea that the built environment might affect informal social control, especially in the form of street surveillance. However, the direction of the relationship hypothesized by Jacobs between, for instance, land use and surveillance, contradicts later suggestions by Newman and others. Jacobs (1961, 1968) suggested that nonresidential land use was helpful in reducing crime in that it provided "eyes on the street" in the form of shopkeepers, workers, and customers.[9] While Newman also recognized the importance of surveillance, he particularly delineated the importance of resident surveillance of the public spaces associated with one's territory. So Newman was interested in the extent to which residents of public housing could view and monitor public play areas, public walkways, etc., from private and semiprivate locations within the housing project. He thus emphasized insiders looking out, not outsiders looking in. He did not necessarily count on outsiders (e.g., nonresidents) to provide surveillance. In fact, he warned against the juxtaposition of the residential public housing projects he studied to certain nonresidential land uses, including high schools and fast-food restaurants. Newman concluded:

> Commercial and institutional generators of activity do not, in and of themselves, necessarily enhance the safety of adjoining streets and areas. The unsupported hypothesis of Jane Jacobs, Shlomo Angel, and Elizabeth Wood must be examined more closely for a better understanding of the nature of their operating mechanisms. The simple decision to locate commercial or institutional facilities within a project in order to increase activity and so provide the safety which comes with numbers must be critically evaluated in terms of the nature of the business, the intended users, their identification with area residents, their periods of activity, the nature and frequency of the presence of concerned authorities and so on. (1973:112)

Newman's suggestions that nonresidential land use might serve to *increase* crime by *decreasing* informal social control has been addressed by others as well. Taylor and his colleagues have suggested that shopkeepers, etc., are "transient residents" of a community.[10] They are there during hours of shop operation, but then they leave. Thus, the area of the street that the shopkeeper "supervises" during business hours is left unattended after the workday is complete, thereby leaving "holes" in the resident-based "fabric." Also, nonresidential land use within a community attracts outsiders, thus diminishing the ability of residents to recognize faces and effectively monitor the legitimacy of one's presence in the community.[11]

Beyond land use, the physical characteristics of street layout and building design can affect surveillance and/or territorial functioning. For instance, neighborhoods containing a high number of accessible through streets are thought to invite outside traffic and thus reduce recognizability and control of strangers. In addition, the placement of buildings, their lobbies, and their windows vis-à-vis the surrounding streets, recreation areas, etc., can be integral in determining whether residents can provide effective guardianship.[12]

Furthermore, certain housing/building designs can disallow for demarcation of private and semiprivate outdoor spaces, thus discouraging residents from taking ownership of the property and defending it from crime. For instance, Newman (1973) was highly critical of high-rise apartment buildings with one or two common entranceways, common elevators, common corridors, and common recreation areas. Newman's view is that such designs create space outside individual apartments that is completely public, therefore diminishing the sense of ownership any one resident has for the space. As a result, the elevators, corridors, and recreation areas quickly become run-down and feared. In contrast, housing developments that utilize building designs that have entranceways and "yards" that are used by one or a few households (e.g., row houses, duplexes, quadplexes) encourage territoriality.[13]

While the presumed role of informal social control has been the predominant theoretical mechanism used to link the physical environment and crime, other possible mechanisms exist. For instance, some work suggests that aspects of the physical environment can affect the emergence of disorder or incivility, and that disorder can serve as the key mechanism linking physical community characteristics and crime.[14] Nonresidential, business-oriented land use, for instance, can create more litter and noise on the streets. This disorder, in turn, can spiral downward into more serious crime.[15] Furthermore, offenders' perceptions of potential targets are important. Taylor and Gottfredson explain, "As perceived by the offender, physical and social elements in a target region or a target site are intertwined"

(1986:389). They continue by stating, "physical features may also influence potential offenders' images of locales even though the features have no effect on resident behavior" (ibid.:399). So, for instance, physical deterioration—itself an aspect of the physical environment—can affect the *perceptions* of offenders regarding residential social control. As such, offenders are likely to perceive disorderly areas as vulnerable.

Finally, aspects of the physical environment may affect more *situational* or *site-level* criminal opportunity (e.g., the convergence of potential offenders, potential targets, and ineffective guardianship), regardless of the levels of physical deterioration or general levels of informal social control characterizing a broader street or neighborhood.[16] So, regardless of area-level territorial functioning (implying guardianship) and physical order, certain sites or targets within areas may be characterized by criminal opportunity as a function of their use or their design. Bars or taverns in communities, for instance, often serve as specific points of criminal opportunity, as a concentration of people gather in one locale (ambient exposure), with money/valuables or other commodities (target suitability), and limited informal social control (people drinking rarely make effective guardians). The prevalence of such "hot spots" and specific vulnerable, attractive targets can impact overall rates of crime within the broader area, though area-level physical and social dynamics might be playing a limited role.

Numerous studies have been conducted in attempt to verify the relationship between physical environment and crime. For instance, substantial evidence supports Newman's conclusions about the effects of certain nonresidential land uses on area crime. Research suggests that proximity to nonresidential land uses such as secondary schools, bars/taverns and alcohol outlets, fast-food restaurants, other businesses, and institutional land have positive effects on crime.[17]

Empirical evidence also exists regarding a connection between street layout and area crime. Most of this evidence has been based upon analysis of small numbers of neighborhoods in single cities, or studies of single neighborhoods as demonstration projects. For instance, Greenberg et al. (1982) examined six Atlanta neighborhoods. They found that the low-crime neighborhoods in their sample had fewer major arteries, more two-lane and one-way streets, less heavily traveled boundary streets, and less on-street or lot-style parking. Demonstration projects in Hartford, Connecticut, and Dayton, Ohio, also provide evidence that street layout is related to area crime. Hartford's Asylum Hill neighborhood underwent considerable physical changes in the mid-1970s, including the closing of certain street entrances into the neighborhood and rerouting traffic to a few major through streets. Follow-up evaluations of the changes revealed that street crime initially declined, except along the major arteries, although it reappeared when certain facets of the demonstration project waned, including community policing and a block watch program.[18]

A similar demonstration project occurred in the Dayton neighborhood of Five Oaks during the early 1990s. Thirty-five streets and 26 alleys were closed within the neighborhood, creating "mini-areas" within the community; the result was that total traffic volume declined by 36 percent and cut-through traffic declined by 67 percent.[19] Follow-up analysis of crime data reveal substantial reductions in crime. Donnelly and Kimble (1997) report that crime dropped 51 percent during the first year after the street closings. While it increased somewhat the following year, it still remained a full 28 percent below the crime figures for the preclosing year. These trends were witnessed across all streets, although they were most pronounced for the closed streets. Scholars studying the Five Oaks projects, however, are hesitant to put too much emphasis on the effects of the physical changes. It has been noted that the Five Oaks community had important facets of social capital going into the project, including cohesive residents who were very involved in the changes as well as access to good nearby parochial schools, including three in the neighborhood itself.

A more comprehensive study of eighty-two Norfolk, Virginia, neighborhoods examined the relationship between neighborhood permeability and neighborhood burglary rates.[20] Permeability was measured as "the number of access lanes leading from each artery into the neighborhood" (White 1990:61). Findings revealed that permeability significantly increased burglary rates, even controlling for social characteristics, including structural density, economic well-being, and residential instability.

There is also empirical evidence that building/housing design, as another aspect of the physical environment, also affects area crime. In his analyses of New York City housing projects, Newman (1973) showed that housing developments with taller buildings tend to be associated with higher rates of crime.[21] Newman also presented evidence that the entry design of New York City housing projects seemed to affect crime. Those projects with lobbies facing the street and with good visibility (e.g., provided by windows) had the lowest rates of crime. Further evidence of the potential crime reduction effects of building/housing design come from Brown and Altman (1983), who showed that the presence of visible neighboring houses lowered burglary. Duffala (1976) extended this notion to the design of commercial establishments; he showed that convenience stores located near vacant lots or situated away from other commerce were at higher risk for robbery.

Given the logic of CPTED, criminal opportunity can seemingly be diminished in a variety of ways through alteration of the physical environment. Rezoning land within a community, closing off streets to cut down on outside traffic, and implementing stricter building codes can all have potential effects on the spatiotemporal convergence of offenders, targets, and absence of guardianship. A growing body of empirical evidence substantiates this logic, and we therefore advocate CPTED strategies as promising practice consistent with the theory presented herein.

School-Based Control. While communities or neighborhoods have been the focus of many of our discussions of environmental contexts throughout this book, we have used schools as a second example of such contexts. Hence, we offer here a few examples of crime reduction initiatives at the school level that are compatible with a multicontextual criminal opportunity theory. As implied above, much of the theoretical and empirical work on CPTED has been done at the neighborhood or subneighborhood level (e.g., street or street block). However, a number of studies also apply the same principles of "defensible space" or "crime prevention through environmental design" to other contexts, including subways,[22] parking facilities,[23] and telephone booths.[24] Secondary schools are clearly additional contexts with potentially important physical/design characteristics that can affect behavior,[25] and scholars have outlined strategies that schools might follow based upon defensible space and CPTED theoretical principles.[26] For instance, Crowe (1999) has suggested that the layout of hallways and locker bays, the positioning of school entrances and windows, and the positioning of high-activity gathering areas (e.g., playgrounds, parking lots, courtyards) can all affect the extent to which students (offenders and targets) can escape the view of school staff and administrators (potential guardians). Despite the clear applicability of CPTED principles to the school environment, relatively few studies have empirically examined the effects of the physical environment on crime with schools as units of analysis. A few noteworthy exceptions include the CPTED school demonstration project in Broward County, Florida, and, more recently, research by Astor and colleagues on several Michigan schools.

In 1980, the National Institute of Justice released its report on the school demonstration project in Broward County, Florida.[27] Four suburban high schools were targeted through the NIJ-sponsored experiment, which included physical modifications to the schools as well as the implementation of police/security activities and organizational involvements from administrators, teachers, and students. Physical modifications included things such as adding windows for surveillance, adding signs/markers of school identity (e.g., supergraphics and border definition), limiting access to isolated areas, relocating informal gathering areas to areas providing natural surveillance (including construction of courtyards or "mini-plazas"), and redesigning bus-loading zones and student parking in order to reduce congestion and improve surveillance. Before-and-after measures of victimization specific to school subenvironments (e.g., loading zones, bathrooms, cafeterias, hallways, parking lots) revealed that: (1) compared to the rest of the schools in the county, the demonstration schools saw larger declines in bathroom theft after the CPTED-related changes; (2) while all schools but one in the county saw declines in assault rates, the largest decline was in the demonstration school receiving the most "effort" in terms of design changes; and (3) project schools reported a reduction in theft that exceeded the reduction experienced countywide (the reduction among nonproject schools was not significant). Interestingly, student perceptions of safety did not change significantly, and territorial attitudes toward the school did not appear to improve among students in project schools. In fact, several cases experienced a lower percentage of students who "felt a part of the school" during the post-CPTED observational period.

Researchers at University of Michigan have been involved recently in a different type of assessment of the physical environment–school crime relationship.[28] Drawing upon the CPTED literature, Astor and his colleagues develop a multimethod approach[29] to explore structural and cultural reasons why students identify certain school subenvironments as dangerous and places that they fear. Supporting the work in Broward County, this research has revealed that more incidents of problem behavior are associated with certain "hot spots" in schools—e.g., hallways, bathrooms, cafeterias, and parking lots—and these areas illicit greater fear among students. These areas often lack the presence of capable guardians and display no clear sign of "ownership" by any of the occupants of the school. This research also suggests that school organization might be related to territorial functioning—that is, middle schools, as compared to elementary schools, have more undefined areas due to their larger size and because there is a sense of specific territoriality that is limited to the boundaries of an individual's classroom or subject area. Taken together, these studies suggest that CPTED strategies could be successfully implemented to promote social order, cohesion, and control in schools.

Individual-Based Control

While we have focused our discussion to this point on environment-centered policies or practices, the dynamic, multicontextual criminal opportunity theory offered here also has implications regarding what individuals can do to lower the likelihood of experiencing criminal acts, including victimization, risk perception, and fear of crime. Elsewhere, Marcus Felson (1998) has eloquently outlined strategies for "everyday life" that relate to low versus high victimization risk. Following the principles of situational crime prevention,[30] Felson identifies very explicit preventive measures that are crime specific. In general, all of the principles

involve one or more of the elements found in our multilevel criminal
opportunity theory: limit exposure to potential offenders, reduce the suitability of targets (people or property), and increase guardianship capaci-
ties. This could include avoiding known hot spots for criminal activity,
recording the identification numbers of portable household goods, locking
doors, installing a home security alarm, and walking in groups. As Felson
and Clarke suggest:

> We all of us, every day, routinely take a wide range of precautions to protect
> ourselves from crime. We lock our doors, secure our valuables, counsel our
> children, and guard our purses and wallets to reduce the risk of victimiza-
> tion. We also try to live in safe neighborhoods, invest in car alarms or
> firearms, and avoid dangerous places and people. (1997:210)

Truly, it seems that desires for security and protection are basic human
needs. Yet, supporting policies and practices aimed at controlling criminal
opportunity raises some ideological and ethical concerns that we will discuss below. Before addressing these ethical issues, however, we will discuss
the policy implications of our dynamic multilevel criminal opportunity
theory in terms of an integration of environmental-level and individual-
level policy.

TOWARD MULTIDIMENSIONAL CRIME POLICY AND PRACTICE

Thus far in this chapter, we have discussed both environmental-level
(community- and school-level) and individual-level crime policy that is
compatible with our theory. Yet, having discussed them separately clouds
an important point of our theory—that individual and environmental factors work simultaneously, additively and multiplicatively, in producing
criminal opportunity and affecting criminal acts. Our multilevel propositions have important implications for crime policy, then, that go beyond
the unidimensional policies typically advocated and adopted. If we are
correct in our theorizing, it is insufficient to propose *either* community-
based interventions (e.g., community corrections, community policing,
CPTED) *or* individual-level situational crime prevention efforts. Since
both would seemingly help limit criminal opportunity,[31] both types of
strategies are seemingly necessary for a more comprehensive approach to
reducing crime. Individual-level target-hardening strategies may be
appropriate, but they often ignore the environmental-level sources of
criminal opportunity. In contrast, macrolevel policy ignores the idea that
individual actions and behaviors can contribute greatly to criminal opportunity, regardless of environment.

So, rather simply, we advocate multidimensional policy, recognizing that since motivated-offender exposure, target suitability, and (in)effective guardianship emerge from multiple spheres (individual and contextual), they can be altered in different spheres as well. However, the notion of person-environment interaction effects introduced in Chapter 5 makes the successful integration of individual-level and environmental-level policy more than simple addition. Merely engaging in both types of endeavors simultaneously is not necessarily the optimal solution. Rather, there must be recognition that these two spheres interact such that individual-level action may be more or less important in particular social environments.

For illustration purposes, let us consider how an environmental policy like community policing might alter individual-level crime prevention practices. Assuming that community policing addresses most clearly the aggregate-level guardianship component of criminal opportunity, the propositions set forth in Chapter 5—Propositions 5.3, 5.6, and 5.9 most notably—suggest that we should expect community-policing efforts to temper the effects of individual-level exposure and individual-level target suitability, while it should exacerbate the effects of individual-level guardianship. Consider first the idea that individual- or object-level characteristics that leave one more exposed or proximate to others may be less suggestive of criminal opportunity in communities with effective community policing. So, something like living in a corner residence may be less risky in such contexts. Also, valuable targets (e.g., expensive cars) are likely to be perceived as less attractive in contexts with community policing as opposed to otherwise-similar communities without such police practices. The aggregate-level guardianship offered by the community policing tempers the opportunity suggested by the target attractiveness. In addition, individuals who engage in self-protective measures including locking doors and installing alarms while living in a neighborhood with community policing will probably get more crime prevention utility from their individual efforts than will individuals engaging in similar efforts in comparable neighborhoods without community policing. In short, the implications stemming from our theory suggest that context-driven policy aimed at enhancing guardianship, such as community-policing efforts, helps to diminish criminal opportunity at both the environmental and individual levels; and conversely, it helps to strengthen or buttress individual-level guardianship (nonopportunity) efforts.

Another example, using schools instead of neighborhoods as the context under consideration, may be useful in delineating the way in which context-based policy interacts with individual-level crime-fighting practices to further reduce criminal opportunity. Suppose that a hypothetical high school recently adopted CPTED principles. With the help of a multidisciplinary team of consultants, the school underwent a major renovation and redesigned locker bays and bathrooms to allow for better traffic flow and increased surveillance potential, added larger interior and exterior windows, reconfigured the front office area so that people entering the building could easily be seen from the inside, and added exterior signs of territoriality, including the construction of a large marquee displayed prominently at the entranceway onto school grounds as well as the planting of decorative shrubbery along the entire perimeter of the property. We would expect that criminal opportunity at this school would be lower than in the pre-CPTED period, holding other factors constant. This presumed decline in crime would occur via two mechanisms. First, the context-based policy would have "direct effects" on criminal acts by reducing ambient criminal opportunity—opportunity presented by the context itself. Second, the context-based policy would reduce criminal acts via moderating effects—by interacting with individual-level opportunity characteristics. We recognize that many factors related to criminal acts are individual level in nature. Certain kids are teased because they are vulnerable, antagonistic, or gratifiable targets, for instance. But, students who were perceived as suitable or attractive targets in the pre-CPTED era may be seen as less suitable. We would argue that the nature of the context— the relative lack of ambient opportunity—alters the quality of individual-level opportunity characteristics.

It is, in fact, this second sort of crime reduction effect—the way in which context conditions or moderates individual-level effects—that may be the most important contribution of macrolevel policy. While most crime studies tend to be single level in nature, the relatively few extant multilevel studies[32] that use appropriate statistical techniques for partitioning variation in crime between individual and contextual units[33] show that the overwhelming bulk of the variance is at the individual as opposed to environmental levels. For example, in most of the multilevel studies conducted by the authors of this book, the typical context-level variation in crime, victimization, risk perception, or fear lies between 3 and 10 percent. Clearly, most of the variation is at the individual level. Microlevel scholars seize upon such findings as evidence that policy needs to be directed at the individual, not the environment. We disagree. Though relatively little reduction in criminal acts may occur via direct macrolevel contextual effects, the decrease brought about by context's altering of the effects of individual-level factors is conceivably quite large. Failure to recognize and estimate the multidimensional effects of community-based policy aimed at reducing criminal opportunity may lead to substantial misspecification. Of course, the examples provided above about how community-based policy works in conjunction with individual-level crime reduction practices are, at this point, largely hypothetical. While we clearly see policy implications

in our theory, we have remained intentionally nonspecific and hypothetical in our recommendations at this point. Future tests of the theory, assuming empirical validation, seem to be the more appropriate foundation for
specific policy recommendations.

ETHICS OF LIMITING CRIMINAL OPPORTUNITY

At first blush, advocating protective measures that reduce criminal opportunity and thereby diminish victimization risk just seems to make good
common sense. However, when such thinking is elevated to the level of
recommended policy strategies, objections arise. Felson and Clarke (1997)
offer an extremely cogent account and response to such objections, which
tend to be ideologically-ethically based. In this section, we borrow heavily
from their insightful essay.

Advocating the control of criminal opportunities manages to produce
criticisms from the entire spectrum of modern political positions. Felson
and Clarke summarize these varied criticisms:

> Critics on the right . . . see situational crime prevention as a deeply irrelevant
> response to crime because it neglects issues of moral culpability and pun-
> ishment. Moreover, it "punishes" the law-abiding by infringing upon free-
> dom and privacy. Those on the left see it as politically and socially naive, in
> that it neglects the role of social and economic inequalities in causation and
> of political muscle in the definition of crime. Liberal critics assert that "tin-
> kering" with symptoms diverts attention from the need to tackle the "root
> causes" of crime, such as unemployment, racial discrimination, substandard
> housing, inadequate schooling, and inconsistent parenting. (1997:198)

The ethical issues that are intertwined with all of these ideological orientations pertain to "social justice, civil liberties, and privacy" (ibid.).

When control of criminal opportunity is elevated to the level of policy
alternatives, concerns over social justice emerge because there is a fear that
certain social strata will have to bear the burden of such control (e.g., the
law-abiding, poor, racial minorities). Generally, there is a sense that an
emphasis on controlling criminal opportunity would blame the victims of
crime, forcing them to take responsibility for their own victimization. In
terms of civil liberties, there is a fear that the control of criminal opportunity could compromise freedom of association (e.g., no loitering on public
streets), access to public spaces (e.g., restricted hours for public parks or the
closing of streets to limit access to certain areas of a city), and rights of personal expression (e.g., jogging before sunrise). Concerning freedom of association, an emphasis on controlling criminal opportunity engenders a fear
that individuals in modern societies will become more and more isolated

and guarded, thereby tearing at the essential *social* fabric of society. It is also feared that in a society that sets out to control criminal opportunity, more and more of our routine activities will be observed, monitored, and recorded (e.g., video cameras in stores, parking lots, and offices, and on city streets), thereby compromising rights of privacy. Thus, regardless of political orientation—left, right, center—advocating the control of criminal opportunity can be construed as a moral threat against social democracy.

In addressing these concerns, Felson and Clarke base their position on three guiding standards of a liberal democracy. Following Felson and Clarke, we believe that crime prevention should be provided "equally to all social strata," "show respect for individual rights," and "share responsibility for crime prevention with all sections of society" (ibid.:199). We concur with Felson and Clarke that even though any policy orientation toward crime prevention can be misused and corrupted, policies and practices aimed at controlling criminal opportunity would not *inherently* undermine liberal democratic commitments. In fact, as Felson and Clarke point out, an emphasis on controlling criminal opportunity could serve social democratic principles "better than other crime policies" (ibid.:199).

According to Felson and Clarke, "fair and equal prevention" revolve around three issues: controlling criminal opportunity "should not serve as a means for one segment of the community to displace its crime risk onto another segment;" it "should not serve just one social class, nor should its costs be borne by another social class or stratum of society;" and it "should be attentive to the victimization risks of minorities and disempowered segments of society" (ibid.:200). The displacement issue suggests that, for example, efforts to control criminal opportunity in one neighborhood might merely divert criminal activity to other neighborhoods, or, at the individual level, one person's efforts to reduce his or her burglary risk might merely direct criminal activity to his or her neighbors. Another concern with displacement is that if criminals are diverted from attempting one particular crime, they may commit another, perhaps more serious crime. For example, having been prevented from committing a burglary, an individual might choose to commit a robbery, which could result in violence or even death.

The displacement criticism, as Felson and Clarke (ibid.:202) point out, does not have empirical support. While displacement is a possibility and actually occurs at times, evidence from situational crime prevention projects suggests it is less of a problem than what critics might imply. Felson and Clarke indicate that in

> Hesseling's (1994) review undertaken for the Dutch Ministry of Justice of 55 situational prevention projects it was concluded that in 22 of the studies there was no evidence of displacement. In none of the remaining 33 studies

was displacement complete and in most there was a considerable net reduction in the amount of crime. (ibid.)

The notion that a potential offender will choose to commit a different crime after being blocked from another type of crime is not empirically supported either. While there is not compelling evidence that crime is displaced due to criminal opportunity control measures, there is some evidence to suggest that there might be a "diffusion of benefits" from such measures.[34] Poyner (1991), for instance, found that placing video surveillance cameras in some university campus parking lots reduced crime risks for *all* lots. It is possible that efforts to reduce victimization at the environmental and individual level may diffuse to benefit others as well.

In addition to avoiding the displacement of crime, controlling criminal opportunity should not serve just one stratum, nor should its costs be borne by another social class. Felson and Clarke (1997:202–3) provide an illuminating example of how controlling criminal opportunity could be misapplied in this regard. Specifically, Felson and Clarke point out that "vehicle-tracking systems that permit stolen cars to be quickly located through signals emitted by transmitters hidden in the body of the car" (ibid.:202) have been introduced to reduce auto theft opportunity. These devices are expensive and therefore used by relatively wealthy auto owners. Some police departments have opted to equip their cruisers with receivers for these transmitters. This sets up the possibility that the police might spend more time trying to recover the stolen cars of those who can afford tracking devices, and thereby ignore the needs of the less affluent. While this potential for misuse of controlling criminal opportunity exists, we do not believe that it is an inherent quality. Indeed, the early work in this area focused on improving environmental conditions in low-income areas. Both Jacobs's (1961) and Newman's (1973) efforts helped to eliminate tower block housing projects and promote the rejuvenation of older, low-income housing as an option to urban renewal, removal, and gentrification. Further, this early work clearly set a tone for an interest and commitment to understanding the particular victimization risks of minority and disempowered members of the community.

Another concern for controlling criminal opportunity relates to respect for individual liberties. We believe that the emphasis on preventing victimization risk (as opposed to controlling or eliminating potential offenders) is firmly grounded in a commitment to basic individual liberty. While some control measures have been abused (e.g., inappropriate uses of surveillance cameras), the goal of attempting to create and maintain an environment that is relatively safe from harm and injury is not to blame. Many of the measures that have been used to reduce criminal opportunity (e.g., the blocking of streets, development of queueing practices, requiring identification to cash a check, restricted hours for public facilities) have created some inconvenience, but has not resulted in egregious loss of individual liberty. Given that everyone is capable of committing criminal acts, it seems the most ethical response might be to reduce victimization by attempting to limit and control opportunities for crime.

CONCLUSION

We have written this book with the explicit purpose of proposing an alternative criminal opportunity theory. Our efforts have been aimed at more fully developing criminal opportunity theory as a dynamic, multilevel, general theory of crime. The components necessary to develop a multicontextual criminal opportunity theory have been gleaned from social control-disorganization and routine activities theories. In some sense, we have merely collected and then assembled these parts into a consistent whole. These traditions highlight the importance of contextual explanations of criminal acts. One of their basic insights is that crime must be understood in terms of individuals acting within and upon social and physical environments. We have thus presented a theory that operates at two levels of analysis—the individual and the environmental—and revolves around three central concepts—motivated offenders, suitable targets, and guardianship. The essence of our theory is that criminal acts can best be explained in terms of criminal opportunity contexts—the convergence in time and place of motivated offenders, suitable targets, and the absence of capable guardians.

In our efforts, we have addressed concerns pertaining to theory, empirical research, and policy. We have identified and clarified key theoretical assumptions, concepts, and propositions, attempting to produce a logically consistent and parsimonious multilevel theory of criminal opportunity contexts. While emphasizing both individual and environmental levels of analysis, we have explored their direct effects as well as their interactions. Our work has considered the relationships between criminal opportunity and criminal acts (i.e., offending and victimization) as well as reactions to crime (e.g., perceived risk, fear, and constrained behavior). After establishing the basic multilevel framework, we incorporated temporal dimensions into our theory by elaborating on the notions of rhythm, tempo, and timing and by exploring developmental changes within individuals across time (i.e., growth curves). To provide a sense of how to test and use our theory, we discussed various methodological approaches. While hierarchical regression modeling represents the best technique for testing our perspective, we endeavored to show how other methods, including qualitative approaches, could also be useful. At the outset, we suggested that a theory can be assessed in terms of its utility for the real world. The focus of this chapter has been to examine the relationship between our dynamic, multilevel, general theory of criminal opportunity and policies and practices. It has been our contention that the kind of crime prevention suggested by our theory is not only consistent with the guiding principles of social-democratic societies, but that they could actually help realize those principles.

We conclude this book where we began, with a hope that our efforts could help focus and advance multilevel scholarship on criminal opportunity. We have not sought to posit a radically new way of thinking about crime. Rather, we have taken some rather tried and true conceptions of criminal opportunity and criminal acts and fashioned a framework that is consistent, systematic, and amenable to empirical investigation. The rewards for our assembling and fashioning efforts will not necessarily lie in results supporting our propositions (although we hope those are forthcoming), but rather in the lines of inquiry our perspective might encourage. Finally, we did not write this book as a response to some perceived crisis in or intellectual fetters upon criminology. To the contrary, this book has been possible because of the robust health of criminology. Over the last century, ecological and individual perspectives have developed in criminology. We have benefited from the riches produced by these approaches, as has criminology generally. These riches have allowed us to advance a theory that synthesizes valuable and varied theoretical, methodological, and empirical insights into a framework that focuses on what we take to be they key to explaining criminal acts—multilevel criminal opportunity contexts.

NOTES

1. It should be noted that the situational crime perspective is committed to the development of very crime-specific theories, whereas our approach has been to develop a general theory of criminal acts. This theoretical difference comes through in our orientation to policy and practice as well. We believe that regardless of the specific crime, the management of exposure to potential offenders, the suitability of targets, and the presence of capable guardians are key to prevention.

2. For example, see Gibbs (1968).

3. The words "in theory" are important here. We do not suggest that there is clear empirical evidence showing that the death penalty is an effective deterrent. In fact, there is conflicting evidence to this effect in the criminological literature. The point of this chapter is not to review this debate. We simply aim to convey that different practices are justified, theoretically, on various grounds.

4. See Chapter 4.

5. See Chapter 2 for a review of studies in the community crime tradition supporting this link.

6. Again, see Chapter 2 for an overview of the studies in the social control-disorganization tradition that find a link between disorder and crime, fear of crime, etc.

7. While police agencies may advocate and cooperate in CPTED initiatives, there is no formal linkage between CPTED and the criminal justice system as is evident in the cases of community policing and community corrections.

8. See Newman (1973, 1996).

9. For example, see Angel (1968) and Wood (1961).

10. For example, see Taylor et al. (1981, 1984), Taylor and Brower (1985), and Taylor (1987, 1988).

11. For example, see Appleyard (1981), Baum et al. (1978), and Brown and Altman (1981).

12. For example, see Crowe (2000) and Newman (1973).

13. See also Stollard (1991).

14. See Kurtz et al. (1998) and Taylor et al. (1995).

15. See Skogan (1990), Taylor (2001), as well as Wilson and Kelling (1982).

16. For example, see Clarke (1997), Heinzelmann (1981), Sherman et al. (1989).

17. For example, see Brantingham and Brantingham (1982), Frisbie, Fishbine, Hintz, Joelson, and Nutter (1977), Harrell and Gouvis (1994), Kurtz et al. (1998), Ley and Cybriwsky (1974), Roncek and Faggiani (1985), Roncek and LoBosco (1983), Roncek and Maier (1991), Roncek and Pravatiner (1989), and Speer et al. (1998).

18. See Fowler and Mangione (1986) and Fowler et al. (1979).

19. See Donnelly and Kimble (1997) and Newman (1996).

20. See White (1990).

21. See also Newman and Franck (1982).

22. See La Vigne (1997).

23. See Smith (1996).

24. See Mayhew, Clarke, Burrows, Hough, and Winchester (1979).

25. See Schneider et al. (1999) and Toby (1994). See also Fisher and Nasar (1992, 1995) for an example of how physical design affects fear and perceptions of crime on a college campus.

26. For example, see Crowe (1999, 2000).

27. See Wallis and Ford (1980).

28. See Astor and Meyer (1999, 2001) and Astor et al. (1999, 2001).

29. The methodological implications of this body of research were discussed in Chapter 8.

30. For example, see Clarke (1980, 1992).

31. See our operationalization of the theory in Chapter 4.

32. See Chapter 2 for a review.

33. See Chapter 8 for a review of HLM.

34. See Clarke and Weisburd (1994).

References

Adams, Kenneth. 1997. Developmental aspects of adult crime. Pp. 309–42 in *Advances in Criminological Theory: Developmental Theories of Crime and Delinquency,* edited by Terence P. Thornberry. New Brunswick, NJ: Transaction.

Akers, Ronald L. 1989. A social behaviorist's perspective on integration of theories of crime and deviance. Pp. 23–36 in *Theoretical Integration in the Study of Deviance and Crime: Problems and Prospects,* edited by Steven F. Messner, Marvin D. Krohn, and Allen E. Liska. Albany: State University of New York Press.

———. 1997. *Criminological Theories: Introduction and Evaluation,* 2d edition. Los Angeles, CA: Roxbury.

———. 1998. *Social Learning and Social Structure: A General Theory of Crime and Deviance.* Boston, MA: Northeastern University Press.

Akers, Ronald L. and John K. Cochran. 1985. Adolescent marijuana use: A test of three theories of deviant behavior. *Deviant Behavior* 6:323–46.

Albrecht, Stan L., Cheryl Amey, and Michael K. Miller. 1996. Patterns of substance abuse among rural black adolescents. *Journal of Drug Issues* 26:751–81.

Alexander, Jeffrey C. 1987. *Twenty Lectures: Sociological Theory Since World War II.* New York, NY: Columbia University Press.

Alwin, Duane F. 1994. Aging, personality, and social change: The stability of individual differences over the adult life-span. Life-Span Development and Behavior 12:135–85.

Anderson, Carolyn S. 1982. The search for school climate: A review of research. *Review of Educational Research* 52:368–420.

Anderson, Elijah. 1990. *Streetwise: Race, Class, and Change in an Urban Community.* Chicago, IL: University of Chicago Press.

Angel, Shlomo. 1968. *Discouraging Crime through City Planning.* Berkeley: University of California, Center for Planning and Development Research.

Appleyard, Donald. 1981. *Livable Streets.* Berkeley: University of California Press.

Astor, Ron Avi and Heather Ann Meyer. 1999. Where girls and women won't go: Female students', teachers', and social workers' views of school safety. *Social Work in Education* 21:201–19.

———. 2001. The conceptualization of violence-prone school subcontexts: Is the sum of the parts greater than the whole? *Urban Education* 36:374–99.

214   References

Astor, Ron Avi, Heather Ann Meyer, and William J. Behre. 1999. Unowned places
    and times: Maps and interviews about violence in high schools. *American Edu-
    cational Research Journal* 36:3–42.
Astor, Ron Avi, Heather Ann Meyer, and Ronald O. Pitner. 2001. Elementary and
    middle school students' perceptions of violence-prone school sub-contexts.
    Elementary School Journal 101:511–28.
Bailey, William C. 1984. Poverty, inequality, and city homicide rates: Some not so
    unexpected findings. *Criminology* 22:531–50.
Bailey, William C. and Ruth D. Peterson. 1990. Murder and capital punishment: A
    monthly time series analysis of execution publicity. *American Sociological
    Review* 54:722–43.
Balkin, Steven. 1979. Victimization rates, safety, and fear of crime. *Social Problems*
    26:343–59.
Bandura, Albert. 1969. *Principles of Behavior Modification.* New York, NY: Holt, Rine-
    hart, and Winston.
Bartusch, Dawn Jeglum and Ross L. Matsueda. 1996. Gender, reflected appraisals,
    and labeling: A cross-group test of an interactionist theory of delinquency.
    Social Forces 75:145–76.
Baum, Andrew, Glenn E. Davis, and John R. Aiello. 1978. Crowding and neighbor-
    hood mediation of urban density. *Journal of Population* 1:266–79.
Beccaria, Cesare. 1764/1963. *On Crimes and Punishment.* Indianapolis, IN: Bobbs-
    Merrill.
Becker, Gary S. 1968. Crime and punishment: An economic approach. *Journal of
    Political Economy* 76:169–217.
———. 1976. *The Economic Approach to Human Behavior.* Chicago, IL: University of
    Chicago Press.
———. 1996. *Accounting for Tastes.* Cambridge, MA: Harvard University Press.
Becker, Gary S. and William M. Landes. 1974. *Essays in the Economics of Crime and
    Punishment.* New York: National Bureau of Economic Research.
Bellair, Paul E. 1997. Social interaction and community crime: Examining the
    importance of neighbor networks. *Criminology* 35:677–703.
———. 2000. Informal surveillance and street crime: A complex relationship. *Crim-
    inology* 38:137–70.
Bellair, Paul E. and Vincent J. Roscigno. 2000. Local labor market opportunity and
    adolescent delinquency. *Social Forces* 78:1509–38.
Bentham, Jeremy. [1789] 1907. *An Introduction to the Principles of Morals and Legisla-
    tion.* London: Athlone.
Beveridge, William Ian Beardmore. 1950. *The Art of Scientific Investigation.* New
    York: Vintage.
Birkbeck, Christopher and Gary LaFree. 1993. The situational analysis of crime and
    deviance. *Annual Review of Sociology* 19:113–37.
Blalock, Hubert M. 1969. *Theory Construction: From Verbal to Mathematical Formula-
    tions.* Englewood Cliffs, NJ: Prentice-Hall.
———. 1984. Contextual-effects models: Theoretical and methodological issues.
    Annual Review of Sociology 10:353–72.
Blau, Judith and Peter M. Blau. 1982. The cost of inequality: Metropolitan structure
    and violent crime. *American Sociological Review* 47:114–29.

Blumer, Herbert G. 1969. *Symbolic Interaction*. Englewood Cliffs, NJ: Prentice-Hall.
Blumstein, Alfred, Jacqueline Cohen, and David P. Farrington. 1988a. Criminal career research: Its value for criminology. *Criminology* 26:1–35.
———. 1988b. Longitudinal and criminal career research: Further clarifications. *Criminology* 26:57–74.
Blumstein, Alfred, Jacqueline Cohen, Jeffrey A. Roth, and Christy A. Visher (Eds.). 1986. *Criminal Careers and Career Criminals*. Washington, DC: National Academy Press.
Blumstein, Alfred, David P. Farrington, and Soumyo Moitra. 1985. Delinquency careers: Innocents, desisters, and persisters. *Crime and Justice: An Annual Review of Research* 6:187–219.
Braga, Anthony A. and Ronald V. Clarke. 1994. Improved radio and more stripped cars in Germany: A routine activities analysis. *Security Journal* 5:154–59.
Braithwaite, John. 1989. *Crime, Shame, and Reintegration*. New York: Cambridge University Press.
Brantingham, Paul J. and Patricia L. Brantingham (Eds.). 1981. *Environmental Criminology*. Beverly Hills, CA: Sage.
———. 1982. Mobility, notoriety and crime: A study of crime patterns in urban nodal points. *Journal of Environmental Systems* 11:89–99.
Brooks-Gunn, Jeanne and Frank F. Furstenberg. 1987. Continuity and change in the context of poverty: Adolescent mothers and their children. Pp. 171–88 in *The Malleability of Children*, edited by James J. Gallagher and Craig T. Ramey. Baltimore, MD: Brooks Publishing.
Brown, Barbara B. and Irwin Altman. 1981. Territoriality and residential crime: A conceptual framework. Pp. 55–76 in *Environmental Criminology*, edited by Paul J. Brantingham and Patricia L. Brantingham. Beverly Hills, CA: Sage.
———. 1983. Territoriality, defensible space and residential burglary: An environmental analysis. *Journal of Environmental Psychology* 3:203–20.
Browning, Katherine and Rolf Loeber. 1999. *Highlights of findings from the Pittsburgh Youth Study: Fact Sheet 95*. Washington, DC: Office of Juvenile Justice and Delinquency Prevention, United States Department of Justice.
Browning, Katherine, Terence P. Thornberry, and Pamela K. Porter. 1999. *Highlights of Findings from the Rochester Youth Developmental Study: Fact Sheet 103*. Washington, DC: Office of Juvenile Justice and Delinquency Prevention, United States Department of Justice.
Bryk, Anthony S. and Mary Erina Driscoll. 1988. *The School as Community: Theoretical Foundations, Contextual Influences, and Consequences for Students and Teachers*. Madison, WI: University of Wisconsin Center on Effective Secondary Schools.
Bryk, Anthony S. and Stephen W. Raudenbush. 1992. *Hierarchical Linear Models: Applications and Data Analysis Methods*. Newbury Park, CA: Sage.
Buck, Andrew J., Simon Hakim, and George F. Rengert. 1993. Burglar alarms and the choice behavior of burglars: A suburban phenomenon. *Journal of Criminal Justice* 21:497–507.
Burkett, Steven and Mervin White. 1974. Hellfire and delinquency: Another look. *Journal for the Scientific Study of Religion* 13:455–62.
Bursik, Robert J. Jr. 1986. Ecological stability and the dynamics of delinquency. Pp.

35–66 in *Communities and Crime,* edited by Albert J. Reiss, Jr. and Michael Tonry. Chicago, IL: University of Chicago Press.

———. 1988. Social disorganization and theories of crime and delinquency: problems and prospects. *Criminology* 30:115–24.

Bursik, Robert J. Jr. and Harold G. Grasmick. 1993. *Neighborhoods and Crime: The Dimensions of Effective Community Control.* New York, NY: Lexington Books.

Bursik, Robert J. Jr., Harold G. Grasmick, and Mitchell B. Chamlin. 1990. The effect of longitudinal arrest patterns on the development of robbery trends at the neighborhood level. *Criminology* 28:431–50.

Bursik, Robert J. Jr. and James Webb. 1982. Community change and patterns of delinquency. *American Journal of Sociology* 88:24–42.

Caspi, Avshalom. 1993. Why maladaptive behaviors persist: Sources of continuity and change across the life-course. Pp. 343–76 in *Studying Lives Through Time: Personality and Development,* edited by David C. Funder, Ross D. Parke, Carol Tomlinson-Keasey, and Keith Widaman. Washington, DC: American Psychological Association.

Caspi, Avshalom, Glen H. Elder, Jr., and Ellen S. Herbener. 1990. Childhood personality and the prediction of life–course patterns. Pp. 13–35 in *Straight and Devious Pathways from Childhood to Adulthood,* edited by Lee N. Robins and Michael Rutter. Cambridge: Cambridge University Press.

Caspi, Avshalom and Terrie E. Moffitt. 1995. The continuity of maladaptive behavior: From description to understanding in the study of antisocial behavior. Pp. 472–511 in *Developmental Psychopathology,* edited by Dante Cicchetti and Donald J. Cohen. New York: Wiley.

Catalano, Richard, Rick Kosterman, J. David Hawkins, Michael Newcomb, and Robert Abbott. 1996. Modeling the etiology of adolescent substance use: A test of the social development model. *Journal of Drug Issues* 26:429–55.

Cerkovich, Stephen A. and Peggy C. Giordano. 2001. Stability and change in antisocial behavior: The transition from adolescence to early adulthood. *Criminology* 39:371–410.

Chiricos, Ted, Michael Hogan, and Marc Gertz. 1997. Racial composition of neighborhood and fear of crime. *Criminology* 35:107–31.

Cisneros, Henry G. 1995. *Defensible Space: Deterring Crime and Building Community.* Washington, DC: Department of Housing and Urban Development.

Clarke, Ronald V. 1980. Situational crime prevention: Theory and practice. *British Journal of Criminology* 20:136–47.

———. 1992. *Situational Crime Prevention: Successful Case Studies.* New York: Harrow and Heston.

———. 1997. Introduction. Pp. 1–43 in *Situational Crime Prevention: Successful Case Studies,* 2d edition, edited by Ronald V. Clarke. Albany, NY: Harrow and Heston.

Clarke, Ronald V. and Derek Cornish. 1985. Modeling offender's decisions: A framework for research and policy. *Crime and Justice: An Annual Review of Research* 6:147–85.

Clarke, Ronald V. and David Weisburd. 1994. Diffusion of crime control benefits: Observations on the reverse of displacement. *Crime Prevention Studies* 2:16–184.

Cline, Hugh F. 1980. Criminal behavior over the life span. Pp. 641674 in *Change in*

Human Development, edited by Orville G. Brimm, Jr., and Jerome Kagan. Cambridge, MA: Harvard University Press.

Cloward, Richard A. and Lloyd E. Ohlin. 1960. *Delinquency and Opportunity: A Theory of Delinquent Gangs*. New York: Free Press.

Cochran, John K. and Ronald L. Akers. 1989. Beyond hellfire: An exploration of the variable effects of religiosity on adolescent marijuana and alcohol use. *Journal of Research in Crime and Delinquency* 26:198–225.

Cohen, Bernard P. 1989. *Developing Sociological Knowledge: Theory and Method*, 2d edition. Chicago, IL: Nelson-Hall.

Cohen, Lawrence E. and David Cantor. 1981. Residential burglary in the United States: Life-style and demographic factors associated with the probability of victimization. *Journal of Research in Crime and Delinquency* 18:113–27.

Cohen, Lawrence E. and Marcus Felson. 1979. Social change and crime rate trends: A routine activity approach. *American Sociological Review* 44:588–608.

Cohen, Lawrence E., James R. Kluegel, and Kenneth C. Land. 1981. Social inequality and predatory criminal victimization: An exposition and test of a formal theory. *American Sociological Review* 46:505–24.

Cohen, Lawrence E. and Kenneth C. Land. 1987. Sociological positivism and the explanation of criminality. Pp. 43–55 in *Positive Criminology*, edited by Michael R. Gottfredson and Travis Hirschi. Newbury Park, CA: Sage.

Cohen, Lawrence E. and Richard Machalek. 1988. A general theory of expropriative crime: An evolutionary ecological approach. *American Journal of Sociology* 94:465–501.

Coleman, James S. 1990. *Foundations of Social Theory*. Cambridge, MA: Harvard University Press.

Colvin, Mark and John Pauly. 1983. A critique of criminology: Toward an integrated structural-marxist theory. *American Journal of Sociology* 89:513–51.

Conger, Rand D. and Ronald L. Simons. 1997. Life-course contingencies in the development of adolescent antisocial behavior: A matching law approach. Pp. 55–100 in *Advances in Criminological Theory: Developmental Theories of Crime and Delinquency*, edited by Terence P. Thornberry. New Brunswick, NJ: Transaction.

Cook, Philip J. 1980. Research in criminal deterrence: Laying the groundwork for the second decade. *Crime and Justice: An Annual Review of Research* 2:211–68.

———. 1986. The demand and supply of criminal opportunities. *Crime and Justice: An Annual Review of Research* 7:1–27.

Cooley, Charles H. 1902. *Human Nature and the Social Order*. New York: Scribner's.

Corbin, Juliet and Anselm L. Strauss. 1998. *Basics of Qualitative Research: Techniques and Procedures for Developing Grounded Theory*. Thousand Oaks, CA: Sage.

Cornish, D. and Ronald V. Clarke (Eds.). 1986. *The Reasoning Criminal*. New York: Springer-Verlag.

Crowe, Timothy D. 1999. Designing safer schools. *School Safety* (fall):9–13.

Crowe, Timothy. 2000. *Crime Prevention Through Environmental Design: Applications of Architectural Design and Space Management Concepts*, 2d edition. Boston, MA: Butterworth-Heinemann.

Crutchfield, Robert D. 1989. Labor stratification and violent crime. *Social Forces* 68:489–512.

218   References

Crutchfield, Robert, Michael Geerken, and Walter Gove. 1982. Crime rate and social integration: The impact of metropolitan mobility. *Criminology* 20:467–78.
Crutchfield, Robert D. and Susan R. Pitchford. 1997. Work and crime: The effects of labor stratification. *Social Forces* 76:93–118.
Cunningham, William C. and Todd H. Taylor. 1984. *The Growing Role of Private Security*. Washington, DC: National Institute of Justice.
D'Unger, Amy, Kenneth C. Land, Patricia McCall, and Daniel S. Nagin. 1998. How many latent classes of delinquent/criminal careers? Results from mixed Poisson regression analyses of the London, Philadelphia, and Racine cohort studies. *American Journal of Sociology* 103:1593–1630.
Dannefer, Dale. 1984. Adult development and social theory: A paradigmatic reappraisal. *American Sociological Review* 49:100–16.
Dannefer, Dale and Ralph R. Sell. 1988. Age structure, the life-course and aged heterogeneity: Prospects for research and theory. *Comprehensive Gerontology* 2: 1–10.
Dash, Leon. 1996. *Rosa Lee: A Mother and Her Family in Urban American* . New York: Basic.
Decker, David, David Schicor, and Robert M. O'Brien. 1982. *Urban Structure and Victimization*. Lexington, MA: Lexington.
Decker, Scott H. and Carol W. Kohfeld. 1985. Crime, crime rates, arrests, and arrest ratios: Implications for deterrence theory. *Criminology* 23:437–50.
DeMarsh, Joseph P. and Karol L. Kumpfer 1986. Family-oriented interventions for the prevention of chemical dependency in children and adolescents. Pp. 117–52 in *Childhood and Chemical Abuse: Prevention and Intervention*, edited by Stephanie Griswold-Ezekoye, Karol L. Kumpfer, and William J. Bukoski. New York: Haworth.
Donnelly, Patrick G. and Charles E. Kimble. 1997. Community organizing, environmental change, and neighborhood crime. *Crime and Delinquency* 43:493–511.
Duffala, Dennis C. 1976. Convenience stores, armed robbery, and physical environment features. *American Behavioral Scientist* 20:227–46.
Durkheim, Emile. [1893] 1964. *The Division of Labor in Society*. New York: Free Press.
———. [1895] 1938. *The Rules of Sociological Method*. Glencoe, IL: Free Press.
Earls, Felton and Christy A. Visher. 1997. *Project on Human Development in Chicago Neighborhoods: A Research Update*. Rockville, MD: U.S. Department of Justice, National Institute of Justice Publication.
Ehrlich, Isaac. 1973. Participation in illegitimate activities: A theoretical and empirical investigation. *Journal of Political Economy* 81:521–65.
Eide, Erling Jörgen Asssness, and Terje Skjerpen. 1994. *Economics of Crime: Deterrence and the Rational Offender*. Amsterdam: North-Holland.
Elder, Glen H. Jr. 1992. The life-course. Pp. 1120–30 in *Encyclopedia of Sociology*, edited by Edgar F. Borgatta and Marie L. Borgatta. New York: Macmillan.
Elder, Glen H. Jr., Cynthia Gimbel, and Rachel Ivie. 1991. Turning points in life: The case of military service and war. *Military Psychology* 3:215–31.
Elder, Glen H. Jr., and Angela M. O'Rand. 1995. Adult lives in a changing society. Pp. 452–75 in *Sociological Perspectives on Social Psychology*, edited by Karen S. Cook, Gary Alan Fine, and James S. House. Needham Heights, MA: Allyn and Bacon.

Elliot, Delbert S. 1994. Serious violent offenders: Onset, developmental course, and termination. *Criminology* 32:1–21.

Elliot, Delbert S., Suzanne S. Ageton, and Rachelle J. Cantor 1979. An integrated theoretical perspective on delinquent behavior. *Criminology* 16:3–27.

Elliot, Delbert S., David Huizinga, and Suzanne Ageton. 1985. *Explaining Delinquency and Drug Use*. Beverly Hills, CA: Sage.

Elliot, Delbert S., William J. Wilson, David Huizinga, Robert J. Sampson, Amanda Elliott, and Bruce Rankin. 1996. The effects of neighborhood disadvantage on adolescent development. *Journal of Research in Crime and Delinquency* 33: 389–426.

Farrington, David P. 1979. Longitudinal research on crime and delinquency. *Crime and Justice: An Annual Review of Research* 1:289–348.

———. 1986a. Age and crime. *Crime and Justice: An Annual Review of Research* 7:189–250.

———. 1986b. Stepping stones to adult criminal careers. Pp. 359–84 in *Development of Antisocial and Prosocial Behavior,* edited by Dan Olweus, Jack Block, and Marian R. Yarow. New York: Academic.

———. 1988a. Psychobiological factors in the explanation and reduction of delinquency. *Today's Delinquent* 7:37–51.

———. 1988b. Studying changes within individuals: The causes of offending. Pp. 158–83 in *Studies of Psychosocial Risk: The Power of Longitudinal Data,* edited by Michael Rutter. Cambridge: Cambridge University Press.

———. 1989a. Early predictors of adolescent aggression and adult violence. *Violence and Victims* 4:79–100.

———. 1989b. Later adult life outcomes of offenders and nonoffenders. Pp. 220–44 in *Children at Risk: Assessment, Longitudinal Research, and Intervention,* edited by M. Brambring, F. Losel, and H. Skowronek. Hawthorne, NY: Aldine de Gruyter.

———. 1991. Antisocial personality from childhood to adulthood. *Psychologist* 4:389–94.

———. 1992. Explaining the beginning, progress, and ending of antisocial behavior from birth to adulthood. Pp. 253–86 in *Facts, Frameworks, and Forecasts,* edited by Joan McCord. New Brunswick, NJ: Transaction.

———. 1993. Childhood Origins of teenage antisocial behaviour and adult social dysfunction. *Journal of Royal Society of Medicine* 86:13–17.

———. 1995. The development of offending and antisocial behaviour from childhood: Key findings from the Cambridge study in delinquent development. *Journal of Child Psychology and Psychiatry* 360:929–64.

Farrington, David P. and J. David Hawkins. 1991. Predicting participation, early onset, and later persistence in officially recorded offending. *Criminal Behaviour and Mental Health* 1:1–33.

Farrington, David P. and Rolf Loeber. 1990. Transatlantic replicability of risk factors in the development of delinquency. Pp. 61–82 in *Where and When: The Influence of History and Geography on Aspects of Psychopathology,* edited by Patricia Cohen, Cheryl Slomkowski, and Lee Robins. Mahwah, NJ: Lawrence Erlbaum.

Farrington, David P., Rolf Loeber, Delbert S. Elliot, David J. Hawkins, Denise B. Kandel, Malcolm W. Klein, David C. Rowe, and Richard E. Tremblay. 1990.

Advancing knowledge about the onset of delinquency and crime. *Advances in Clinical Child Psychology* 13:283–342.

Farrington, David P., Rolf Loeber, and Welmoet B. Van Kammen. 1990. Long-term criminal outcomes of hyperactivity-impulsivity-attention deficit and conduct problems in childhood. Pp. 62–80 in *Straight and Devious Pathways from Childhood to Adulthood*, edited by Lee N. Robins and Michael Rutter. Cambridge: Cambridge University Press.

Farrington, David P. and Donald West. 1981. The Cambridge study in delinquent development. Pp. 179–95 in *Prospective Longitudinal Research*, edited by Sarnoff A. Mednick and André E. Baert. Oxford: Oxford University Press.

Featherman, David L. and Richard M. Lerner. 1985. Ontogenesis and sociogenesis: Problematics for theory and research about development and socialization across the lifespan. *American Sociological Review* 50:659–76.

Felson, Marcus. 1998. *Crime and Everyday Life*, 2d edition. Thousand Oaks, CA: Pine Forge.

Felson, Marcus and Ronald V. Clarke. 1997. The ethics of situational crime prevention. Pp. 197–218 in *Rational Choice and Situational Crime Prevention*, edited by Graeme Newman, Ronald V. Clarke, and S. Giora Shoham. Brookfield, VT: Ashgate.

Felson, Marcus and Lawrence E. Cohen. 1980. Human ecology and crime: A routine activity approach. *Human Ecology* 8:389–405.

———. 1981. Modeling crime rate trends: A criminal opportunity perspective. *Journal of Research in Crime and Delinquency* 18:138–64.

Felson, Richard B., Allen E. Liska, Scott J. South, and Thomas L. McNulty. 1994. The subculture of violence and delinquency: Individual versus school context effects. *Social Forces* 73:155–73.

Fergusson, David M., L. John Harwood, and Daniel S. Nagin. 2000. Offending trajectories in a New Zealand birth cohort. *Criminology* 38:525–52.

Ferraro, Kenneth F. 1995. *Fear of Crime: Interpreting Victimization Risk*. Albany: State University of New York Press.

Ferraro, Kenneth F. and Randy L. LaGrange. 1987. The measurement of fear of crime. *Sociological Inquiry* 57:70–101.

Finkelhor, David and Nancy J. Asdigian. 1996. Risk factors for youth victimization: Beyond a lifestyle/routine activities approach. *Violence and Victims* 11:3–19.

Fisher, Bonnie and Jack L. Nasar. 1992. Fear of crime in relation to three exterior site features: Prospect, refuge, and escape. *Environment and Behavior* 24:35–65.

Fisher, Bonnie and Jack L. Nasar. 1995. Fear spots in relation to microlevel physical cues: Exploring the overlooked. *Journal of Research in Crime and Delinquency* 32:214–39.

Fisher, Bonnie S., John J. Sloan, Francis T. Cullen, and Chunmeng Lu. 1998. Crime in the ivory tower: The level and sources of student victimization. *Criminology* 36:671–710.

Fowler, Floyd J., Mary Ellen McCalla, and Thomas Mangione. 1979. *Reducing Residential Crime and Fear: The Hartford Neighborhood Crime Prevention Program*. Washington, DC: U.S. Government Printing Office.

Fowler, Floyd J. and Thomas Mangione. 1986. A three-pronged effort to reduce crime and fear of crime: The Hartford Experiment. Pp. 87–108 in *Community Crime Prevention*, edited by Dennis P. Rosenbaum. Newbury Park, CA: Sage.

Frisbie, Doug, Glenn M. Fishbine, Robert Hintz, Mitchell R. Joelson, and James B. Nutter. 1977. *Crime in Minneapolis: Proposals for Prevention*. Minneapolis, MN: Community Crime Prevention Project, Governor's Commission on Crime Prevention and Control.

Furstenberg, Frank F., Jr., Thomas D. Cook, Jacquelynne Eccles, and Jacqueline Eccles. 1999. *Managing to Make It: Urban Families Adolescent Success*. Chicago, IL: University of Chicago Press.

Gamson, William. 1992. *Talking Politics*. New York: Cambridge University Press.

Garofalo, James. 1981. The fear of crime: Causes and consequences. *Journal of Criminal Law and Criminology* 72:839–57.

Garofalo, James and John Laub. 1979. The fear of crime: Broadening our perspective. *Victimology* 3:242–53.

Geertz, Clifford. 1973. *The Interpretation of Cultures: Selected Essays*. New York: Basic.

Gibbs, Jack P. 1968. Crime, punishment, and deterrence. *Social Science Quarterly* 48:515–30.

———. 1972. *Sociological Theory Construction*. Hinsdale, IL: Dryden.

———. 1975. *Crime, Punishment, and Deterrence*. New York: Elsevier.

———. 1989. Three perennial issues in the sociology of deviance. Pp. 179–95 in *Theoretical Integration in the Study of Deviance and Crime: Problems and Prospects*, edited by Steven F. Messner, Marvin D. Krohn, and Allen E. Liska. Albany: State University of New York Press.

Glaser, Barney G. and Anselm L. Strauss. 1967. *The Discovery of Grounded Theory: Strategies for Qualitative Research*. Hawthorne, NY: Aldine de Gruyter.

Glueck, Sheldon and Eleanor Glueck. 1930. *500 Criminal Careers*. New York: Knopf.

———. 1934. *One Thousand Juvenile Delinquents*. Cambridge, MA: Harvard University Press.

———. 1950. *Unraveling Juvenile Delinquency*. Cambridge, MA: Harvard University Press.

———. 1964. *Ventures in Criminology*. Cambridge, MA: Harvard University Press.

———. 1967. *Predicting Delinquency and Crime*. Cambridge, MA: Harvard University Press.

———. 1968. *Delinquents and Nondelinquents in Perspective*. Cambridge, MA: Harvard University Press.

Goldstein, Harvey, Michael Healy, and Jon Rasbash. 1994. Multilevel models with applications to repeated measures data. *Statistics in Medicine* 13:1643–55.

Gottfredson, Denise. 1986. An empirical test of school-based environmental and individual interventions to reduce the risk of delinquent behavior. *Criminology* 24:705–31.

———. 1987. An evaluation of an organization development approach to reducing school disorder. *Evaluation Review* 11:739–63.

———. 2001. *Schools and Delinquency*. New York: Cambridge University Press.

Gottfredson, Denise C., Gary D. Gottfredson, and Lois G. Hybl. 1993. Managing adolescent behavior: A multi-year, multi-school study. *American Educational Research Journal* 30:179–215.

222   References

Gottfredson, Gary D. and Denice C. Gottfredson. 1985. *Victimization in Schools.* New York: Plenum.
Gottfredson, Michael and Travis Hirschi. 1986. The true value of lambda would appear to be zero: An essay on career criminals, criminal careers, selective incapacitation, cohort studies, and related topics. *Criminology* 24:213–34.
———. 1987. The methodological adequacy of longitudinal research on crime. *Criminology* 25:581–614.
———. 1988. Science, public policy, and the career paradigm. *Criminology* 26: 37–55.
———. 1990. *A General Theory of Crime.* Stanford, CA: Stanford University Press.
Greenberg, David F. 1985. Age, crime, and social explanation. *American Journal of Sociology* 91:1–21.
Greenberg, David F., Ronald C. Kessler, and Charles H. Logan. 1981. Aggregation bias in deterrence research: An empirical analysis. *Journal of Research in Crime and Delinquency* 18:128–37.
Greenberg, Stephanie W., William M. Rohe, and Jay R. Williams. 1982. *Safe and Secure Neighborhoods: Physical Characteristics and Informal Territorial Control in High and Low Crime Neighborhoods.* Washington, DC: National Institute of Justice.
Hackler, James C., Kwai-Yiu Ho, and Carol Urquart-Ross. 1974. The willingness to intervene: Differing community characteristics. *Social Problems* 21:328.
Hagan, John. 1997. Crime and capitalization: Toward a developmental theory of street crime. Pp. 287–308 in *Advances in Criminological Theory: Developmental Theories of Crime and Delinquency,* edited by Terence P. Thornberry. New Brunswick, NJ: Transaction.
Hagan, John and Alberto Palloni. 1988. Crimes as social events in the life-course: Reconceiving a criminological controversy. *Criminology* 26:87–100.
Harrell, Adele and Caterina P. Gouvis. 1994. *Community Decay and Crime.* Washington, DC: Urban Institute.
Hawkins, J. David., Michael W. Arthur, and Richard. F. Catalano. 1995. Preventing substance abuse. Pp. 343–428 in *Building a Safer Society: Strategic Approaches to Crime Prevention,* edited by Michael Tonry and David P. Farrington. Chicago, IL: University of Chicago Press.
Hawkins, J. David., Richard F. Catalano, Diane M. Morrison, Julie O'Donnell, Robert D. Abbott, and L. Edward Day. 1992. The Seattle Social Development Project: Effects of the first four years on protective factors and problem behaviors. Pp. 141–61 in *Preventing Antisocial Behavior: Interventions from Birth Through Adolescence,* edited by Joan McCord and Richard E. Tremblay. New York: Guilford:). Press.
Hawkins, J. David., Howard J. Doueck, and Denise M. Lischner. 1988. Changing teaching practices in mainstream classrooms to improve bonding and behavior of low achievers. *American Educational Research Journal* 25:31–50.
Hawkins, J. David., Elizabeth Von Cleve, and Richard F. Catalano. 1991. Reducing early childhood aggression: Results of a primary prevention program. *Journal of the American Academy of Child and Adolescent Psychiatry* 30:208–17.
Hawley, Amos H. 1950. *Human Ecology: A Theory of Community Structure.* New York: Ronald.

Hechter, Michael and Satoshi Kanazawa. 1997. Sociological rational choice theory. *Annual Review of Sociology* 23:191–214.

Heimer, Karen. 1995. Gender, race and the pathways in delinquency: An interactionist explanation. Pp. 140–73 in *Crime and Inequality,* edited by John Hagan and Ruth Peterson. Stanford, CA: Stanford University Press.

———. 1996. Gender, interaction, and delinquency: Testing a theory of differential social control. *Social Psychology Quarterly* 59:39–61.

Heimer, Karen and Ross L. Matsueda. 1994. Role-taking, role commitment, and delinquency: A theory of differential social control. *American Sociological Review* 59:365–90.

Heineke, John M. 1978. *Economic Models of Criminal Behavior.* Amsterdam: North-Holland.

Heinzelmann, Fred. 1981. Crime prevention and the physical environment. Pp. 87–101 in *Reactions to Crime,* edited by Dan A. Lewis. Beverly Hills, CA: Sage.

Heitgard, Janet L. and Robert J. Bursik, Jr. 1987. Extracommunity dynamics and the ecology of delinquency. *American Journal of Sociology* 92:775–87.

Hellman, Daryl A. and Susan Beaton. 1986. The pattern of violence in urban public schools: The influence of school and community. *Journal of Research in Crime and Delinquency* 23:102–27.

Hesseling, Rene B. P. 1994. Displacement: A review of the empirical literature. *Crime Prevention Studies* 3:197–230.

Hindelang, Michael, Michael Gottfredson, and James Garofalo. 1978. *Victims of Personal Crime.* Cambridge, MA: Ballinger.

Hirschi, Travis. 1969. *Causes of Delinquency.* Berkley: University of California Press.

———. 1979. Separate and unequal is better. *Journal of Research in Crime and Delinquency* 16:34–38.

———. 1989. Exploring alternatives to integrated theory. Pp. 37–50 in *Theoretical Integration in the Study of Deviance and Crime: Problems and Prospects,* edited by Steven F. Messner, Marvin D. Krohn, and Allen E. Liska. Albany: State University of New York Press.

Hirschi, Travis and Michael Gottfredson. 1983. Age and the explanation of crime. *American Journal of Sociology* 89:552–84.

———. 1995. Control theory and the life-course perspective. *Studies on Crime and Crime Prevention* 4:131–43.

Hogan, Dennis P. and Nan Marie Astone. 1986. The transition to adulthood. *Annual Review of Sociology* 12:109–30.

Homans, George C. 1967. *The Nature of Social Science.* New York: Free Press.

Hooks, Bell. 1984. *Feminist Theory: From Margin to Center.* Boston, MA: South End.

Horney, Julie D., Wayne D. Osgood, and Ineke H. Marshall. 1995. Criminal careers in the short-term: Intra-individual variability in crime and its relation to local life circumstances. *American Sociological Review* 60:655–73.

Horowitz, Ruth. 1987. Community tolerance of gang violence. *Social Problems* 34:437–50.

Hough, Mike. 1987. Offenders' choice of target: Findings from victim surveys. *Journal of Quantitative Criminology* 3:355–69.

Hox, Joop and Ita G. Kreft. 1994. Multilevel analysis methods. *Sociological Methods and Research* 22:283–99.

Huizinga, David, Finn-Aage Esbensen, and Delbert S. Elliot. 1988a. *The Denver Youth Survey: Project Overview—Denver Youth Survey, Project Report Number 2.* Boulder: University of Colorado Press.

———. 1988b. *The Denver Youth Survey: Social Ecology Analysis—Denver Youth Survey, Project Report Number 8.* Boulder: University of Colorado.

Hunter, Albert J. 1985. Private, parochial and public orders: The problem of crime and incivility in urban communities. Pp. 230–42 in *The Challenge of Social Control: Citizenship and Institution Building in Modern Societies,* edited by Gerald D. Suttles and Mayer N. Zald. Norwood, NJ: Ablex.

Inciardi, James A., Ruth Horowitz, and Anne E. Pottieger. 1993. *Street Kids, Street Drugs, Street Crime: An Examination of Drug Use and Serious Delinquency in Miami.* Belmont, CA: Wadsworth.

Iversen, Gudmund R. 1991. *Contextual Analysis.* New York: Sage.

Jacobs, Jane. 1961. *The Death and Life of the American City.* New York: Vintage.

———. 1968. Community on the city streets. Pp. 74–93 in *The Search for Community in Modern America,* edited by D. Baltzell. New York: Harper and Row.

Jang, Sung Joon. 1999. Age-varying effects of family, school, and peers on delinquency: A multilevel modeling test of interactional theory. *Criminology* 37:643–85.

Jang, Sung Joon and Carolyn A. Smith. 1997. A test of reciprocal causal relationships among parental supervision, affective ties, and delinquency. *Journal of Research in Crime and Delinquency* 34:307–36.

Jang, Sung Joon and Terence P. Thornberry. 1998. Self-esteem, delinquent peers, and delinquency: A test of the self-enhancement thesis. *American Sociological Review* 63:587–99.

Jargowsky, Paul A. and Mary Jo Bane. 1991. Ghetto poverty in the United States, 1970–1980. Pp. 253–73 in *The Urban Underclass,* edited by Christopher Jencks and Paul E. Peterson. Washington, DC: Brookings Institution.

Jarjoura, G. Roger. 1993. Does dropping out of school enhance delinquent involvement? Results from a large-scale national probability sample. *Criminology* 24:65–80.

Jencks, Christopher and Susan E. Mayer. 1990. The social consequences of growing up in a poor neighborhood, Pp. 111–86 in *Inner-City Poverty in the United States,* edited by Laurance E. Lynn, Jr. and Michael G. H. McGreary. Washington, DC: National Academy Press.

Jenkins, Patricia H. 1997. School delinquency and the school social bond. *Journal of Research in Crime and Delinquency* 34:337–67.

Jensen, Gary F. and David Brownfield. 1986. Gender, lifestyles, and victimization: Beyond routine activity theory. *Violence and Victims* 1:85–99.

Jessor, Richard. 1976. Predicting time of onset of marijuana use: A developmental study of high school youth. *Journal of Consulting and Clinical Psychology* 44:125–34.

Jessor, Richard and Shirley L. Jessor. 1977. *Problem Behavior and Psychosocial Development: A Longitudinal Study of Youth.* New York: Academic.

Johnson, Richard E. 1979. *Juvenile Delinquency and Its Origins.* Cambridge: Cambridge University Press.

Johnson, Richard E., Anastasios C. Marcos, and Stephen J. Bahr. 1987. The role of peers in the complex etiology of adolescent drug use. *Criminology* 25:323–39.

Johnson, Valerie and Robert J. Pandina. 1991. Effects of family environment on adolescent substance use, delinquency, and coping styles. *American Journal of Drug and Alcohol Abuse* 17:71–88.

Kagan, Jerome. 1980. Perspectives on continuity. Pp. 26–74 in *Constancy and Change in Human Development,* edited by Orville G. Brim, Jr., and Jerome Kagan. Cambridge, MA: Harvard University Press.

Kandel, Denise B., and Kenneth Andrews. 1987. Processes of adolescent socialization by parents and peers. *International Journal of the Addictions* 22:319–42.

Kandel, Denise B., Ronald C. Kessler, and Rebecca Z. Margulies. 1978. Antecedents of adolescent initiation into stages of drug use: A developmental analysis. *Journal of Youth and Adolescence* 7:13–40.

Kandel, Denise B., Ora Simcha-Fagan, and Mark Davies. 1986. Risk factors for delinquency and illicit drug use from adolescence to young adulthood. *Journal of Drug Issues* 16:67–90.

Kaplan, Abraham. 1964. *The Conduct of Inquiry.* San Francisco, CA: Chandler.

Kaplan, Howard B. 1980. *Deviant Behavior in Defense of the Self.* New York: Academic.

Kaplan, Howard B., Steven S. Martin, Robert J. Johnson, and Cynthia Robbins. 1986. Escalation of marijuana use: Application of a general theory of deviant behavior. *Journal of Health and Social Behavior* 27:44–61.

Kaplan, Howard B., Steven S. Martin, and Cynthia Robbins. 1984. Pathways to adolescent drug use: Self-derogation, weakening of social controls, and early substance use. *Journal of Health and Social Behavior* 25:270–89.

Kapsis, Robert E. 1978. Residential succession and delinquency: A test of Shaw and McKay's theory of cultural transmission. *Criminology* 15:459–86.

Kasarda, John D. and Morris Janowitz. 1974. Community attachment in mass society. *American Sociological Review* 39:328–39.

Kennedy, Leslie W. and David R. Forde. 1990. Routine activities and crime: An analysis of victimization in Canada. *Criminology* 28:137–51.

Kinch, John W. 1963. A formalized theory of the self-concept. *American Journal of Sociology* 68:481–86.

Klepper, Steven and Daniel Nagin. 1989. The deterrent effect of perceived certainty and severity of punishment revisited. *Criminology* 27:721–46.

Kornhauser, Ruth Rosner. 1978. *Social Sources of Delinquency: An Appraisal of Analytic Models.* Chicago, IL: University of Chicago Press.

Krivo, Lauren J. and Ruth D. Peterson. 1996. Extremely disadvantaged neighborhoods and urban crime. *Social Forces* 75:619–50.

Krohn, Marvin D. and James L. Massey. 1980. Social control and delinquent behavior: An examination of the elements of the social bond. *Sociological Quarterly* 21:529–43.

Kurtz, Ellen, Barbara Koons, and Ralph Taylor. 1998. Land use, physical deterioration, resident-based control, and calls for service on urban streetblocks. *Justice Quarterly* 15:21–149.

LaGrange, Randy L., Kenneth F. Ferraro, and Michael Supancic. 1992. Perceived risk and fear of crime: Role of social and physical incivilities. *Journal of Research in Crime and Delinquency* 29:311–34.

Laird, Nan M. and James H. Ware. 1982. Random effects models for longitudinal data. *Biometrics* 38:963–74.

Land, Kenneth C. 2001. Models and indicators. *Social Forces* 80:381–410.

226 References

————. 1992. Models of criminal careers: Some suggestions for moving beyond the current debate. *Criminology* 30:149–55.

Land, Kenneth C., Patricia L. McCall, and Lawrence E. Cohen. 1990. Structural covariates of homicide rates: Are there any invariances across time and social space? *American Journal of Sociology* 95:922–63.

Land, Kenneth C. and Daniel S. Nagin. 1996. Micro-models of criminal careers: A synthesis of the criminal careers and life course approaches via semiparametric mixed Poisson regression models, with empirical applications. *Journal of Quantitative Criminology* 12:163–91.

Larzelere, Robert E. and Gerald E. Patterson. 1990. Parental management: Mediator of the effect of socioeconomic status on early delinquency. *Criminology* 28:301–23.

Laub, John H. 1983. Urbanism, race, and crime. *Journal of Research in Crime and Delinquency* 20:183–98.

Laub, John H., Daniel S. Nagin, and Robert J. Sampson. 1998. Good marriages and trajectories of change in criminal offending. *American Sociological Review* 63:225–38.

Laub, John H. and Robert J. Sampson. 1988. Unraveling families and delinquency: A reanalysis of the Gluecks' data. *Criminology* 26:355–80.

————. 1991. The Sutherland-Glueck debate: On the sociology of criminological knowledge. *American Journal of Sociology* 96:1402–40.

————. 1993. Turning points in the life course: Why change matters to the study of crime. *Criminology* 31:301–25.

————. 1995. Crime and context in the lives of 1,000 Boston men, circa 1925–1955. Pp. 119–39 in *Current Perspectives on Aging and Life Cycle*, edited by Zena Smith Blau and John Hagan. Greenwich, CT: JAI.

————. 2001. Understanding desistance from crime. *Crime and Justice: An Annual Review of Research* 28:1–69.

Lauritsen, Janet. 1998. The age-crime debate: Assessing the limits of longitudinal self-report data. *Social Forces* 77:127–55.

Lauritsen, Janet L., Robert J. Sampson, and John H. Laub. 1991. The link between offending and victimization among adolescents. *Criminology* 29:265–91.

La Vigne, Nancy G. 1997. Visibility and vigilance: Metro's situational approach to preventing subway crime. *National Institute of Justice Research in Brief, NCJ 166372*. Washington, DC: U.S. Department of Justice.

LeBlanc, Marc. 1997. A generic control theory of the criminal phenomenon: The structural and dynamic statements of an integrative multilayered control theory. Pp. 215–86 in *Advances in Criminological Theory: Developmental Theories of Crime and Delinquency*, edited by Terence P. Thornberry. New Brunswick, NJ: Transaction.

Lee, Min Sik and Jeffery T. Ulmer. 2000. Fear of crime among Korean Americans in Chicago communities. *Criminology* 38:1173–1206.

Lefkowitz, Bernard. 1998. *Our Guys*. New York: Vintage.

Lewis, Dan A. and Greta Salem. 1986. *Fear of Crime: Incivility and the Production of a Social Problem*. New Brunswick, NJ: Transaction.

Ley, David and Roman Cybriwsky. 1974. The spatial ecology of stripped cars. *Environment and Behavior* 6:53–68.

Liska, Allen E. 1990. The significance of aggregate dependent variables and contextual independent variables for linking macro and micro theories. *Social Psychological Quarterly* 53:292–301.

Liska, Allen E. and Baccaglini, William. 1990. Feeling safe by comparison: Crime in the newspapers. *Social Problems* 37:360–74.

Liska, Allen E., Marvin D. Krohn, and Steven F. Messner. 1989. Strategies and requisites for theoretical integration in the study of crime, law and deviance. Pp. 1–19 in *Theoretical Integration in the Study of Deviance and Crime: Problems and Prospects,* edited by Steven F. Messner, Marvin D. Krohn, and Allen E. Liska. Albany: State University of New York Press.

Liska, Allen E., Joseph J. Lawrence, and Andrew Sanchirico. 1982. Fear of crime as a social fact. *Social Forces* 60:760–70.

Liska, Allen E., Andrew Sanchirico, and Mark D. Reed. 1988. Fear of crime and constrained behavior: Specifying and estimating a reciprocal effects model. *Social Forces* 66:827–37.

Liska, Allen E. and Barbara D. Warner. 1991. Functions of crime: A paradoxical process. *American Journal of Sociology* 96:1441–63.

Little, Daniel. 1991. *Varieties of Social Explanation: An Introduction to the Philosophy of Social Science* . Boulder, CO: Westview.

Loeber, Rolf. 1982. The stability of antisocial child behavior: A review. *Child Development* 53:1431–46.

———. 1990. Development and risk factors of juvenile antisocial behavior and delinquency. *Clinical Psychology Review* 10:1–41.

Loeber, Rolf and Dale Hay. 1997. Key issues in the development of aggression and violence from childhood to early adulthood. *Annual Review of Psychology* 48:371–410.

Loeber, Rolf and Marc LeBlanc. 1990. Toward a developmental criminology. *Crime and Justice: An Annual Review of Research* 12:375–437.

———. 1998. Developmental Criminology Updated. *Crime and Justice: An Annual Review of Research* 23:115–98.

Loeber, Rolf and Magda S. Stouthammer-Loeber. 1986. Family factors as correlates and predictors of juvenile conduct problems and delinquency. *Crime and Justice: An Annual Review of Research* 7:29–149.

———. 1998. Development of juvenile aggression and violence: Some common misconceptions and controversies. *American Psychologist* 53:242–59.

Loeber, Rolf, Magda S. Stouthammer-Loeber, Welmoet Van Kammen, and David P. Farrington. 1991. Initiation, escalation, and desistance in juvenile offending and their correlates. *Journal of Criminal Law and Criminology* 13:231–66.

Loeber, Rolf, Phen Wung, Kate Keenan, Bruce Giroux, Magda S. Stouthammer-Loeber, Welmoet Van Kammen, and Barbara Maughan. 1993. Developmental Pathways in disruptive behavior. *Development and Psychopathology* 5:12–48.

Lofland, John. 1969. *Deviance and Identity.* Englewood Cliffs, NJ: Prentice-Hall.

Loftin, Colin and David McDowall. 1982. The police, crime, and economic theory: An assessment. *American Sociological Review* 47:393–401.

Lynam, Donald R. 1996. Early identification of chronic offenders: Who is the fledgling psychopath? *Psychological Bulletin* 120:209–34.

Lynch, James P. and David Cantor. 1992. Ecological and behavioral influences on property victimization at home: Implications for opportunity theory. *Journal of Research in Crime and Delinquency* 26:378–400.

Lyotard, Jean-Francois. 1984. *The Postmodern Condition*. Minneapolis: University of Minnesota Press.

Macoby, Eleanor E., Joseph P. Johnson, and Russell M. Church. 1958. Community integration and the social control of juvenile delinquency. *Journal of Social Issues* 14:38–51.

Malvin, Janet J., Joel M. Moskowitz, Gary A Schaeffer, and Eric Schaps. 1984. Teacher training in affective education for the primary prevention of adolescent drug abuse. *American Journal of Drug and Alcohol Abuse* 10:223–35.

Marcos, Anastasios C., Stephen J. Bahr, and Richard E. Johnson. 1986. Test of bonding/association theory of adolescent drug use. *Social Forces* 65:135–61.

Massey, Douglas S. and Nancy A. Denton. 1993. *American Apartheid: Segregation and the Making of the Underclass*. Cambridge, MA: Harvard University Press.

Massey, James L. and Marvin D. Krohn. 1986. A longitudinal examination of an integrated social process model of deviant behavior. *Social Forces* 65:106–34.

Massey, James L., Marvin D. Krohn, and Lisa M. Bonati. 1989. Property crime and the routine activities of individuals. *Journal of Research in Crime and Delinquency* 26:378–400.

Matsueda, Ross L. 1992. Reflected appraisals, parental labeling, and delinquency: Specifying a symbolic interactionist theory. *American Journal of Sociology* 97:1577–1611.

Matsueda, Ross L. and Karen Heimer. 1997. A symbolic interactionist theory of role-transitions, role-commitments, and delinquency. Pp. 163–214 in *Advances in Criminological Theory: Developmental Theories of Crime and Delinquency*, edited by Terence P. Thornberry. New Brunswick, NJ: Transaction.

Mawby, Russel I. 1977. Defensible space: A theoretical and empirical appraisal. *Urban Studies* 14:169–79.

Maxfield, Michael G. 1987a. Lifestyle and routine activity theories of crime: Empirical studies of victimization, delinquency, and offender decision-making. *Journal of Quantitative Criminology* 3:275–82.

Maxfield, Michael G. 1987b. Household composition, routine activity, and victimization: A comparative analysis. *Journal of Quantitative Criminology* 3:301–20.

Mayhew, Patricia, Ronald V. Clarke, John N. Burrows, John M. Hough, and Stuart W. C. Winchester. 1979. *Crime in Public View*. London: Her Majesty's Stationery Office.

McCord, Joan. 1979. Some child-rearing antecedents of criminal behavior in adult men. *Journal of Personality and Social Psychology* 37:1477–86.

———. 1991. Family relationships, juvenile delinquency, and adult criminality. *Criminology* 29:397–417.

———. 1995. Relationship between alcoholism and crime over the life-course. Pp. 129–41 in *Drugs, Crime, and Other Deviant Adaptations*, edited by Howard B. Kaplan. New York: Plenum.

McGahey, Richard M. 1986. Economic conditions, neighborhood organization, and urban crime. Pp. 231–70 in *Communities and Crime*, edited by Albert J. Reiss, Jr., and Michael Tonry. Chicago, IL: University of Chicago Press.

---. 1994. *Crime and Its Social Context*. Albany: State University of New York Press.

Mead, George Herbert. 1934. *Mind, Self, and Society*. Chicago, IL: University of Chicago Press.

Merry, Sally E. 1981. Defensible space undefended: Social factors in crime control through environmental design. *Urban Affairs Quarterly* 16:397–422.

Messner, Steven F. and Judith R. Blau. 1987. Routine leisure activities and rates of crime: A macro-level analysis. *Social Forces* 64:1035–52.

Messner, Steven F., Marvin D. Krohn, and Allen E. Liska (eds.). 1989. *Theoretical Integration in the Study of Deviance and Crime: Problems and Prospects*. Albany, NY: State University of New York Press.

Messner, Steven F. and Marvin D. Krohn. 1990. Class compliance structures and delinquency: Assessing integrated structural-Marxist theory. *American Journal of Sociology* 96:300–28.

Messner, Steven F. and Reid M. Golden. 1992. Racial inequality and racially disaggregated homicide rates: An assessment of alternative theoretical explanations. *Criminology* 30:421–45.

Messner, Steven F. and Kenneth Tardiff. 1985. The social ecology of urban homicide: An application of the "routine activities" approach. *Criminology* 23:241–67.

Miethe, Terance D. 1992. *Testing theories of criminality and victimization in Seattle, 1960–1990*. Ann Arbor, MI: Inter-University Consortium for Political and Social Research.

Miethe, Terance D. and David McDowall. 1993. Contextual Effects in models of criminal victimization. *Social Forces* 71:741–59.

Miethe, Terance D. and Robert F. Meier. 1990. Criminal opportunity and victimization rates: A structural-choice theory of criminal victimization. *Journal of Research in Crime and Delinquency* 27:243–66.

---. 1994. *Crime and Its Social Context: Toward an Integrated Theory of Offenders, Victims, and Situations*. Albany: State University of New York Press.

Moffitt, Terrie E. 1990. Juvenile delinquency and attention-deficit disorder: Developmental trajectories from ages 3 to 15. *Child Development* 61:893–910.

---. 1993. Life-course persistent and adolescence-limited antisocial behavior: A developmental taxonomy. *Psychological Review* 100:674–701.

---. 1997a. Adolescence-limited and life-course persistent offending: A complementary pair of developmental theories. Pp. 11–54 in *Advances in Criminological Theory: Developmental Theories of Crime and Delinquency*, edited by Terence P. Thornberry. New Brunswick, NJ: Transaction.

---. 1997b. Neuropsychology, antisocial behavior, and neighborhood context. Pp. 116–70 in *Violence and Childhood in the Inner City*, edited by Joan McCord. Cambridge: Cambridge University Press.

Moffitt, Terrie E., Avshalom Caspi, Nigel Dickson, Phil A. Silva, and Warren Stanton. 1996. Childhood-onset versus adolescent-onset of antisocial problems in males: Natural history from ages 3 to 18 years. *Development and Psychopathology* 8:399–424.

Moffitt, Terrie E. and Phil A. Silva. 1988. Self-reported delinquency: Results from an instrument for New Zealand. *Australian and New Zealand Journal of Criminology* 21:227–40.

Morenoff, Jeffrey D. and Robert J. Sampson. 1997. Violent crime and the spatial dynamics of neighborhood transition: Chicago, 1970–1990. *Social Forces* 76: 31–65.

Morgan, David L. 1988. *Focus Groups as Qualitative Research*. Newbury Park, CA: Sage.

Murray, Charles. 1995. The physical environment. Pp. 349–62 in *Crime*, edited by James Q. Wilson and Joan Petersilia. San Francisco, CA: ICS.

Mustaine, Elizabeth Ehnhardt and Richard Tewksbury. 1998. Predicting risks of larceny theft victimization: A routine activity analysis using refined lifestyle measures. *Criminology* 36:829–57.

Nagel, Ernest. 1961. *The Structure of Science*. New York: Harcourt Brace World.

Nagin, Daniel. 1978. General deterrence: A review of the empirical evidence. Pp. 95–139 in *Deterrence and Incapacitation: Estimating the Effects of Criminal Sanctions on Crime Rates*. Washington, DC: National Academy Press.

Nagin, Daniel S. and David P. Farrington. 1992a. The stability of criminal potential from childhood to adulthood. *Criminology* 30:235–60.

———. 1992b. The onset and persistence of offending. *Criminology* 30:501–23.

Nagin, Daniel S., David P. Farrington and Terrie E. Moffitt. 1995. Life-course trajectories of different types of offenders. *Criminology* 33:111–39.

Nagin, Daniel S. and Kenneth C. Land. 1993. Age, criminal careers, and population heterogeneity: Specification and estimation of a nonparametric mixed Poisson model. *Criminology* 31:327–62.

Nagin, Daniel S. and Raymond Paternoster. 1991. On the relationship of past to future participation in delinquency. *Criminology* 29:163–89.

Nagin, Daniel S. and Richard Tremblay. 1999. Trajectories of boys' physical aggression, opposition, and hyperactivity on the path to physically violent and nonviolent delinquency. *Child Development* 70:1181–96.

Needle, Richard H., Susan S. Su, and William J. Doherty. 1990. Divorce, remarriage, and adolescent substance use: A prospective longitudinal study. *Journal of Marriage and Family* 52:157–69.

Neuendorf, Kimberly A. 2002. *The Content Analysis Guidebook*. Thousand Oaks, CA: Sage.

Newman, Oscar. 1973. *Defensible Space: Crime Prevention through Urban Design*. New York: Macmillan.

Newman, Oscar. 1995. Defensible space: A new physical planning tool for urban revitalization. *Journal of the American Planning Association* 61:149–55.

———. 1996. *Creating Defensible Space*. Washington, DC: U.S. Department of Housing and Urban Development.

Newman, Oscar. and Karen A. Franck. 1982. The effects of building size on personal crime and fear of crime. *Population and Environment* 4:203–20.

Nielson, Amy. 1999. Testing Sampson and Laub's life-course theory: Age, race/ethnicity, and drunkenness. *Deviant Behavior* 20:129–51.

Norem-Hebeisen, Ardyth, David W. Johnson, Douglas Anderson, and Roger Johnson. 1984. Predictors and concomitants of changes in drug use patterns among teenagers. *Journal of Social Psychology* 124:43–50.

O'Donnell, Julie, J. David Hawkins, Richard F. Catalano, Robert D. Abbott, and L. Edward Day. 1995. Preventing school failure, drug use, and delinquency among low-income children: Long-term intervention in elementary schools. *American Journal of Orthopsychiatry* 65:87–100.

O'Rand, Angela M. 1990. Stratification and the life course in sociology. Pp. 130–48 in *Handbook of Aging and the Social Sciences,* edited by Robert H. Binstock and Linda K. George. New York: Academic.

Opp, Karl-Dieter. 1997. "Limited Rationality" and Crime. Pp. 47–63 in *Rational Choice and Situational Crime Prevention,* edited by Graeme Newman, Ronald V. Clarke, and S. Giora Shoham. Brookfield, VT: Ashgate.

Parker, Karen F. and Matthew V. Pruitt. 2000. How the West was one: Explaining the similarities in race-specific homicide rates in the West and South. *Social Forces* 78:1483–1508.

Paternoster, Raymond and Robert Brame. 1997. Multiple routes to delinquency? A test of developmental and general theories of crime. *Criminology* 35:49–84.

Paternoster, Raymond, Charles Dean, Alex Piquero, Paul Mazerolle, and Robert Brame. 1997. Continuity and change in offending careers. *Journal of Quantitative Criminology* 12:231–66.

Paternoster, Raymond, Linda E. Saltzman, Theodore G. Chiricos, and Gordon P. Waldo. 1983. Perceived risk and social control: Do sanctions really deter? *Law and Society Review* 17:457–79.

Patillo, Mary E. 1998. Sweet mothers and gangbangers: Managing crime in a black middle-class neighborhood. *Social Forces* 76:747–74.

Patterson, E. Britt. 1991. Poverty, income inequality, and community crime rates. *Criminology* 29:755–76.

Patterson, Gerald R., Barbara DeBaryshe, and Elizabeth Ramsey. 1989. A developmental perspective on antisocial behavior. *American Psychologist* 44:329–35.

Patterson, Gerald R. and Dishion, T. J. 1985. Contributions of families and peers to delinquency. *Criminology* 23:63–79.

Patterson, Gerald R., John B. Reid, and Thomas J. Dishion. 1995. *Antisocial Boys.* Eugene, OR: Castilia.

Pearl, Judea. 2000. *Causality: Models, Reasoning, and Inference.* New York: Cambridge University Press.

Perkins, Douglas D. and Ralph B. Taylor. 1996. Ecological assessments of community disorder: Their relationships to fear of crime and theoretical implications. *American Journal of Community Psychology* 24:63–107.

Petee, Thomas, Gregory S. Kowalski, and Trudie F. Milner. 1991. Ecological context and crime. Paper presented at the 43rd Annual Meeting of the American Society of Criminology, San Francisco, 1991.

Petersilia, Joan. 1980. Criminal career research: A review of recent evidence. *Crime and Justice: An Annual Review of Research* 2:321–79.

Piquero, Alex R., Alfred Blumstein, Robert Brame, Rudy Haapanen, Edward Mulvey, and Daniel S. Nagin. 2001. Assessing the impact of exposure time and incapacitation on longitudinal trajectories of criminal offending. *Journal of Adolescent Research* 16:54–74.

Piquero, Alex R., Robert Brame, Paul Mazerolle, and Rudy Haapanen. 2002. Crime in emerging adulthood. *Criminology* 40:137–69.

Piquero, Alex R. and Paul Mazerolle. 2001. Introduction. Pp. viii–xx in *Life-Course Criminology*, edited by Alex R. Piquero and Paul Mazerolle. Belmont, CA: Wadsworth.

Polakowski, Michael. 1994. Linking self- and social control with deviance: Illuminating the structure underlying a general theory of crime and its relation to deviant activity. *Journal of Quantitative Criminology* 10:41–78.

Popper, Karl. 1965. *Logic of Scientific Discovery*. New York: Harper and Row.

Poyner, Barry. 1991. Situational prevention in two car parks. *Security Journal* 2:96–101.

Pyle, David J. 1983. *The Economics of Crime and Law Enforcement*. London: Macmillan.

Rand, Alicia. 1987. Transitional life events and desistance from delinquency and crime. Pp. 134–62 in *From Boy to Man: From Delinquency to Crime*, edited by Marvin Wolfgang, Terence P. Thornberry, and Robert M. Figlio. Chicago: University of Chicago Press.

Rankin, Joseph H., and Roger Kern. 1994. Parental attachment and delinquency. *Criminology* 32:495–515.

Rasbash, Jon and Harvey Goldstein. 1994. Efficient analysis of mixed hierarchical and cross-classified random structures using multilevel model. *Journal of Educational and Behavioral Statistics* 19:337–50.

Rasbash, Jon and Geof Woodhouse. 1995. *Mln Command Reference*. London: Institute of Education, University of London.

Raudenbush, Stephen W. and Robert J. Sampson. 1999. Ecometrics: Toward a science of assessing ecological setting, with application to the systematic social observation of neighborhoods. *Sociological Methodology* 29:1–41.

Reiss, Albert J., Jr. 1971. Systematic observation of natural social phenomena. *Sociological Methodology* 1:3–33.

Riley, Matilda White. 1987. On the significance of age in sociology. *American Sociological Review* 52:1–14.

Robinson, Matthew B. and Christine E. Robinson. 1997. Environmental characteristics associated with residential burglaries of student apartment complexes. *Environment and Behavior* 29:657–75.

Roncek, Dennis. 1981. Dangerous places: Crime and residential environment. *Social Forces* 60:74–96.

Roncek, Dennis and Ralph Bell. 1981. Bars, blocks and crimes. *Journal of Environmental Systems* 11:35–47.

Roncek, Dennis and Donald Faggiani. 1985. High schools and crime: A replication. *Sociological Quarterly* 26:491–505.

Roncek, Dennis and Antoinette LoBosco. 1983. The effect of high schools on crime in their neighborhood. *Social Science Quarterly* 64:598–613.

Roncek, Dennis and Pamela Maier. 1991. Bars, blocks, and crimes revisited: Linking the theory of routine activities to the empiricism of "hot spots." *Criminology* 29:725–54.

Roncek, Dennis and Mitchell A. Pravatiner. 1989. Additional evidence that taverns enhance nearby crime. *Sociology and Social Research* 73:185–88.

Rose, Dina R. and Todd R. Clear. 1998. Incarceration, social capital, and crime: Implications for social disorganization theory. *Criminology* 36:411–79.

Saltzman, Linda E., Raymond Paternoster, Gordon P. Waldo, and Theodore G.

Chiricos. 1982. Deterrent and experiential effects: The problem of causal order in perceptual deterrence research. *Journal of Research in Crime and Delinquency* 19:172–89.

Sampson, Robert J. 1983. Structural density and criminal victimization. *Criminology* 21:276–93.

———. 1985. Neighborhood and crime: The structural determinants of personal victimization. *Journal of Research in Crime and Delinquency* 22:7–40.

———. 1987. Communities and crime. Pp. 91–114 in *Positive Criminology*, edited by Michael R. Gottfredson and Travis Hirschi. Newbury Park, CA: Sage.

———. 1988. Local friendship ties and community attachment in mass society: A multilevel systemic model. *American Sociological Review* 53:766–79.

———. 1991. Linking the micro- and macrolevel dimensions of community social organization. *Social Forces* 70:43–64.

———. 1992. Family management and child development: Insights from social disorganization theory. Pp. 63–93 in *Facts, Frameworks, and Forecasts: Advances in Criminological Theory*, Volume 3, edited by Joan McCord. New Brunswick, NJ: Transaction.

———. 1997. The embeddedness of child and adolescent development: A community-level perspective on urban violence. Pp. 31–77 in *Violence and Childhood in the Inner City*, edited by Joan McCord. New York: Cambridge University Press.

Sampson, Robert J. and Thomas C. Castellano. 1982. Economic inequality and personal victimisation. *British Journal of Criminology* 22:363–85.

Sampson, Robert. J. and W. Byron Groves. 1989. Community structure and crime: Testing social disorganization theory. *American Journal of Sociology* 94:774–802.

Sampson, Robert J. and John H. Laub. 1990. Crime and deviance over the life-course: The salience of adult social bonds. *American Sociological Review* 55:609–27.

———. 1993. *Crime in the Making: Pathways and Turning Points through Life*. Cambridge, MA: Harvard University Press.

———. 1995. Understanding variability in lives through time: Contributions of life-course criminology. *Studies on Crime and Crime Prevention* 4:143–58.

———. 1996. Socioeconomic achievement in the life course of disadvantaged men: Military service as a turning point, circa 1940–1965. *American Sociological Review* 61:347–67.

———. 1997. A life-course theory of cumulative disadvantage and the stability of delinquency. Pp. 133–62 in *Advances in Criminological Theory: Developmental Theories of Crime and Delinquency*, edited by Terence P. Thornberry. New Brunswick, NJ: Transaction.

———. 1998. Integrating quantitative and qualitative data. Pp. 213–30 in *Methods of Life Course Research: Qualitative and Quantitative Approaches*, edited by Janet Z. Giele and Glen H. Elder, Jr. Thousand Oaks, CA: Sage.

Sampson, Robert J. and Janet L. Lauritsen. 1990. Deviant lifestyles, proximity to crime, and the offender-victim link in personal violence. *Journal of Research in Crime and Delinquency* 27:110–39.

Sampson, Robert J. and Stephen W. Raudenbush. 1999. Systematic social observation of public spaces: A new look at disorder in urban neighborhoods. *American Journal of Sociology* 105: 603–51.

Sampson, Robert J., Stephen W. Raudenbush, and Felton Earls. 1997. Neighborhoods and violent crime: A multilevel study of collective efficacy. *Science* 277:918–24.

Sampson, Robert J. and John D. Wooldredge. 1987. Linking the micro- and macrolevel dimensions of lifestyle-routine activity and opportunity models of predatory victimization. *Journal of Quantitative Criminology* 3:371–93.

Sasson, Theodore. 1995. *Crime Talk: How Citizens Construct a Social Problem.* Hawthorne, NY: Aldine de Gruyter.

Schneider, Mark, Melissa Marschall, Christine Roch, and Paul Teske. 1999. Heuristics, low information rationality, and choosing public goods: Broken windows as shortcuts to information about school performance. *Urban Affairs Review* 34:729–41.

Schroyer, Trent. 1970. Toward a critical theory of advanced industrial society. *Recent Sociology* 2:210–34.

Schuerman, Leo and Solomon Kobrin. 1986. Community careers in crime. Pp. 67–100 in *Communities and Crime,* edited by Albert J. Reiss, Jr., and Michael Tonry. Chicago, IL: University of Chicago Press.

Seidman, Steven. 1994. *Contested Knowledge: Social Theory in the Postmodern Age.* Oxford: Blackwell.

Shannon, Lyle W. 1988. *Criminal Career Continuity: Its Social Context.* New York: Human Sciences.

Shaw, Clifford R. and Henry D. McKay. 1942. *Juvenile Delinquency and Urban Areas.* Chicago, IL: University of Chicago Press.

Sherman, Lawrence, Patrick R. Gartin and Michael E. Buerger. 1989. Hot spots and predatory crime: Routine activities and the criminology of place. *Criminology* 27:27–56.

Shibutani, Tamotsu. 1955. Reference groups as perspectives. *American Journal of Sociology* 60:562–69.

Shihadeh, Edward S. and Nicole Flynn. 1996. Segregation and crime: The effect of black social isolation on the rates of black urban violence. *Social Forces* 74:1325–52.

Shihadeh, Edward S. and Graham C. Ousey. 1996. Metropolitan expansion and black social dislocation: The link between suburbanization and center-city crime. *Social Forces* 75:649–66.

———. 1998. Industrial restructuring and violence: The link between entry-level jobs, economic deprivation, and black and white homicide. *Social Forces* 77: 185–206.

Shover, Neal and Carol Y. Thompson. 1992. Age, differential expectations, and crime desistance. *Criminology* 30:89–104.

Simcha-Fagan, Ora, Joseph C. Gersten, and Thomas S. Langer. 1986. Early precursors and concurrent correlates of patterns of illicit drug use in adolescents. *Journal of Drug Issues* 16:7–28.

Simcha-Fagan, Ora and Joseph E. Schwartz. 1986. Neighborhood and delinquency: An assessment of contextual effects. *Criminology* 24:667–703.

Simons, Ronald L., Rand D. Conger, and Leslie B. Whitbeck. 1988. A multistage social learning model of the influences of family and peers upon adolescent substance abuse. *Journal of Drug Issues.* 3:293–315.

Simons, Ronald L., Christine Johnson, Rand D. Conger, and Glen Elder, Jr. 1998. A test of latent trait versus life-course perspectives on the stability of adolescent antisocial behavior. *Criminology* 36:217–43.

Simons, Ronald L., Chyi-In Wu, Rand Conger, and Frederick Lorenz. 1994. Two routes to delinquency: Differences between early and late starters in the impact of parenting and deviant peers. *Criminology* 32:163–96.

Singer, Simon I. 1981. Homogeneous victim-offender populations: A review and some research implications. *Journal of Criminal Law and Criminology* 72:779–88.

Sjoberg, Gideon and Roger Nett. 1997. *A Methodology for Social Research*. Prospect Heights, IL: Waveland.

Skinner, B. F. 1953. *Science and Human Behavior*. New York: Macmillan.

Skogan, Wesley G. 1990. *Disorder and Decline*. New York: Free Press.

Skogan, Wesley G. and Michael G. Maxfield. 1981. *Coping with Crime: Individual and Neighborhood Reactions*. Beverly Hills, CA: Sage.

Smith, Douglas A. and Robert Brame. 1994. On the initiation and continuation of delinquency. *Criminology* 32:607–29.

Smith, Douglas A. and G. Roger Jarjoura. 1988. Social structure and criminal victimization. *Journal of Research in Crime and Delinquency* 25:27–52.

———. 1989. Household characteristics, neighborhood composition and victimization risk. *Social Forces* 68:621–40.

Smith, Douglas A. and Raymond Paternoster. 1990. Formal processing and future delinquency: Deviance amplification as selection artifact. *Law and Society Review* 24:1109–31.

Smith, Mary S. 1996. Crime prevention through environmental design in parking facilities. *National Institute of Justice Research in Brief, NCJ 157310*. Washington, DC: U.S. Department of Justice.

Smith, William R., Sharon Glave Frazee, and Elizabeth L. Davison. 2000. Furthering the integration of routine activity and social disorganization theories: Small units of analysis and the study of street robbery as a diffusion process. *Criminology* 38:489–523.

Speer, Paul W., D. M. Gorman, Erich W. Labouvie, and Mark Ontkush. 1998. Violent crime and alcohol availability: Relationships in an urban community. *Journal of Public Health Policy* 19:303–38.

Stafford, Mark C. and Omer R. Galle. 1984. Victimization rates, exposure to risk, and fear of crime. *Criminology* 22:173–85.

Stark, Rodney. 1987. Deviant places: A theory of the ecology of crime. *Criminology* 25:893–909.

Steffensmeier, Darrell J., Emilie Anderson Allen, and Cathy Streifel. 1989. Modernization and female crime: A cross-national test of alternative explanations. *Social Forces* 68:262–83.

Steffensmeier, Darrell J., Emilie Anderson Allen, Miles D. Harer, and Cathy Streifel. 1989. Age and the distribution of crime. *American Journal of Sociology* 94:803–31.

Steffensmeier, Darrell J. and Cathy Streifel. 1991. Age, gender, and crime across three historical periods: 1935, 1960, 1985. *Social Forces* 69:869–94.

Stinchcombe, Arthur L. 1968. *Constructing Social Theories*. New York: Harcourt, Brace, World.

Stollard, Paul (Ed.). 1991. *Crime Prevention through Housing Design: Designing to Deter*. London: E. & F.N. Spons.

Stryker, Sheldon. 1980. *Symbolic Interactionism*. Menlo Park, CA: Benjamin/Cummings.

Sucoff, Clea A. and Dawn M. Upchurch. 1998. Neighborhood context and the risk of childbearing among metropolitan-area black adolescents. *American Sociological Review* 63:571–85.

Suttles, Gerald D. 1968. *The Social Order of the Slum: Ethnicity and Territory in the Inner City*. Chicago, IL: University of Chicago Press.

Taylor, Ralph B. 1987. Toward an environmental psychology of disorder. Pp. 951–86 in *Handbook of Environmental Psychology*, edited by D. Stokols and I. Altman. New York: Wiley.

———. 1988. *Human Territorial Functioning*. Cambridge, MA: Cambridge University Press.

———. 2001. *Breaking Away from Broken Windows: Baltimore Neighborhoods and the Nationwide Fight against Crime, Grime, Fear, and Decline*. Boulder, CO: Westview.

Taylor, Ralph B. and Sidney Brower. 1985. Home and near-home territories. Pp. 83–122 in *Human Behavior and Environment: Current Theory and Research: Home Environments*, Volume 8, edited by I. Altman and C. Werner. New York: Plenum.

Taylor, Ralph B. and Jeanette Covington. 1988. Neighborhood changes in ecology and violence. *Criminology* 26:553–89.

———. 1993. Community structural change and fear of crime. *Social Problems* 40:374–95.

Taylor, Ralph B. and Stephen D. Gottfredson. 1986. Environmental design, crime, and prevention: An examination of community dynamics. Pp. 387–416 in *Communities and Crime*, edited by Albert J. Reiss, Jr., and Michael Tonry. Chicago, IL: University of Chicago Press.

Taylor, Ralph B., Stephen D. Gottfredson, and Sidney Brower. 1981. Territorial cognitions and social climate in urban neighborhoods. *Basic and Applied Social Psychology* 2:289–303.

Taylor, Ralph B., Stephen D. Gottfredson, and Sidney Brower. 1984. Block crime and fear: Local social ties and territorial functioning. *Journal of Research in Crime and Delinquency* 21:303–31.

Taylor, Ralph B. and Margaret Hale. 1986. Testing alternative models of fear of crime. *Journal of Criminal Law and Criminology* 77:151–89.

Taylor, Ralph B. and Adele V. Harrell. 1996. *Physical Environment and Crime: A Final Summary Report Presented to the National Institute of Justice*. Washington, DC: U.S. Department of Justice.

Taylor, Ralph B., Barbara A. Koons, Ellen M. Kurtz, Jack R. Greene, and Douglas D. Perkins. 1995. Street blocks with more nonresidential land use have more physical deterioration: Evidence from Baltimore and Philadelphia. *Urban Affairs Review* 31:120–36.

Taylor, Ralph B., Sally Ann Shumaker, and Stephen D. Gottfredson. 1985. Neighborhood-level link between physical features and local sentiments: Deterioration, fear of crime, and confidence. *Journal of Architectural Planning and Research* 2:261–75.

Thompson, Carol Y. and Bonnie Fisher. 1996. Predicting household victimization utilizing a multi-level routine activity approach. *Journal of Crime and Justice* 19:49–66.

Thornberry, Terence. 1987. Toward an interactional theory of delinquency. *Criminology* 25:863–91.

———. 1989. Reflections on the advantages and disadvantages of theoretical integration. Pp. 51–60 in *Theoretical Integration in the Study of Deviance and Crime: Problems and Prospects,* edited by Steven F. Mesner, Marvin D. Krohn, and Allen E. Liska. Albany: State University of New York Press.

———. 1997. Introduction: Some advantages of developmental and life-course perspectives for the study of crime and delinquency. Pp. 1–10 in *Advances in Criminological Theory: Developmental Theories of Crime and Delinquency,* edited by Terence P. Thornberry. New Brunswick, NJ: Transaction.

Thornberry, Terence P., Alan J. Lizotte, Marvin D. Krohn, Margaret Farnworth, and Sung Joon Jang. 1991. Testing interactional theory: An examination of reciprocal causal relationships among family, school, and delinquency. *Journal of Criminal Law and Criminology* 82:3–35.

———. 1994. Delinquent peers, beliefs, and delinquent behavior: A longitudinal test of interactional theory. *Criminology* 32:47–83.

Tittle, Charles R. 1988. Two empirical regularities (maybe) in search of an explanation: Commentary on the age/crime debate. *Criminology* 26:75–85.

———. 1995. *Control Balance: Toward a General Theory of Deviance.* Boulder, CO: Westview.

Toby, Jackson. 1994. Everyday school violence: How disorder fuels it. *American Educator* 17(4):4–9, 44–48.

Tracy, Paul E., Marvin E. Wolfgang, and Robert Figlio. 1990. *Delinquency in Two Birth Cohorts.* New York: Plenum.

Tucker, Melvin L. and Bill Starnes. 1993. Crime prevention through environmental design: The Tallahassee model. *Police Chief* (October):130–33.

Uggen, Christopher. 2000. Work as a turning point in the life course of criminals: A duration model of age, employment, and recidivism. *American Sociological Review* 67:529–46.

Vila, Bryan J. and Lawrence E. Cohen. 1993. Crime as strategy: Testing an evolutionary ecological theory of expropriative crime. *American Journal of Sociology* 98:873–912.

Wallis, Allan and Daniel Ford. 1980. *Crime Prevention through Environmental Design: The Demonstration in Broward County, Florida, Executive Summary.* Washington, DC: U.S. Department of Justice.

Warner, Barbara D. and Glenn L. Pierce. 1993. Reexamining social disorganization theory using calls to police as a measure of crime. *Criminology* 31:493–517.

Warner, Barbara D. and Pamela Wilcox Rountree. 1997. Local social ties in a community and crime model: Questioning the systemic nature of informal social control. *Social Problems* 44:423–39.

———. 2000. Implications of ghetto-related behavior for a community-and-crime model: Defining the process of cultural attenuation. *Sociology of Crime, Law and Deviance* 2:39–62.

Warr, Mark. 1990. Dangerous situations: Social context and fear of victimization. *Social Forces* 68:891–907.

———. 1998. Life-course transitions and desistance from crime. *Criminology* 36:183–216.

Warr, Mark and Mark Stafford. 1983. Fear of victimization: A look at the proximate causes. *Social Forces* 61:1033–43.

Weber, Max. 1949. *The Methodology of the Social Sciences.* Glencoe, IL: Free Press.

Weis, Joseph G. and J. David Hawkins. 1981. Preventing delinquency. *Report of the National Justice Assessment Centers.* Washington, DC: U.S. Government Printing Office.

West, Donald J. and David P. Farrington. 1973. *Who Becomes Delinquent?* London: Heinemann Education.

Westinghouse Electric. 1977a. *Crime Prevention through Environmental Design: CPTED Program Manual,* Volume 1, *Planning and Implementation Manual.* Arlington, VA: Author.

———. 1977b. *Crime Prevention through Environmental Design: CPTED Program Manual,* Volume 2, *CPTED Strategies and Directives Manual.* Arlington, VA: Author.

White, Garland F. 1990. Neighborhood permeability and burglary rates. *Justice Quarterly* 7:57–67.

Wilcox, Pamela. 2002. Self Help? Examining the anti-crime effectiveness of citizen weapon possession. *Sociological Focus* 35:145–167.

Wilcox Rountree, Pamela. 1994. *The Antecedents and Effects of Criminal Victimization in Seattle.* Unpublished Ph.D. dissertation, Duke University, Raleigh, North Carolina.

———. 1998. A reexamination of the crime-fear linkage. *Journal of Research in Crime and Delinquency* 35:341–72.

———. 2000. Weapons at school: Are the predictors generalizable across context? *Sociological Spectrum* 20:291–324.

Wilcox Rountree, Pamela and Richard R. Clayton. 1999. A contextual model of adolescent alcohol use across the rural-urban continuum. *Substance Use and Misuse* 34:495–519.

Wilcox Rountree, Pamela and Kenneth C. Land. 1996a. Burglary victimization, perceptions of crime risk, and routine activities: A multilevel analysis across Seattle neighborhoods and census tracts. *Journal of Research in Crime and Delinquency* 33:147–80.

———. 1996b. Perceived risk versus fear of crime: Empirical evidence of conceptually distinct reactions in survey data. *Social Forces* 74:1353–76.

———. 2000. The generalizability of multilevel models of burglary victimization: A cross-city comparison. *Social Science Research* 29:284–305.

Wilcox Rountree, Pamela, Kenneth C. Land, and Terance D. Miethe. 1994. Macro-micro integration in the study of victimization: A hierarchical logistic model analysis across Seattle neighborhoods. *Criminology* 32:387–414.

Wilcox Rountree, Pamela, Neil Quisenberry, Debra T. Cabrera, and Shayne Jones. 2000. Busy places and broken windows: The role of land use in the production of fear of crime. Paper presented at the 52d Annual Meeting of the American Society of Criminology, San Francisco.

Wilcox Rountree, Pamela and Barbara D. Warner. 1999. Social ties and crime: Is the relationship gendered? *Criminology* 37:401–25.

Williams, Kirk and Richard Hawkins. 1986. Perceptual research on general deterrence: A critical overview. *Law and Society Review* 20:545–72.

Wilson, James Q. and Richard Herrnstein. 1985. *Crime and Human Nature.* New York: Simon and Schuster.

Wilson, James Q. and George L. Kelling. 1982. Broken windows. *Atlantic Monthly* (March):29–38.

Wilson, William J. 1987. *The Truly Disadvantaged: The Inner City, the Underclass, and Public Policy.* Chicago, IL: University of Chicago Press.

———. 1996. *When Work Disappears.* Chicago, IL: University of Chicago Press.

Wolfgang, Marvin E., Terence P. Thornberry, and Robert M. Figlio. 1987. *From Boy to Man, from Delinquency to Crime.* Chicago, IL: University of Chicago Press.

Wong, George Y. and William M. Mason. 1985. The hierarchical logistic regression model for multilevel analysis. *Journal of the American Statistical Association* 80:513–24.

Wood, Elizabeth. 1961. *Housing Design: A Social Theory.* New York: Citizens' Housing and Planning Council of New York, Inc.

Wright, Bradley R., Avshalom Caspi, Terrie E. Moffitt, and Phil A. Silva. 1999. Low self-control, social bonds, and crime: Social causation, social selection, or both? *Criminology* 37:479–514.

———. 2001. The effects of social ties on crime vary by criminal propensity: A life-course model of interdependence. *Criminology* 39:321–52.

Zetterberg , Hans Lennart. 1965. *On Theory Verification in Sociology.* Totowa, NJ: Bedminster.

Zucker, Robert A. 1989. Is risk for alcoholism predictable? A probabilistic approach to a developmental problem. *Drugs and Society* 3:69–92.

Index